And Five Were Foolish

Dornford Yates

Alpha Editions

This Edition Published in 2021

ISBN: 9789355348432

Design and Setting By
Alpha Editions
www.alphaedis.com
Email – info@alphaedis.com

As per information held with us this book is in Public Domain. This book is a reproduction of an important historical work. Alpha Editions uses the best technology to reproduce historical work in the PR-same manner it was first published to preserve its original nature. Any marks or number seen are left intentionally to preserve its true form.

TABLE OF CONTENTS

SARAH	- 1 -
MADELEINE	- 31 -
KATHARINE	- 54 -
SPRING	- 85 -
ELIZABETH	- 114 -
JO I JANUARY 7TH, 1926	- 139 -
II NOVEMBER 22ND, 1926	- 142 -
III MARCH 3RD, 1928	- 144 -
IV FEBRUARY 20TH, 1929	- 148 -
V MARCH 11TH, 1929	- 153 -
VI SEPTEMBER 5TH, 1929	- 161 -
ATHALIA	- 163 -
ANN	- 190 -
ELEANOR	- 232 -
SUSAN	- 259 -

SARAH

SARAH VULLIAMY stared at her pink finger-tips.

"But," she protested, "I wanted to marry George Fulke."

"I can't help that," said Pardoner gloomily, filling her glass with champagne. "I didn't make the rotten Will."

"Well, you needn't be so ungallant about it," retorted Sarah. "And it's no use giving me any more champagne, because I shan't drink it. Filthy stuff."

Her companion raised his eyes to heaven.

"□'Filthy stuff,'□" he breathed. "And I brought you here, because this is the only place in London that's got any left. 'Filthy stuff.' I daresay it doesn't appeal to you, but why blaspheme? Never mind. When we're married, I'll——"

"I tell you," said Sarah, "I want to marry George Fulke."

"I'm not surprised," said Pardoner. "George Fulke is a most desirable young man. I should think, as a husband, he'd feed right out of your hand. But there you are. You've refused him three times—on your own confession: and now it's too late."

"It's not too late at all," said Miss Vulliamy. "I'm lunching with him to-morrow, and, if I'm nice to him——"

"For heaven's sake," said Pardoner, "don't go and play with fire. I know what these lawyers are. If you went and got engaged to somebody else, there'd be the devil to pay before we could straighten it out. Which reminds me—the sooner our engagement's announced——"

"But I don't want to marry you," wailed Sarah.

Pardoner clasped his head in his hands.

"Look here," he said. "I don't know how many proposals you've had, but——"

"Thirty-nine," said Sarah, "to date."

"Well, do those thirty-nine include one from me?"

Sarah shook her fair head.

"I've often wondered why they didn't," she said.

Pardoner felt inclined to scream. Instead, he emptied his glass. Then he leaned forward.

"Shall I tell you?" he said.

"Oh, do."

"Because I'm—I'm already in love with somebody else."

"Oh, Virgil, how exciting. Who is it?"

Pardoner swallowed.

"It isn't exciting at all," he said aggrievedly. "It's very tragic. Here have I been waiting and waiting for old James Tantamount to pass to a well-earned rest, and now he's done it—and fairly cramped my style."

"But who is it, Virgil?"

"You wouldn't know her," protested Pardoner.

"Tell me her name."

"Townshend. June Townshend. One of the Lincolnshire lot."

Sarah knitted her brows.

"June Townshend," she said musingly. "I never heard of her. Does she——"

"I told you you hadn't," said Pardoner. "But that's neither here nor there. There's my skeleton or cross, or whatever you like to dress it in. You see, my lady, we're both in the same sad boat. You want George, and I want June. And we can't have 'em."

Sarah stretched out her hand.

"Let me look at the Will," she said.

Pardoner produced and handed her a paper.

. . . . subject to the aforesaid legacies give devise and bequeath all my real and personal property of every sort and description as follows to be divided equally between my nephew Virgil Pardoner of 79 St. James's Street, S.W. and my ward Sarah Cust Vulliamy at present of Palfrey in the New Forest upon the absolute condition that my aforesaid nephew and ward are married the one to the other within three months of my death. But should my aforesaid nephew and ward or either of them fail to observe this condition or dispute this Will then I devise and bequeath the whole of my aforesaid property equally to the undermentioned Institutions. . . .

Sarah read the words thoughtfully.

"It doesn't say how much, does it?"

"Wills don't," said Virgil. "That's where the lawyers come in. Forsyth tells me that, when everything's paid, the money alone will be over six hundred thousand."

"It's a shame," cried Sarah. "A beastly shame. They say the Law's just, but it isn't. Men always get the best. Here I get three hundred thousand and lose my freedom. You get your share and me into the bargain. And what about poor George? I shan't know how to tell him."

As soon as Pardoner could speak—

"What about June?" he demanded. "She'll—she'll never forgive me."

"Oh, blow June," said Sarah. "Besides, it's not settled yet, and I'm not at all sure I'm going to do it. Money isn't everything."

"That," said Virgil, "depends upon the amount. Besides, I daresay after a bit we shall—we shall be—er—quite happy."

"Ugh," shuddered Sarah. "We shan't. We shall be miserable. No," she added suddenly. "It's a great temptation, but we'd better not."

She handed the paper back.

"'Better not'?" cried Pardoner. "What d'you mean—'better not'?"

"Better not marry," said Sarah. "It'ld be selling ourselves."

Virgil took a deep breath.

"My dear child, you don't know what you're saying. You can't go and throw away three hundred thousand pounds. Besides, what about my share? If you chuck up yours, you chuck up mine too."

"That," said Sarah deliberately, "does not weigh with me. I came to dinner to-night to decide whether I could possibly do it. And now I know I can't."

"My dear Sarah," said Pardoner, "be reasonable. By the mercy of heaven, neither of us is already married. To complete our good fortune, neither of us is even pledged to marry anybody else."

"What about June?" said Sarah.

"She's got nothing in writing," said Virgil shortly. "Listen. If either of us had been engaged, it would have complicated everything, especially for me. The damages, for instance, would have been painfully easy to assess. So we've much to be thankful for. Of course, it would have been nicer if we'd been left the money unconditionally, but there you are. We might be worse off. Supposing I had false teeth or a long matted beard or something.... And I've always thought, Sarah, that you were very charming, and I shouldn't be surprised if, after a year or two, you got quite crazy about me."

Miss Vulliamy sighed.

"I feel very uneasy about June," she declared. "George'll find somebody else, I expect. Men are like that. But poor June Townshend ... I should hate her to think that my ... my husband——"

"June's very intelligent," said Virgil. "I'll write and explain the position. Don't worry about that. She's most sympathetic. I'm sure she'd be the first to——"

"Congratulate you?"

"Well, almost," said Pardoner. "She's an awful good sort, June."

"What brutes men are," said Sarah. "However, if you must have your wretched money, I suppose I shall have to give way. Incidentally, you might begin by choosing me a peach, will you?"

Virgil selected one carefully. Then he looked at Sarah.

"Tell me the worst," he said. "Shall it be rough or smooth?"

"Smooth, of course. And don't rush it. Peel it properly. Remember—you're my slave now. Oh, and I'd like some grenadine. I'm thirsty."

Pardoner set down his knife.

"I beg," he implored, "I beg that you will not disgrace me by supplanting this nectar by a tumbler of—of Schoolgirl's Joy. I mean, I'd rather order you a pint of draught stout. Stout may be coarse, but, at least, it's got some body."

"Grenadine," said Sarah relentlessly. "All nice and red and sweet. I love it."

Physically and mentally, the epicure writhed. . . . Then he gave the order.

Sarah smiled maddeningly.

"That was very sweet of you, Virgil—darling."

"Not at all, my love"—shakily. "When we're—er married—blast this peach!" he added savagely, plunging his hands in water. "I suppose you couldn't do with a walnut?"

"Get down to it," said Sarah shortly. "'When we're married,' you were saying."

"Was I? Oh, yes. Well, when——By the way, I'd better announce it, hadn't I?"

"I suppose so," said Sarah.

"Right," said Virgil. "The usual thing, I take it. 'A marriage has been arranged, and——'"

He stopped short and looked at her.

Sarah smiled back.

"It has, with a vengeance," she flashed. "Hasn't it?"

Virgil wiped his hands and lifted his glass.

"Your very good health, Sarah. I'm sorry you can't marry George. But I'll do my best."

He drank luxuriously.

Sarah lifted her grenadine.

"And yours, Virgil. I know your feelings exactly. As for poor June, words fail me. But, since it can't be helped, I'll do what I can."

"We shall get through—dear," said Pardoner stoutly. "And—and you've got a very sweet way."

"That," said Sarah, "is thanks to the grenadine. And now get on with that peach. Where shall we live?" she added artlessly. "Lincolnshire?"

Pardoner choked. Then—

"I'm sure," he said stiffly, "it would have been your guardian's——"

"—and your uncle's——"

"—wish that we should live at Palfrey."

"Is there any reason why we should consider his wishes?"

"Hang it," said Virgil. "The old fellow's left us six hundred thousand."

"And blighted our lives."

"Oh, not 'blighted,'□" said Pardoner. "You can't blight three hundred thousand quid. You can make it a bit sticky, but you can't blight a sum like that. It's—it's invulnerable."

"I was speaking of our lives," said Miss Vulliamy. "Not our legacies."

"Same thing," said Pardoner comfortably, passing a somewhat rugged sculpture across the table. "Same thing. You see. The two are indistinguishable. Supposing another Will turned up, leaving the lot to me." Sarah shuddered. "Exactly. Your life would become a blank—same as your bank balance."

"Not for long," said Miss Vulliamy.

"Why?"

"Because," said Sarah, with a dazzling smile. "I should sue you for breach of promise." Her companion paled. "The damages would be—er—painfully easy to assess, wouldn't they?"

Pardoner frowned. Then his face cleared.

"The contingency," he said, "is happily remote. If it ever happened, I should give you half, because you've the sporting instinct."

"How much," said Sarah dreamily, "shall you give June?"

The other started.

"June? Oh, June's all right. She—she wouldn't expect anything. I—I shouldn't like to offer it. It'ld be—er—indelicate."

Miss Vulliamy sighed.

"Well, well," she said, "I expect you know best. Any way, we've had a nice straight talk, haven't we? I mean, we haven't minced matters. I've told you that, but for the money, I wouldn't be seen dead with you; and you've been equally frank."

Pardoner shifted upon his chair.

"I said," he protested, "I said you'd a very sweet way. I remember it perfectly."

"That," said Miss Vulliamy, "was your only lapse." She raised her straight eyebrows and a faint smile hung upon her red lips. "But for that, you have been disconcertingly honest."

Pardoner lighted a cigarette.

"You're a strange girl," he said. "One minute you talk like an infant, and the next like a woman of forty. Which are you?"

"That," said Sarah, "will be for my husband to discover."

James Tantamount, Esquire, had died at San Francisco.

The direct cause of death was his consumption of iced melon. The physician, who travelled with him mainly to pull his stomach out of the disorders into which the *bon vivant* was constantly haling that valuable member, had besought him again and again to eschew the delicacy. On each occasion James Tantamount had asked him what he thought he was there for. "Any fool," he insisted, "can prevent. I can prevent myself. But I'm not going to. I'm not going to earn your money. Your job's to cure—when I'm sick. Stick to it." It was indeed, I fancy, as much with the idea of giving his attendant work as with that of indulging his appetite that he had upon the tenth day of June devoured two more slices of melon than he was accustomed to consume. If I am right, his ghost must have been disappointed. The man himself did not have time. In a word, he had consumed the delicacy, and pausing only to make a long nose at his physician upon the other side of the table, had laid down his life and his spoon at the same moment.

His secretary had cabled to London for instructions.

Forsyth and Co., Solicitors, had referred to the Will and replied that their client was to be buried forthwith, adding that, by the terms of that remarkable document, if his doctor and secretary desired to receive the year's salary apiece which it offered them, they must be prepared to produce credible testimony that they had followed the coffin attired as convicts and playing vigorously upon harps.

The heat prevailing at San Francisco had not only precluded any discussion of the provision, but had made the asportation of the harps a perfectly hellish business, and only the hilarious encouragement of an enormous crowd had enabled the two contingent legatees to stagger into possession.

There, then, you have the late James Tantamount—bluff, greedy, generous, but blessed or cursed with an incorrigible love of what are called 'practical' jokes. It was not his fault. He had been bred upon them. To the day of his death he could recall with tearful relish the memory of his father, amid roars of laughter, pursuing the vicar round the dining-room, while the doctor blew frantically upon a hunting horn and other guests arranged recumbent chairs as timber to be leaped. . . .

If such a passionate propensity had not asserted itself in death, it would have been surprising. To lovers of fun, riches and a Will offer the chance of a lifetime. The tragedy of it is, they are not alive to enjoy the jest. When James Tantamount, of Palfrey, left his vast fortune to his nephew and his ward upon the condition that they should marry, he knew he was being funny. He had no conception, however, that he was perpetrating the joke of his career.

The news of the old fellow's death had sent hopes soaring. It was generally assumed that his nephew and ward would each receive half of his fortune. For a few days, therefore, the two enjoyed undreamed-of popularity, as a highly desirable couple, and frantic efforts were made by countless matrons to catch their respective eyes. All wrote: some called: others sent flowers. The hearts that 'went out' to them in their 'irreparable loss' argued an esteem for the late James Tantamount hitherto too deep to be expressed.

There is a grief, wrote Mrs. Closeley Dore to Virgil, too *deep to talk about.... As soon as you feel able, come and spend a few days at Datchet. You shall do as you please, and use the house as an hotel. Bring your man, of course....*

The Closeley Dores had four daughters.

My child, wrote Mrs. Sheraton Forbes to Sarah, *I know so well that dreadful sense of loneliness, which gnaws the aching heart. Come back to Fairlands with us on Saturday. We will leave you entirely to yourself, but I should like to think that my dear old friend's sweet ward had someone to turn to in this darkest hour. The world is so hard....*

Mrs. Sheraton Forbes had three sons.

It was a dreadful business....

Then the announcement appeared, and the sympathy died down. It was generally, if grudgingly, admitted that Virgil and Sarah had done the right thing. Crestfallen mothers, consoled by the reflection that, even if they had lost the prize, nobody else had won it, agreed that it was what 'that old Tantamount' would have wished. Some said, sniffing, that his death had drawn the two together.

Finally, the contents of the Will had become public property.

The effect upon the matrons of Mayfair was electrical. With, I think, the slightest encouragement, the late millionaire would have been burned in effigy. As for the two legatees, the outburst of execration with which their determination was posthumously and somewhat illogically received, beggars description.

"My dear," said Mrs. Closeley Dore to Mrs. Sheraton Forbes, "my dear, I can stand worldliness, but I detest indecency. Only a man with the mind of a Nero could have conceived such an infamous idea. But then he was always gross. My father, you know, would never have him inside the house." She shuddered. "But, for an old relic of the Roaring Forties to make a degrading suggestion is one thing; for a decently brought up young man and woman to adopt it is quite another. Those two have no excuse. It is the apotheosis of immorality. I don't pretend I'm not worldly—I am, and I know it. But deliberately to abet one another in debasing one of the Sacraments of the Church——"

In a voice shaken with emotion, Mrs. Sheraton Forbes replied with a misquotation from the Solemnization of Matrimony.

It was a dreadful business. . . .

In the Clubs the affair got the laugh of the season. Virgil Pardoner, who had always been liked, was openly chaffed out of his life and secretly voted 'a devilish lucky chap.' As for the deceased, he was declared a fellow of infinite jest, and his scheme for 'keeping the goods in the family' boisterously applauded. The sluice-gates of Reminiscence were pulled up, and memories of 'Old Jimmy Tantamount' were manufactured and retailed by the hour.

In my lady's chamber Miss Vulliamy was frankly envied.

"I don't mind admitting," said Margaret Shorthorn, "that I could have done with Virgil. They talk about Sarah's selling herself. Well, what if she is? We're all trying to do it. The only difference is that in Sarah's case the conditions of sale have been announced in the Press. Besides, Virgil's no monster . . . I only wish to heaven I'd had such a chance."

"I agree," said Agatha Coldstream. "If I had to face love in a cottage, I'd as soon face it with Virgil as with most men I know. But Virgil plus half a million...." She raised her black eyes to heaven expressively. "Besides, I like Sarah. And I'll tell you one thing—her pals won't be the worse off for her good fortune. Those two'll give their friends the time of their lives. You see if they don't."

So much for Society's reception of the news.

The attitude of Lincoln's Inn Fields was not advertised, but, since John Galbraith Forsyth was a sound judge of character, his opinion may be recorded.

"Tantamount had no right to make such a Will. I told him so at the time, and I've often regretted since that I didn't refuse to draw it. He was playing with fire—hell fire. He might have messed up four lives. And, if he had, he'ld've paid for it. That sort of thing isn't forgiven.... Now that I've seen the parties, my mind's at rest. They're out of the top drawer, both of 'em; and they're splendidly matched. They don't know it—yet, and they don't like their hands being forced. For that's what it is. One's only human, you know, and in these lean years six hundred thousand's a bait you can't ignore. But they'll come through all right. I'm not at all certain, myself, that we couldn't have upset the Will. I'd always got the possibility up my sleeve. But now I shan't use it."

Upon the night of their betrothal, neither Miss Vulliamy nor Pardoner had been at their best. They were uncomfortable and suspicious. They felt their position. To my mind, it does them real credit that they were not exceedingly sour. The circumstances were affording a unique occasion for the expression of irony and distaste. Each was, indeed, a mill stone about the other's neck. Add to this that they had been brought up as brother and sister, and had never looked upon one another in any other light, when you will see how easily Bitterness might have taken her seat at the board. The two had seen each other in the making—without any frills....

But Sarah and Virgil were two very charming people. After ten minutes with either of them you felt refreshed. I do not think I can pay them a higher compliment.

Somebody once said that Miss Vulliamy always looked as though she had just had a cold shower. It was a good description. Her big blue eyes were always alight with expectancy, her eager face glowing, her pretty red mouth upon the edge of laughter. Her little way, too, of raising a delicate chin stuck fast in your memory, while the length of her exquisite lashes was almost unfair. Her figure and the slimness of her legs belonged to idylls. Looking upon the lady, you thought first of the dawn and then of dew and cool meadows. Sarah would have made an arresting Naiad. Shepherds who repaired to her fountain would have been constantly crowded out.

Pardoner was tall, and conveyed the idea of laziness. It was his soft brown eyes that gave this impression. His thick dark hair and his high colour had earned him at Oxford the sobriquet of *Rouge et Noir*. An aquiline nose, and a firm, well-shaped mouth distinguished a handsome face. The way in which he wore his clothes brought his tailor much hardly merited custom. His most attractive voice delighted the ear. It was, in fact, hereby that his personality emerged. When he was silent, he passed in a well-mannered crowd; when he opened his mouth, other people stopped talking.

The two met in Bond Street a fortnight later.

"Good morning," said Virgil. "I bet I've been cut by more people than you."

"Four," said Sarah, "since half-past ten."

"Five and a half," said her fiancé. "Mrs. Sheraton Forbes had a child with her under fourteen. This ostracism amuses me to death. Never mind. How's Fulke?"

"Desperate," said Miss Vulliamy. "I knew he would be. He bucked up a lot when I said he should be our first guest."

"Did he, indeed?" said Virgil. "Truly a forgiving nature."

"Yes, he is very sweet," agreed Sarah. "Couldn't he be your best man?"

Pardoner fingered his chin.

"I'm afraid he's too young," he said slowly. "I must have a compeer."

"Very well, then," said Sarah. "He can give me away."

"That," said Virgil, "will be a most becoming rôle."

Miss Vulliamy frowned. Then—

"As we're here," she said, "what about an engagement ring?"

"Of course," said Virgil. "Come on. We'll get it at once."

The two repaired to a jeweller's and bought a beauty.

"And while we're about it," said Pardoner, "a wedding ring too."

A wedding ring was selected.

"And we might as well get our presents," said Sarah, staring at a tiara composed of diamonds and emeralds. "You know: 'The bridegroom's presents to the bride included. . .'"

"Right," said Virgil. "Have what you like. I'm in a generous mood. Besides, my turn's coming. In fact I'll just have a look round."

Before they left the shop, the bride had given the bridegroom a gold cigarette-box, four pearl pins, six pairs of sleeve links, and a green crocodile dressing-case, which, with its gold-mounted fittings, cost her eight hundred pounds.

On being acquainted with the lengths to which her generosity had gone—

"They will think I love you," said Miss Vulliamy, as soon as she could speak.

"Remembering that tiara," said Pardoner, "they'll say I'm doting. I didn't know they made such expensive things. But for my brain-wave about that dressing-case, I should have been left standing."

In a shaking voice Sarah demanded luncheon.

"Not that I want to presume upon your hospitality, but we've many things to discuss," she concluded coldly.

"On condition," said Pardoner, "that you do not drink grenadine, I'll do you a treat."

"I don't see why," said Miss Vulliamy, "I should give up my staple drink."

Virgil shuddered.

"I'll try and explain some day. For one thing it's bad for the heart."

"It's never affected mine," said Sarah.

"No," said Virgil, "I daresay it hasn't. To be frank, I was thinking of my own. But never mind. Give it a miss till we're married—a sort of interim injunction. We can argue it out later."

"Very well," said Sarah reluctantly.

That the table which was offered them at Claridge's should lie directly between one presided over by Mrs. Closeley Dore and another at which Mrs. Sheraton Forbes was entertaining two stylish Americans was sheer good fortune..... Virgil and Sarah had the time of their lives. Placidly to browse under their enemies' noses was delightful enough. The reflection that the more they vented their good humour, the higher must rise the fever of indignation raging on either side, made the two positively festive.... When the two Americans asked their hostess the identity of 'that most attractive couple,' and seemed surprised to learn that they were not of the Blood Royal, Mrs. Sheraton Forbes' cup began to overflow....

At length—

"Ah," said Pardoner, "the rot's set in. The tumult and the shouting dies, The Closeleys and the Dores depart. I'll bet old Chippendale doesn't last two minutes alone."

"Got it in one," said Sarah. "She's up. Her guests haven't finished, but she hasn't seen that. She's ordering coffee in the lounge. I'm afraid she's terribly upset."

"Good," said Virgil. "And we've shortened 'Slam It's' life. When I called you 'darling' just now, I thought she was going to founder. Incidentally, I said it very well, didn't I?"

"Like a professional," said Miss Vulliamy. "You must have said it before."

"Never, darling."

"O-o-oh," said Sarah. "Any way, you needn't say it now. The audience has dispersed."

"But it comes so natural."

Sarah tilted her chin.

"We are not amused," she said stiffly. "And now to business. We'd better be married about the end of the month. What about the twenty-fifth?"

Virgil consulted a note-book.

"Can't be done," he said. "I'm playing polo. I can manage the twenty-fourth."

"Don't be a fool," said his fiancée. "What about the honeymoon?"

After a lot of argument, Pardoner agreed to waive the polo, on the understanding that the wedding-trip was restricted to fourteen days.

"Well, that's that," said Sarah. "Now then, where shall it be? I may say that I insist upon a church."

A church was at last selected and Pardoner promised to make the necessary arrangements.

"The next thing," said Miss Vulliamy, "is where to go. What about Dinard?"

"As you please," said Virgil. "I suppose that's where Fulke's going," he added carelessly.

Sarah shook her sweet head.

"Not till the first," she replied. "Which brings us to June."

"August," corrected Virgil. "August. July—August—Sept——"

"June Townshend," said Sarah shortly.

Pardoner started and dropped his cigarette.

"What about her?" he said uneasily. "She wouldn't like Dinard. She's a—a clergyman's daughter."

Sarah bowed before a little gust of laughter.

Then—

"Have you written to her?" she demanded.

"Er, no. Not yet. I mean, it's a delicate matter."

"Virgil," said Miss Vulliamy. "Unless you write to her to-day, I won't marry you."

"But——"

"That's flat," said Sarah. "I mean what I say. After all this time, to let that poor girl see our engagement in the paper and nurse her sorrow without one word of explanation or regret.... I confess I'm disgusted. No honourable man——"

"I'm not an honourable man," said Pardoner. "I'm a loathsome and venomous worm. Ask Mrs. Closeley Dore."

"You will write to her now," said Sarah. "You will send for a sheet of notepaper and write to her now—in the lounge. I'll help you."

By the time the document was settled, it was a quarter to four.

> My Dear June,
>
> Possibly by now you will have seen the announcement of my engagement in the papers. Had I been able, I should have wished to tell you of it myself, but a recent bereavement has not only kept me in London, but has affected my brain. The marriage I am contracting is one which you would have been the first to wish me to make. Indeed, I have often fancied that I could hear your soft voice urging me to go forward. My poor uncle is dead, dear, and I have reason to believe that it was his earnest desire that I should wed his ward. I feel, therefore, that the least I can do is to respect his wishes. Nothing, however, can take away the memory of the many happy, happy hours we have spent together, and I look forward confidently to bringing my wife to see you, as soon as we are settled. I am sure that you and she will get on together, and perhaps one day you will come and stay with us at Palfrey, which we shall make our home.
>
> Your affectionate friend,

"Now address it," said Sarah, "and send for a stamp."

Pardoner hesitated.

"I'ld, er, I'ld like to sleep on it," he said. "I mean, it's—it's a ticklish business."

Miss Vulliamy indicated an envelope with a firm pointed finger.

"Pretty hands you've got," said Virgil musingly. "Pretty nails, too."

"What are June's like?"

"Oh, very good," said Virgil. "Full of character, you know. But yours are bewitching. That left one——"

"Apostate," said Sarah. "And now address this envelope."

Virgil did so laboriously.

Miss June Townshend,

The Rectory,

Roughbridge,

Lincolnshire.

They posted the letter together, before they parted.

It was two days later that Mrs. Purdoe Blewitt was seriously annoyed.

"Such impudence," she said, bristling. "As if she were the daughter of the house...."

The Reverend Purdoe Blewitt, Rector of Loughbridge, laid down his pen.

"What is the matter, my dear?"

His wife stabbed at the bell and flounced into a chair before replying.

"Jane, of course," she snorted. "Fortunately, I met the postman, or I should never have known." She tapped a letter with meaning. "She's still doing it."

The Rector knew better than to inquire the nature of the iniquity. Mrs. Blewitt believed in remembering her servants' offences and expected this belief to be shared. He assumed an aggravated look.

"How very trying," he said, playing for safety. "I should say to her that the next time she does it——"

"Does what?" said his wife.

The Rector started guiltily.

"I understood you to say, my dear," he faltered, "that she was still doing it."

"So she is," said his wife.

The Reverend Purdoe Blewitt put a hand to his head.

"It's not nice of her," he said, blindly endeavouring to avoid collision. "Not at all nice. I mean——"

Here he observed that his wife was surveying him with a profound contempt, and quailed accordingly.

The appearance of a pert parlourmaid postponed his chastisement.

"Jane," said Mrs. Blewitt, at once averting her face and stretching forth the letter as though it were some contagious body, "I suppose it is not the slightest good desiring you to remember that your address is not *The Rectory, Loughbridge*, but *c/o The Rev. Purdoe Blewitt, The Rectory, Loughbridge*. However, for what it is worth, I will again point out that, even if you were here as a guest—which you are not—it would be the essence of bad taste to omit the Rector's name from the head of your notepaper."

"An' if," sweetly rejoined Miss Townshend, taking the letter, "if your gues's frien's—not knowin' you—didn't take no notice of what was wrote at the 'ead of the notepaper, I s'pose your gues's 'ld still get it in the neck." Mrs. Purdoe Blewitt recoiled, and the Rector emitted a protesting noise. "You know, you're too particular to live, you are;

and p'raps you'll take this as notice. Servants aren't no good to you. What you want is 'alf a dozen Archangels—and then you'd show 'em 'ow to wear their wings."

Apparently unable to speak, Mrs. Blewitt, crimson with fury, clawed at the air, while the Rector, feeling that something must be done, rose to his feet and cleared his throat.

Ere words came, however, Miss Townshend was out of the room.

The look of her letter was promising.

This had been addressed to 'Roughbridge,' but, there being no such place, the Post Office had risen to the occasion and above the mistake.

Five days had gone by since Mrs. Purdoe Blewitt had been so annoyed, and Pardoner and Miss Vulliamy were dining together, ostensibly to discuss arrangements for their alliance, actually because they enjoyed each other's company.

"I wonder she hasn't replied," said Sarah, obediently sipping her champagne.

Virgil shrugged his shoulders.

"I daresay she won't," he said. "She's very considerate. I mean, it's delicate ground, and it'ld be just like June if she sank her own feelings and, er, let bygones be bygones."

His fiancée shook her head.

"If she doesn't answer," she said, "I shall be really worried. Silence can only mean one of two things: either that she doesn't know how to behave——"

"Oh, she knows how to behave all right."

"—or that she's almost beside herself."

"No, no," said Virgil. "June's not that kind of girl. I shan't be at all surprised, if she doesn't reply. In fact, I should be rather surprised, if she did. You know, I had a feeling, when I wrote that letter, that it would never be answered. You see, June——"

"But you used to kiss her, you know."

Pardoner pulled his moustache.

"Once in a while," he said. "But I never made a meal of it. It was more of a salute."

Miss Vulliamy stared across the room.

"I think," she said softly, "your love for her is very beautiful."

"Was," said Virgil uneasily. "I've—I've trodden it under."

Sarah shuddered.

"Hush," she said. "Hush. Don't talk like that, Virgil. It's—it's blasphemy."

As she spoke, a page came to the table.

"Mr. Pardoner, sir?"

"Yes," said Virgil.

"Miss Townshend would like to speak to you, sir, on the telephone."

Pardoner started. Then he turned to Sarah with a sheepish smile.

"Who's come in on this little deal?" he demanded.

"Whatever d'you mean?" said Miss Vulliamy, striving to keep her voice steady.

"Nothing doing," said Virgil, continuing to smile. "Admit it's a plant."

"By all that's solemn," said Sarah. "I swear I've nothing to do with it."

"But you've——"

"I haven't, Virgil. I swear I haven't, I'ld—I'ld be ashamed," she added tearfully.

Three times did her betrothed endeavour to speak.

At the fourth attempt—

"Must be some mistake," he muttered, wiping his brow. Then he turned to the page. "All right. I'll come."

He bowed an apology to Sarah and followed his executioner out of the room....

Of the two, Sarah was, if possible, the more dumbfounded.

Upon the very first evening she had made up her mind that Miss June Townshend was non-existent. She could have sworn that Pardoner had invented the lady, to be a foil to George Fulke. Gleefully, she had decided to turn the foil into a lash to be laid mischievously about her fiancé's shoulders. The laborious drafting of the letter to June had afforded her the highest gratification, and her searching cross-examinations of Virgil upon his associations with the lady had never failed to bear her most refreshing fruit. Now, without a word of warning, the Palace of Fun had fallen, and out of the ruins were sticking some extremely ill-favoured truths. The very least of these was suggesting that the edifice had been erected upon a foundation of distasteful fact.

It was while she was staring at Virgil's empty place, considering these things, that for the first time she realized something which was still more to the point. This was that with her future husband she was most heartily in love....

Pardoner walked down the hall, thinking furiously. Arrived at the box, he took the spare receiver and told the page to speak for him.

"Say you can't find me," he said, "and ask her to leave a message."

The boy did so.

A voice, which was anything but gentle, replied:

"All right, I'll come round."

Virgil blenched.

"Say I'm not living here, and you don't know my address."

"Then why you ask me to leave a message," flashed Miss Townshend.

"Er—on the chance," stammered the page.

"Well, 'ere it is—on the chance," said Jane. "I'll be round in 'alf an hour."

The receiver was slammed into place.

Virgil and the page stared at one another in dismay.

Then the former said an extremely unpleasant word under his breath and erupted violently from the box. . .

Miss Vulliamy greeted him with a cold smile.

"Get on all right?" she said acidly.

"We must leave at once," said Virgil. "Go on to the Berkeley, or my rooms, or somewhere. We can't stay here. She says she's coming at once—may be here any moment."

"Then why go?" said Sarah.

"Well, we can't be here when she comes. You don't want a scene, do you? Screams and yells in the hall, and all that sort of thing?" He mopped the sweat from his face. "It's all that blinking letter you made me write," he added savagely. "I might have known——"

"But, of course, you must see her," said Sarah, rising. "I'll go, if you like: but you must stay. Poor, wretched girl, you can't——"

"Stay?" cried Virgil. "You're mad. I don't want to be blackmailed."

"But you said that June——"

"It—it *isn't* June," wailed Pardoner. "I mean, it can't be. It—it isn't her voice. It's an impostor—that's the word—impostor, Sarah. Someone or other's got hold of that blasted letter, and now they're trying it on."

"But it must be June," said Sarah. "The telephone's very deceptive. Sometimes those very soft voices——"

"I tell you it's *not*," raged Virgil. "*June doesn't drop her 'h's'.*"

With a bright red spot upon either cheek, Miss Vulliamy preceded him to the door.

While she was getting her cloak, Pardoner gave the porter instructions too definite to be mistaken. These he reinforced with two pounds.

Then a taxi was summoned, and a moment later the two were flying up Brook Street....

Pardoner entered that cab with the determined intention of telling Miss Vulliamy the truth. He meant to humble himself. He intended to apologize for his reception of his amazing luck. He meant to ask her to do her best to love and to confess there and then that "if the Will went west to-morrow morning, I'd beg and humbly pray you to become my wife."

Fate ruled otherwise.

The tone in which his fiancée cut short his opening sentence with a request to be taken home, would have silenced anyone. After a second effort, which was met by the lady with a true flash of temper, Pardoner told the cabman to drive to Rutland Gate.

The journey was completed without a word.

Arrived at the house, Sarah was handed out with her head in the air. Virgil's offer to ring or use her latchkey might not have been made. His presence was ignored utterly. My lady let herself in, and closed the door behind her exactly as if she were alone. The broad white step without, might have been empty. Then she went to her room and burst into tears.

Virgil repaired to a Club and ordered a brandy and soda. This he imbibed in the library, where no one may speak, cursing all women with a deep and bitter curse....

After a perfectly poisonous hour and a half, he went to bed.

Upon the following morning he received two several communications.

The first was from the hall-porter at Claridge's and made his hair rise.

The second was from Sarah and desired him to meet her at noon at Lincoln's Inn Fields.

Pardoner agreed, but went early, proposing to have Forsyth to himself for a valuable quarter of an hour. Miss Vulliamy went early also, with the same idea. They met on the doorstep and, as Forsyth was engaged, spent an awkward ten minutes in the same waiting-room. . . .

At last they were shown into the presence.

The solicitor, who had been hoping to congratulate them as lovers, was much disappointed. Still, his hopes were not dashed, and, wisely making no attempt to thaw the atmosphere, begged to be told the nature of the trouble.

Virgil stammered the facts. He was careful to tell nothing but the truth. But for Sarah's presence, he would have gone further, and told the whole truth . . . but for Sarah's presence . . .

Forsyth heard him out gravely. Then he rang for a clerk.

"Get me on to Claridge's," he said.

In silence the three awaited the connection.

Presently a bell throbbed.

Forsyth picked up the receiver.

"Is that Claridge's? Put me on to the hall-porter. . . . Hullo! . . . This is Forsyth and Co., solicitors. . . . Yes, Mr. Forsyth. . . . I understand a lady calling herself 'Miss Townshend,' has been asking for Mr. Pardoner. . . . Yes? . . . Sitting in the hall now, is she? Good. Tell her that he will be there to see her at three o'clock. . . . Right. . . . Good-bye."

"But, look here," said Virgil, "I'm not going to——"

"Yes, you are," said Forsyth. "You're going to be in the lounge. Two of my clerks are going to be there also. One of these is going to take your name in vain. He's going to meet the lady and say he's you. Of course, it may not come off, but it's worth trying. If it does, we've got her cold. There's the evidence of a spare clerk and the hall-porter, to say she took John Snooks for Virgil Pardoner. You must be there yourself, to have a look at her. If, having seen her, you've anything more to say, say it to the spare clerk. And to-night you must leave for

Lincolnshire. The real Miss Townshend must know the facts of the case, and we obviously can't trust the post. If all goes well, she won't be needed, but if there's any hitch, she'll have to be produced."

Pardoner broke into a sweat.

Then—

"Need she be mixed up in it? I mean . . ."

The solicitor shrugged his shoulders.

"If A say's she's B," he said shortly, "when she isn't, the obvious thing to do is to produce B, isn't it?"

"I'd better come back here at four," said Virgil, positively. "After I've seen the woman."

Forsyth shook his head.

"I'm leaving for Paris," he said, "at two o'clock. Can't get out of it. Back in a week, I hope. But don't worry. When's the wedding?" he added pleasantly.

"Twenty-fou—fifth," said Virgil, with a sickly smile. "Soon be here now."

Sarah moistened her lips.

"I think," she said slowly, "I think I ought to say that I'm rather unsettled." Her fiancé paled, and Forsyth shot her a swift glance. "I don't say here and now that I won't go through with it, but——"

"But you must," cried Virgil. "You must. Why, that tiara alone——"

"—unless and until this matter is cleared right up, I'm sorry, but . . ." She drew off her engagement ring and laid it upon the table. "I think perhaps, if Mr. Forsyth would put this in his safe . . ."

There was a dreadful silence.

At length—

"I'm sure," said Forsyth, turning to look at Pardoner, "we both understand. It's very natural. The wretched business places you both in a false position." He picked up the ring and slid it into an envelope.

"I may add that I look forward confidently to restoring this pretty thing to you, directly I'm back." He rose and walked to the door. "And now, good-bye. Don't worry, because I'm away. My managing clerk, Maple, will be at your service."

As in a dream, Virgil followed Miss Vulliamy down the stairs and out into the broad square. There she gave him her hand and bade him farewell.

At half-past ten the next morning Pardoner received a letter of some importance.

Private.

DEAR MR. PARDONER,

From the clerk who attended you yesterday, I understand that you are not proposing at present to leave for Lincolnshire. I write to beg you to do this without delay.

What took place at Claridge's yesterday afternoon makes it abundantly clear that the person, who called there to meet you, is no fool. Thanks, no doubt, to the periodicals in which your photograph has recently so often figured, she is well acquainted with your looks, and from the papers, which, I understand she produced, I see no reason to disbelieve that she is, in fact, Miss Jane Townshend, late of The Rectory, Loughbridge or Roughbridge, Lincolnshire. It is, of course, a most unfortunate coincidence that there should be two ladies bearing the very same name and address, but since such a coincidence exists, it is not at all easy successfully to contend that this woman's possession of your letter is unlawful and was never intended.

In these circumstances, you will surely appreciate the extreme desirability of your seeing the other Miss Townshend without delay, explaining to her the position, and, if possible, inducing her to come to London at once. Indeed, in my opinion, her production alone can now snuff this matter out.

Yours faithfully,

F. S. MAPLE.

Virgil fell upon the telephone.

After a maddening delay—

"Is that Mr. Maple?" he said.

"Speaking," said a brusque voice.

"I'm Virgil Pardoner."

"Yes?"

"The name isn't *Jane*. It's *June*."

"Ah. I thought Mr. Forsyth said 'June,' but I wanted to see what you said. That's splendid. She's altered your letter, of course—changed the 'u' into 'a.' That was easy. And now we *have* got her—tight. All you've got to do is to trot out Miss *June* Townshend and, if she has any letters of yours—she probably has—to see that she brings them with her. There's a train at——"

"She hasn't," yelled Virgil. "She hasn't. I know she hasn't."

"Oh, but she may. Lots of women promise to destroy——"

"She can't. I never wrote any. There's—*there's no such woman.*"

"No such *what*?" cried Maple.

"Woman," said Virgil, calmly. Now that the murder was out, he felt much better. "You know. Female of man. June Townshend is a creation of my lightning brain. I also invented Stoughbridge, or whatever the rotten place is, complete with Rectory. I pictured an old-world garden, with a hammock and croquet-nets. Oh, and a bamboo cake-stand. June was there, feeding the aspodestras with crumbs of rock-cake. The letter, I may say, was written to substantiate the fantasy. It was a beautiful piece of prose. . . ."

There was a long silence.

Presently—

"Are you serious?" said Maple. "I mean, d'you mean what you say?"

"Absolutely."

"Well, this is a facer," said Maple. "Of course, I'll do what I can, but you've disarmed me. If the thing's to be kept quiet it looks as if that beautiful piece of prose——"

"Will prove extremely expensive?" said Virgil, cheerfully.

"Exactly."

"An action for breach of promise couldn't succeed?"

"Good heavens, no. But she'll be a nuisance."

"Let her," said Virgil. "I won't pay a blinkin' cent."

"But what will Miss Vulliamy say?"

"That," said Virgil sweetly, "remains to be seen. I may tell you I wrote the letter under duress. *She made me do it.* Of course, if she likes to buy my literature back, she's at liberty to do so. She's plenty of money—or can have. Besides, it'ld be a pretty compliment. So please do nothing for me. And just acknowledge these instructions, will you? Before you lunch. I'd like her to know the worst this afternoon."

"Very good," said Maple, laughing. "I'll dictate a letter at once."

Private.

DEAR MR. PARDONER,

I have carefully considered the conversation, which we had upon the telephone this morning, and I have come to the conclusion that, in the circumstances, your wisest course is, as you suggest, to take no further action.

Since the Miss June Townshend, to whom you addressed your letter, has never in fact existed outside your imagination, and there is, therefore, no one with whom we can confront the woman, into whose hands that letter has fallen, the only possible move we could make would be to offer to buy the document back.

As, however, your hands are perfectly clean, I agree that to make such a move would be beneath your dignity and that you can well afford to ignore such petty molestation as that to which this person may resort.

An action for breach of promise could not possibly succeed.

As I have already pointed out, her alteration of "June" to "Jane" has, in the absence of "the original," no bearing upon the case.

Yours faithfully,
F. S. MAPLE.

This note and its predecessor reached Sarah Vulliamy while she was dressing to dine tête-à-tête with George Fulke.

Beyond that Sarah was unusually pensive, the dinner calls for no remark.

Exactly a month had slipped by.

There had been rain in the night, and Luchon was looking her best.

So was Mrs. Pardoner. She had just had a cold shower.

Seated upon the edge of the breakfast table, one bare leg dangling from the folds of an apricot kimono, her curls in a disorder more lovely than any array, she periodically frowned upon a letter, regarded her new wedding-ring, and gazed at the sunlight upon the mountain-side.

Presently she raised her voice.

"Virgil."

A lapping noise in the bathroom was suspended.

"Yes, darling."

"George Fulke says I've blighted his life."

"So you have," said Virgil.

"By not going to Dinard," added Sarah.

"Serve him right," said Virgil.

"He says he quite understood that ours was a marriage of convenience."

"So it was," said Virgil. "Great convenience."

"But what shall I do?" said Sarah. "He says that his heart is 'aching for a vivid, stimulating personality to fill the emptiness of life.'□"

Her husband appeared, swathed in a bath dressing-gown.

"My dear," he said, "it's too easy. Take a fresh envelope and pass the letter on."

"Who to?" said his wife.

Virgil fingered his chin.

"The trouble is," he murmured, "I'm not quite sure of her address. I think it was Bloughbridge."

MADELEINE

IT was upon the seventh day of September that Madeleine Peyre, of Ruffec, made a mistake. This was notable; first, because the lady was justly accounted wise, and, secondly, because, as errors go, the mistake was a bad one.

Madeleine was the Silvia of Ruffec. She went faithfully to Mass, and what she believed to be proper, that unobtrusively she endeavoured to do. She spoke ill of no one. Her exquisite pink-and-white complexion, her raven hair, her steady grey eyes, were three great several beauties. Add that her features were regular, her teeth most white, and her figure graceful, when you will understand that the swains of Ruffec commended her with cause. As I have said already, Madeleine's judgment also was unusually sound. To ram home my comparison, it was, I think, the light in her wonderful eyes which you forgot last of her comeliness, while the flowers she was constantly receiving gave her actual distress. She never would wear them. No other girl in Ruffec received any flowers.

When, therefore, Madeleine Peyre, the Silvia of Ruffec, married the wrong man, the town pulled her down from her pedestal and let her lie.

It is the way of the world.

The announcement of the betrothal aroused consternation. People were amazed—staggered. You could have knocked them down. That Pierre Lacaze was a brute was common knowledge. They said his first wife had been bullied into her grave.... The astonishment was succeeded by sickness of heart. Discussion of the tragedy dissolved into sighs and tears.... Finally came Anger. Madeleine Peyre was denounced for an ungrateful fool. Where sighs had been heaved, fingers were wagged and snapped. Ruffec told Ruffec that Mademoiselle Peyre would soon find out her error, and that the discovery would serve her right. People began to gloat upon the disillusionment which was awaiting their darling. Upon the wedding day itself leers were exchanged....

It is the way of the world.

Had her parents lived, the mistake would not have been made. But they had been killed together, five years before. Madeleine, aged sixteen, had seen no reason why the little creamery they had been keeping should close its aged hatch. As a result, this had remained open ever since. Out of the profits of the little enterprise its girlish governor and her two young brothers had been lodged and fed and clothed decently. Now the brothers were come to men's estate, while the goodwill of the business was a legacy worth having. Moreover, Jean and Jacques Peyre were no fools. About their future Madeleine felt easy enough.

For the matter of that, up to the very last she had no qualms about her own. *Quos Deus vult perdere prius dementat.* Every one—her brothers included—disliked Lacaze. The man was so obviously a brute. Madeleine clung to him steadfastly. . . .

Then the day came, and the Silvia of Ruffec cast her pearls before swine.

Be sure Lacaze rent her.

Nearly ten months had trailed by, and Madeleine had aged ten years.

The two lived in Paris, where Lacaze plied his trade of steeple-jack and made good money. The work suited him. The hours were short, the pay high. Fearless as a lion, the danger delighted his heart. The respect his prowess inspired tickled his vanity.

So much for his public life.

Lacaze married Madeleine Peyre as other men buy a fine horse. The only difference was that he got her for nothing.

In the Silvia of Ruffec he had seen a fine stamp of animal, intelligent, well-made, good to look upon. He had judged her strong, courageous, and obedient. Her possession would be something to be proud of. Others would covet such a prize. . . .

The fellow was perfectly right.

Physically and mentally Madeleine was all that could be desired. When he took her out and about, everyone stared in admiration. When he showed her off to his friends they made no secret of their envy. His house was always in order, such as he had not dreamed of. There was, however, a fretful fly in the ointment. It was this. Madeleine's manners were perfect, but they were the manners of Silvia, and not the manners of a show horse.

Within twenty-four hours of her wedding it was all over, and Madeleine had realized her plight. Of course the blow had been frightful ... stunning ... too terrible to describe. The first blinding flash of perception had exploded a second: the second, a third. ... Her poor brain had staggered under this fearful appulse, her spirit fainted, her heart sunk to her shoes. Her love for Lacaze had shrivelled and died then and there. Not so her obedience. ... So soon as she could think clearly, Madeleine resolved to do her best to dovetail her principles into her husband's demands.

The result was unsatisfactory—to Madame Lacaze. You cannot make a fair wallet out of a silk purse and a sow's ear. The ways of Lacaze were not Madeleine's. The grace the heaven had lent her, meant nothing to him. More—the man had a will. The grace the heaven had lent her, he made her discard.

The result was unsatisfactory—to Monsieur Lacaze. Madeleine bowed to his will, but not to his liking. She discarded her precious loan, if and when she was urged—never unless she was urged. His will had to be expressed—*always*. That was where her manners, as a horse, were so imperfect. Her rider's heels ached. ...

Never once did Lacaze lose his temper. Better for his wife if he had. Instead, he smiled a quiet smile, set his strong teeth and—stuck to his spurs. After a month or two his heels developed new muscles and stopped aching. From then on, the blood upon his rowels was never dry.

Her spirit had to be broken. Well, that was easy enough. It had been done before. A pair of aching heels, however, had to be paid for. Lacaze determined to break his wife's spirit by eighths of an inch.

Fortune favours the brute.

Nine months after their marriage, a pair of spurs of a sharpness he could never have compassed fell into his lap.

A letter arrived for Madeleine while she and Lacaze sat at meat. It came from her brother Jean.

> DEAREST MADELEINE,
>
> *I write to say that René Dudoy has taken a job in Paris. It is a good thing for him, but he will be lonely. He has said absolutely that he will not go to see you. I expect you can guess why. But we have told him not to be silly, and that you will be a good friend, if you can be nothing else. We think you would have wished us to do this. It is true, is it not? If so, look him up. His address will be 66 rue Castetnau.*
>
> *Jacques and I are well, but still miss our only sister very much. The shop flourishes. We took twenty-six francs more last week than the week before, though a storm on Wednesday robbed us of six good litres.*
>
> *Your loving brother,*
>
> JEAN.

Covertly Lacaze watched her read it and lay it down. Something—Heaven knows what—told him that here was matter she did not wish him to see. He went to work delicately.

"Ah!" he cried of a sudden. "The thing had escaped me. My dear, to-morrow put on your very best gown. We are going to the wedding of Robert and José Tuyte."

Madeleine winced.

"Must we, Pierre? José Tuyte is awfully clever, I know. But she is an actress, and—and I do not go well with the stage. I am too slow for them."

(If to appear nightly in the costume of a child of seven at *The Dead Rat*, there to accept cigarettes and encourage the purchase of champagne, is to be an actress, Madeleine was perfectly right. That she was too slow for such a 'stage' was unarguable.)

"My dear, what would you? Robert is a good friend, and I knew José before I knew you. They would be most hurt. Besides, marriage is like a wet sponge. It wipes clean the slate. You need not, you know, dance all the time."

"Dance?"

"Have I forgotten again? We are to have supper that night at *Le Parapluie*. The big room has been engaged. I tell you, it will be festive. A little below us, perhaps, but we must descend, my dear. It behoves us to descend. Their feelings must not be hurt."

Madeleine paled.

Once before she had subscribed to festivity under the shelter of *Le Parapluie*. The revels had haunted her ever since. . . .

She was about to protest—beg to be excused—when she remembered her letter. Mercifully, this seemed to have escaped notice—so far. It occurred to her that pleasant, bright conversation might save it inviolate. Desperately she strove to keep the ball rolling. . . .

Lacaze saw her anxiety, and let her strive.

When the meal was over, he pushed back his chair. For the next five minutes he debated audibly whether he should go forth to buy tobacco, or send the servant. Madeleine wanted him to go—terribly, but dared not put in her oar. She was, of course, quite satisfied that he had forgotten her letter. Her only fear was that he would catch sight of it again.

At last Lacaze decided to go himself. He rose, sought for his hat, chucked her under the chin and left the room.

Madeleine thrust the letter into her dress and thanked God.

Then the door opened and her husband put in his head.

"I quite forgot," he said, smiling. "What does young Jean have to say?"

His wife took the letter from her bosom and gave it into his hand.

He read it deliberately. At length—

"Poor René," he said gaily. "So I put a spoke in his wheel. Dear, dear. We must try to make up for it. I seem to remember him faintly—a calf with curly fair hair. '66 rue Castetnau.' Good." He handed the letter back. "We'll call there next Sunday morning. The better the day, sweeting, the better the deed. 'Lonely.' Poor clod, what a shame! But for Lacaze, the steeple-jack, he might have been watching your pink little hands ladle cream into pots, while he counted the takings and gave out the change. Certainly we must make up for it—so far as we can. . . ."

He sighed and went out.

As he closed the door, his eyes lighted. He walked down the passage thoughtfully, licking his lips. . . .

Madeleine sat staring at the disordered cloth.

Long ago Misery had repaired to her eyes. Now Despair had come also. She was really frightened.

Lacaze was perfectly right. But for him, she would have married René. Ever since her disastrous wedding she had tried not to think about the past—the old days. As for what might have been, this she had shut most rigidly out of her thoughts. As if to mock her pains, here was Fate flaunting it under her very nose. . . .

Again, God knows she was patient—to a fault. But her husband's derision of René had set her cheeks flaming. That it had made her heart warm towards her old swain, she did not realize. *That it had been intended so to do*, only another Lacaze could have guessed. The man was evil.

Finally, Madeleine knew in her heart that she had always loved René, and never Lacaze . . . that she had loved René very much . . . that at the present moment she loved him more than ever.

All things considered, then, that Silvia was thoroughly frightened is not surprising. There were breakers ahead.

Lacaze knew that he could trust his wife. He knew that she was loyal, incorruptible, holy. Trading upon this holiness, he fairly thrust the lovers into each other's arms. Before his dominant will the two poor wretches were helpless. . . .

The climax came one beautiful July evening.

Dudoy had been bidden to call for Madeleine and take her to the Café de la Forêt Noire. There the two were to wait till the steeple-jack joined them.

"You know my corner," he had said. "Take it and sip your syrup until I arrive. I shall not be long, but Notre Dame is ailing. She has a crack, poor lady, in one of her horns. To be frank, it is an awkward business. I hope I shan't slip. If I did—well, you two would take care of each other, would you not?" He pinched his wife's ear. "Still, we will hope and pray my poor life may be spared."

At a quarter to seven, therefore, honest curly-haired René strode down the Rue de Tocqueville, to fold sweet sorrow in his arms. Madame Lacaze was ready, and the two left at once.

On their way through the bustling streets they spoke very little. Matter-of-fact conversation was difficult enough to come by. They kept what reserve they had for the table without the window at the Café de la Forêt Noire.

This appeared soon enough.

René saw Madeleine settled, and called for drink. Then they began to talk—artificially. Madeleine laboured hard and met with success. After a little, Dudoy began to dance to her piping. . . .

Then a laughing-eyed rogue of a child came and snapped the poor pipe in two.

What happened exactly was this. The tot had escaped from its parents three tables away. Liking the look of the lovers, it came to them straight, showed them its sixpenny watch, made them both free of its lips and, finally, desired them to draw a castle forthwith. Lack of a pencil and paper made it impossible to comply. Madeleine pointed this out gently enough. Pharaoh-like, the child waved aside the objection, demanding a castle tearfully. The two sought to distract him for all they were worth. . . . Here the parents suspended a bubbling colloquy to look for their offspring. Madeleine and René were rescued in the nick of time. . . .

The radiant father and mother were full of apologies.

"I pray you, forgive us. We were talking, and for a moment, we forgot. It is at this age that they must be watched all the time. *When you have a fine fat boy, you will understand.*"

Hats were raised, smiles and bows were exchanged, and the incident closed.

Madeleine and René Dudoy sat ready to burst into tears.

At length—

"*Mon Dieu!*" said René hoarsely. "*Mon Dieu*, it is not to be borne! I am a man, am I not? With blood in my veins? I am not a stock or a stone. I have a heart, Madeleine, a broken heart—that cries and cries and cries. All the time we are making our small talk my heart is crying. All the time——"

"René, René," wailed Madeleine, "why do you come? Why did you come to-day? Why yesterday? Why the day before that?"

"He makes me!" cried René. "You know it. I have no choice. Besides, the hours he offers me are of pure gold. I cannot throw them away. That evening I did not come, I nearly died. I sat and drank absinthe and wept till they asked me to go. The proprietor was very kind. He understood perfectly. But it was bad for the house."

"It was very bad for you," said Madeleine gravely. "But listen, René. You are wrong. The hours my husband offers you are not of gold at all. They are of cold, sharp steel, that——"

"Gold or steel," breathed René, "I do not care. They are spent in your company. There is a fence between us, I know—a hell of a fence—but we can peer through the bars. It is permitted to touch you . . . watch your mouth move . . . hear the music of your voice—and, when you are gone to embrace a memory."

"Hush, René, hush! *Mon Dieu*, will you have me faint?"

"Madeleine, Madeleine, why did you marry Pierre? A-a-ah, I do not blame you! Do not think that. It was your own affair. Only . . . we could have been happy, I think, and . . . and I can draw quite good castles, such as that little one desired. . . ." His voice broke, and a bright tear rolled down Madeleine's cheek. She swept it away swiftly. Dudoy pulled himself together. "Bah! The milk is spilled. I watched you spill it at Ruffec that autumn day. Now, alas, you go thirsty! I feared you would. And I am thirsty too, sweet; for I would have drunk of that milk. Consider, then. Since we both thirst, it is better to share our misfortune. Besides, if the past is dead, there is always the future. The good God, perhaps, will give us another pitcher." He paused and looked down at his feet. "A steeple-jack's work," he muttered, "is very dangerous." Madeleine shivered. "One day, perhaps—perhaps this very evening—he will not come back."

The girl shook her head.

"Yes, he will," she said dully. "Pierre will never slip." She started violently. "*Mon Dieu*, what have I said? Ah, René, believe me, I have been dreaming. The heat, perhaps. . . ." She laughed hysterically. " 'The past is dead,' you were saying. 'The past is dead.' "

The man had no ears to hear. His eyes were burning with hope.

"I love you," he said uncertainly. "I love your beautiful hands. I love your soft dark hair. I cannot play with it now, because of the bars. But one day the bars will be broken, and then I shall come and fill these arms with its glory. Be sure, my heart, I shall wait and wait always . . . until the bars fall. Ah, see how the good God has given light to our darkness. He has shown us the way to go. Now, when we are together, we shall never be sad. We will remember always that we are waiting . . . just waiting . . . until the bars fall. . . ."

Head up, rigid, white-faced, Madeleine sat staring and seeing nothing. Her ears, however, were hearing perfectly. After a moment she braced herself, drawing a deep breath. Holy, fair and wise, her resolve was taken.

"I do not see," she said slowly, "that we have anything to share— you and I. A year ago, perhaps, there might have been something. But, as you said just now, the past is dead. And since we have nothing to share, René, it would be so much better if . . . if . . ."

She hesitated and passed a hand across her eyes.

René Dudoy stared.

"But what are you saying?" he cried. "You go back to where we began. We have thrashed all this out. You said our hours were not golden. I have shown you——"

"You have shown me that it is better, René, that we two should not meet any more."

"Not alone, perhaps. I think you are right, sweetheart. I will arrange that somehow. Now that we have our understanding——"

"I wish," said Madeleine steadily, "that you would leave Paris."

The other recoiled.

"What!" he screamed. "What! Leave Paris? *Mon Dieu!* This is more than I can stand." He leaned back in his chair and wiped the sweat from his face. "I think you are ill," he said. "To hear you, anyone would think that you did not care," he added desperately.

"I do not care," said Madeleine.

The young man started as though she had stabbed him with a knife. Then he went very white.

"I do not care," she repeated. "I do not want to hurt you, but you have made a mistake. Jean wrote to me, you know, and said you were very sad. He said you would not come to see me because—because you could not forget. I showed the letter to Pierre, and we agreed that we must be kind to you. We thought, perhaps, when you saw how—how happy we were, you would join in our happiness, and so become cured. Instead, you have grown worse. More—you have involved me terribly. I have tried to be kind, and you have mistaken my kindness for something else. It is really very difficult, René, but, you see, we are not at all in the same boat. I ought, of course, I see now, to have told you at once. But I didn't, I didn't want to hurt you, and—it was doing no harm. It is an awkward thing, you know, to tell any man—let alone an old friend. But now it is getting beyond . . . beyond a joke. . . ."

René winced at the word piteously. With white lips and a bleeding heart, Madeleine struggled on.

"You see, I have not told Pierre. . . . And I do not want Pierre, my husband, to make the same mistake. I do not think that he would, but you never know. And if he did, it would be very awkward for me. I do not know how I should show him that he was wrong. . . .

"And so, you see, my friend, that when I said that the hours we spend together are of sharp steel, I was perfectly right. They pierce your heart, I fear, and they—they—embarrass me. . . . Don't look like that, René! I tell you, I hoped——"

"Hope?" cried René, with a wild laugh. "Hope? I do not know what you mean. What is hope?"

Here Lacaze appeared, smiling and nodding good will.

"Did you think I was dead?" he crowed. "I think that you must have. As a matter of fact, I've never been off the ground. Notre Dame was not ready for me. Instead, to tell you the truth, I have been talking business." He jerked his head at the window directly behind them. "Sitting in there. I became so absorbed that I forgot our engagement. Then I heard your voices, you know, and that reminded me." He took his seat between them and looked benignantly round. "And now about supper. . . . I think a nice little *ragoût*, with potatoes *en robe de chambre*."

The party was not a success.

René Dudoy pleaded night-work and left at once.

As for Madeleine, she fainted before the *ragoût* was served.

All things considered, I am inclined to think that when Madame Lacaze deceived the man she loved, because he was not her husband, she made another mistake. But then I am of the earth, earthy. What cannot possibly be denied is that it was a most splendid action. 'So shines a good deed in a naughty world.' Probably the trouble was that she did not trust herself. René's desire to make the word 'wait' their watchword was dangerous, because it was sweet. It would have been the thin edge of the wedge. Madeleine was determined to play the game. It was not Lacaze she stood by, but the office he filled. It was not Dudoy she sent packing, but the devil himself. That her lover did not stand in her husband's shoes was her misfortune. As such, however, it did not affect the case. She was a good girl.

Ten days after that dreadful evening at the Café de la Forêt Noire, the War came with a crash.

The electrical atmosphere of the next three months saved Madeleine's life. No spirit, however sick, could have failed to respond to such exciting treatment.

Lacaze, the steeple-jack, the lion, welcomed the War with flashing eyes. From the moment the storm broke, his one idea was to kill. When the time came, he fought with twice the ardour with which he had reduced high places. He soon became sergeant; he was worth ten ordinary men. In all his pride, however, he never forgot how once his heels had ached. Besides, his wife's dismissal of Dudoy had made him frown....

Before he left for the battle he had arranged everything.

In reply to the questions which every soldier is asked, he stated that he was unmarried, and gave the name of Madame José Beer (*née* Tuyte) as that of his next-of-kin.

Then he visited the trull and told her her new estate.

José was flattered, but curious. Lacaze enlightened her.

"Now, if I should be killed, the news will come to you."

"I shall mourn," said José.

"As you please," said Lacaze. "But burn the paper at once and keep your mouth shut. Tell no one. You know, I fear, that Madeleine is very stuck up." He sighed. "It is no good mincing matters. Her pride has caused me much grief. You and I are not good enough. She would, I think, like to be free. If she were free...." He broke off and shrugged his shoulders. "There is a young officer somewhere. They correspond...."

"The jade!" raged José. "The jade! The graceless minx! Trust me." Her voice vibrated. "She shall never be free. Never!" Here she became maudlin. "But, Pierre dear, I shall not receive the news. It is not to be thought of..."

"Perhaps not," said Pierre shortly, taking his leave. "But remember my words. I trust you to see justice done."

"Never fear," cried José, her pig eyes gleaming....

Finally, the steeple-jack spoke with his wife.

He chose their last night together.

It was a stifling evening: such air as found its way into their apartment seemed to be stale: odours of neighbouring kitchens rose up stagnant. Out of the roar of the traffic continual cries of newsvendors stood as syrens out of a gale.

Madeleine sat by a window, sewing hard. Lacaze lounged upon a settee, smoking calmly and oiling a pair of boots.

My lady finished her stitching and cut the thread. Then she held up her work and turned it about. After a moment she rose and crossed to her husband.

"Is that what you want, Pierre? It does not look very well, but I think it will wear. If it is right, I will do the other shoulder."

Lacaze examined the shirt.

This was a cotton affair of green and grey stripes. Over one shoulder strips of fine linen had been laid, by way of a pad. These had been quilted beautifully.

"But this is charming," he said, putting his head on one side. "Ah, me, what it is to be loved! If René could only see this he would jump into the Seine. You know I shall be chaffed—devilishly. No one will ever believe that this was the work of a wife. Never mind. I am content. Now I shall be cool these hot days, yet my shoulders will not be sore." He peered at the linen. "Where did you find this stuff?"

"I cut up a chemise."

"Sweeter and sweeter," he crowed. "The soldier goes off to the war with his girl on his shoulder. My dear, you are getting quite gay. How did you think of such a charming conceit?"

"I did not," said Madeleine coldly. "I had nothing else."

"Use nothing else," said Lacaze. "But always have a new shirt—I have six—with just the same delicate straps awaiting the day I return. For I shall return, sweeting. Never fear that I shan't." His voice rang out boldly. "Never fear, madame. Nothing will happen to me. I shall always come back." He caught her arm in his hand and smiled up into her eyes. "Do you hear, my beautiful wife? Do you realize that? Poor Pierre will always return. Jean may lie out in the mud. What can be collected of Jacques may be dumped in a grave. René may writhe out his life with a bullet inside. But poor old Pierre, your husband, will always return." He let go her arm and sank back in his seat. "Now, is that not good news? That widowhood is not for you? Believe me, my dear, you are a lucky woman. . . . Of course I may not always come back to you. We poor soldiers are so easily led. . . . . But I shall not be killed. You see. And in the end you will triumph, and I—shall—come—back. . . ."

So soon as Madame Lacaze could find her voice, she asked her smiling husband what money she was to have to maintain herself and the apartment.

His reply was definite.

"The apartment is given up and the furniture sold. I have done that to-day. You will lodge with the Marats and go out to work. I have been wondering what you could do, my sweet, but you have shown me. If you sew hard, you will make quite a lot of money."

Madeleine walked to the window and picked up the remains of her chemise. The garment tugged at her thoughts. She let them go. . . .

In an instant she was at Ruffec, stepping the cool, quiet streets. There was old Monsieur Laffargue, the doctor, getting down from his gig. Now he was smiling broadly and rallying her about her cheeks. 'You must do something,' he said. She could hear his jolly old voice.

'Something. I don't know what. No one will ever believe there's no paint there.' She passed on smiling.... A voice called from a window. Madame Durand, of course, the postman's wife. 'Madeleine, Madeleine, my sister has had a son. A great fat rogue, they say, four kilos at birth. Is it not wonderful?' Madeleine rejoiced with her, and went her way. Then Père Fréchou stopped her, to give her five great peaches—two for each of her eyes and one for her pretty red lips ... She came to the Rue de l'Image, all decked with the evening sun. The awnings of the little shops made it absurdly narrow, like a toy street. And there, striding into the sunlight, came René Dudoy. His healthy young face lighted up. 'I was on my way, Madeleine, to tell you how lucky I am. The *patron* has been given the order for three mantelpieces in stone at the Château St. Pol, and I am to do the work and to put them in.' 'Oh, René, I am so glad—so awfully glad. Go on and tell Jean and Jacques. Or stay—go home and get Marie and bring her to supper with us. See what Père Fréchou has given me. Did ever you see such beauties? We'll eat them to-night in your honour. There's plenty of cream.' René's face was a picture. Madeleine passed on thoughtfully.... At the draper's she laid out her money—some thirty-two francs—not without much hesitation and plucking at stuffs. Madame Bidart was kindness itself, and made her a price. Indeed, the old lady refused to sell her the linen she chose. It was not good enough, she declared. Now this was superb—fit for a king's daughter. 'But I am not a king's daughter,' protested Madeleine, laughing. 'You are an angel from heaven,' said Madame Bidart. 'I tell you——'

"How long will you be?" said Lacaze yawning luxuriously. "I mean, it is getting late, and I must be up at five."

"A quarter of an hour," said his wife, and bent to her work.

The night was stifling.

Madeleine's younger brother was killed that fateful August. Ere September was old, Jean had been taken prisoner. Of René, no news reached her.

For the matter of that, she heard naught of Lacaze, either. He had not told her his regiment. He never wrote. The man might have been dead . . . might have. . . .

He came to see her at last, one dark December morning. . . .

When he went back, he took a shirt with him.

Twice more he came to see her, and each time took back a shirt. He swore by these garments—called them his mascots, his charms—declared he could never be killed while she sat on his shoulders. . . .

The idea stuck.

Madeleine began to believe her linen was preserving his life.

She tried to be grateful.

Two shirts remained to be strapped. Setting to work one Sunday, she found her chemise was gone. She had used all its stuff. Her impulse, of course, was to purchase a piece of fresh linen. Without a thought she would have done so, but for his idle words. As it was. . . .

The temptation was frightful.

Why should she cut up her own clothes? Besides, faith put in mascots was vain—heathenish. What could they profit a man? Supposing they could. . . . Supposing there was some curious guardian virtue in linen she wore. . . . Well, *what—if—there—was?*

She thrust the shirt away and went for a walk.

The next morning she bought some new linen. . . .

She came back from Mass a week later and cut up another chemise.

The third winter of the War stole upon a frantic world, stumbling and striking. Lacaze did not come. He had not returned since April—April of 1916. Madeleine began to wonder . . . wonder why he did not appear.

When the New Year was in, she went to the War Office.

She did not get far.

"You are his wife?" said the clerk.

"Yes."

"What is his regiment?"

"I do not know. He has never told me."

"Show me a letter of his."

"I have none. He never writes."

"Nor you to him?"

"Never. He was sergeant, I think."

Two shoulders were shrugged.

"So are many. You are sure you are married?"

"Of course."

"Well, then, Madame, he is safe. No news is good news. You would have heard, certainly. There is no doubt about it. Calm yourself, Madame. He will come back."

But Lacaze did not come.

Again, in June, she went to the War Office.

She saw the same clerk. He asked the same questions, shrugged the same shoulders, gave her the same reply. . . .

That Autumn her orders fell off. People, I suppose, were beginning to sew for themselves. Madeleine could hardly find work for two days a week. The Marats—the people she lodged with—saw what was coming, and, meeting her trouble half-way, diverted it from their path. In a word, they gave her notice. This, thanks to their foresight, they were able to do without any compunction at all. It would not have been nice to turn out a soldier's wife—possibly 'relict'—because she could not pay her way. As it was, they could look the world in the face. They did so defiantly. They also cancelled, with sighs, their subscription to an orphanage on the ground that they had lost a valuable paying guest. . . . .

Madeleine entered the service of an English officer's wife.

Early in 1918 she received a letter from Jean.

DEAREST MADELEINE,

> *I have come back alive out of death. I have been a prisoner, you know, for nearly four years. Now I have been exchanged—because I am useless to France. I am rather run down, you see, and my right arm is gone. But take heart, dearest. I can do nothing just yet, and the Army has sent me home, but old Monsieur Laffargue says I shall be as strong as ever in ten or twelve months. I am with the Dudoys. René has been back some time. Do you know he is blind?..*

Blind....

Those gentle grey eyes sightless.... Those strong brown fingers picking and feeling their way....

Madeleine was at the War Office within the half-hour.

The clerk she had seen was gone, and another attended to her case. This was a kindly fellow, who had dried many eyes.

He heard her out gravely. Then—

"Madame, be happy. Absolutely your husband is safe. Take it from me. He has not even a scratch. Always the wife hears at once. That he has not been to see you is easily explained. Ten to one he is in the East—Salonica, making fat Bulgars perspire. He wrote and told you, of course, but the letter was sunk. These Germans! Madame, believe and be happy. Your husband is safe. I tell you he will come back."

Madeleine stole out of the building as she would have stolen out of a dock. She had committed a crime, and had been given judgment.

She would have given anything to go to Ruffec ... anything—except the one thing she had. This was her self-respect. If she went to Ruffec, if once she saw those strong brown fingers groping their pitiful way, the flesh might spoil the spirit of its only hoard. And that meant poverty she could not face. She was a good girl.

Eighteen months had gone by, when Lady Joan Satinwood told her French maid that it was her determined intention to winter in France.

"We shall go down by car, Madeleine—the Major and I, and you and the chauffeur. It'll be great fun, and I expect you'll be thrilled to see your country again."

"Yes, madame."

"I suppose you've—you've no news?"

"Of my husband? No, madame."

"I'm sorry. But don't despair. Remember my cousin, Sir George. And he was reported 'killed.' Two and a half years afterwards, Madeleine, he came walking in...."

"Yes, madame."

When Madeleine learned in mid-Channel, some three weeks later, that they were to go by Poitiers she felt very faint....

Poitiers lies north of Ruffec, just forty-one miles.

"*Et de Poitiers?* .... After we 'ave lef' Poitiers? ..."

"Angoulême," said the chauffeur, thumbing his itinerary. "That's right. Vivonne, Chaunay, Ruffec, Angoulême. Sleep Angoulême. Nex' day—Barbézieux, Bordeaux. Sleep Bor—— 'Elp!"

He dropped his paper and caught his companion as she swayed. Then he carried her into the saloon and sought for a stewardess....

Later that day he recounted his experience to a friend.

"I arst 'er if she was a good sailor, too," he concluded aggrievedly.

Four days later, as they were entering Poitiers, a brake-rod snapped. No resultant damage was done, but the car was stopped at a garage that Terry—the chauffeur—might see if an adjustment could be made. By good fortune, it could.

The car was backed over a pit, and Terry got out of his coat and into his overalls. He was a good chauffeur. Where his car was concerned, he fancied his own fingers more than a hireling's.

The Major got out and went strolling. Lady Joan stayed in the car. Madeleine stood in the garage, translating for Terry.

Half an hour's work, and the connection was made.

Terry heaved himself out of the pit and called for waste.

The mechanics stared.

"Cotton waste," said the chauffeur. "Comprenny? Pour wiper the hands."

Madeleine smiled and asked for a rag.

A mechanic went shuffling. A moment later he returned with a rectangular cardboard box.

"*Voilà*," he said.

"Wot's this?" said Terry, staring. "Dog biscuits?"

The mechanic pointed to the label.

Essuyages Aseptisés

"We use nothing else," he explained. "They are all manner of rags, quite clean and sterilized. This boxful will last a long time."

The chauffeur asked the price, ripped open the box, and pulled out the first piece of stuff. Madeleine took the box from him and stowed it away in the car.

When she returned, Terry had wiped his hands and was looking curiously at his duster.

"'Ere's a present from Flanders all right," he said slowly. "See? That's where some pore bloke stopped one."

Madeleine peered at the stuff.

This was the left breast of what had been a man's shirt. Immediately over the heart there was a rough hole. The cotton thereabouts was all stained to a dull brown, so that the green and grey stripes were indistinguishable. The shoulder was gone, but hanging from the top of the fragment was a strip of quilted linen.

Let me quote from Lady Joan's letter, dated some five days later and written from St. Jean-de-Luz.

. . . I saw the shirt myself. It was a terrible document. Poor girl! The shock was frightful. As luck would have it, the very next town on our route—a place called Ruffec—was her old home. Her brother was there. We found him and handed her over. Whether she'll ever come back to me, I haven't the faintest idea. . . .

Again let me quote from a letter her ladyship wrote when two months had gone by.

P.S.—You remember Madeleine? I've just had a note from her saying she's married again! No wonder France is recovering more quickly than England. Most English girls would still be upon slops. However, that's her affair. But isn't it just my luck? She was a perfect maid.

Which was a true saying.

Two years later Lacaze alighted at Ruffec from the Paris train.

The man was changed terribly. Five years in the German mines had left their mark. He had been broken down.

His hair was grisled, his broad, square shoulders were bowed, his carriage mean. None would have known the shrunken shambling figure for that of the mighty steeple-jack. His countenance, however, was unmistakable. This was ravaged, too, but the old faint smile still hung about those merciless lips, and the old insolent scorn still smouldered in the big black eyes.

Lacaze pulled his hat over his face and stood waiting till such travellers as had also alighted should have left the platform.

A horn brayed, and the train began to move.

"Good bye!" cried a voice. "Good-bye! If you see René Dudoy, ask him if he remembers Fernand Didier, and say I was sorry I had no time to visit him. Good-bye!"

The train gathered speed and rumbled out of the station.

Lacaze moved towards the gates thoughtfully.

Half an hour later he darkened the creamery's hatch.

René looked up from his work. He was making a basket.

"Enter, monsieur," he said. "And sit down, please. My wife will be back in a moment, and then she will serve you."

Slowly Lacaze came in, looking down on the ground.

"You are married, then?" he said quietly.

The other stared.

"Yes," he said, "monsieur. Why not?"

"No reason at all," said Lacaze, smiling. "And how is your wife?"

René returned to his work.

"She is very well, thank you."

"I am glad of that," said Lacaze. "Very glad."

René Dudoy looked up.

"Monsieur's interest is unusually kind. Would it be indiscreet to ask why?"

Lacaze gave a short laugh.

"I know her," he said. "She was a friend of mine. But I thought that she married Lacaze—Lacaze, the steeple-jack."

"She did," said Dudoy. "But he was killed in the War. And, after, she married me. But, monsieur, tell me your name. If you are a friend of hers, you must have been mine also."

"I was," said Lacaze softly, his chin on his chest. "I knew you well." The other set down his basket and rose to his feet. "We were both at her wedding. You sent her roses, I think. And I sent her—violets."

"Not violets," said René. "You must have sent something else. You forget. Lacaze sent her violets."

In a flash Lacaze had stepped forward and pulled off his hat.

"Your servant," he breathed, smiling.

Dudoy wrinkled his brow.

"I cannot think who you are," he said. "Do tell me your name." The other's smile faded into a stare. "There are times, you know, when one misses one's sight terribly." Lacaze started. "When Madeleine's here, I can see. We share her beautiful eyes." He threw back his curly head. "Then, if you offered me sight, I would not take it. My blindness is a bond between us which those who have eyes of their own can never know. But—when she leaves me, then sometimes the old darkness returns—that awful darkness which, when she came to me, Madeleine did away ... And now, I pray you, monsieur, tell me your name."

Lacaze turned his head and stared into the sunlit street.

Then—

"I am Fernand Didier," he said. "And—and I must go, or I shall miss my train."

He pulled his hat over his eyes and blundered out of the shop.

René cried to him to stay.

"Fernand! Fernand!"

Lacaze took no notice.

Ten minutes later he was clear of the town.

KATHARINE

DREAMILY, MRS. FESTIVAL regarded the ceiling.

"I frequently wonder," she said, "what possessed me to marry you."

"My beauty of soul," said her husband pleasantly. "You were all dazzled."

"I think," continued his wife, "it was out of pity. You know. When you see people laughing at someone, and the someone joins in, never dreaming that they're the object of the mirth, one feels sorry for them."

Captain Giles Festival swallowed before replying.

Then—

"I know," he said. "Like when we were dining with the Mascots, and you kept talking about soap."

Katharine Festival flushed.

The reminiscence was not one which she cherished.

Lady Mascot's father and soft soap had been mutually constructive.

At length—

"I might have known," she observed, "that you wouldn't appreciate it. Gratitude is not among your attributes."

"If you mean," said Giles, "that I don't feel impelled to fall down and worship you for taking my name—in vain, you're perfectly right. I gave you a blinkin' good chance, and you blinkin' well took it."

Katharine drew in her breath.

"Do you imagine," she demanded, "that the chance you were kind enough to give me was the only chance I had?"

"If," said her husband, "I imagined anything, I should imagine you considered it the best. If one can only have one strawberry, one doesn't deliberately take a bad one, does one? Not even out of pity?"

"No," said Katharine sweetly. "Only by mistake."

There was a pregnant silence.

Then—

"Sold," murmured Giles, "the very deuce of a pup—by Mistake, out of Pity. No flowers, by request."

"Let me at once admit," said Katharine coldly, "that I did not select you for your good taste."

"'Select'?" cried her husband. "'Select'?" He laughed wildly. Then he covered his eyes. "Oh, give me strength."

"I suppose you consider that you selected me."

"I did. In a weak moment——"

"Are you," said Katharine shakily, "are you going to say you were blind?"

"I am not," said Giles. "I was not blind. I was—well—er—just nicely."

"Well, I wasn't," said his wife hotly. "I was blind. I thought I was accepting a gentleman. I find I accepted a——"

"I know," said Giles mercilessly. "I know, teacher. A foul and loathsome worm."

"No," said his wife calmly. "Just an ordinary cad."

Captain Festival rubbed his nose thoughtfully. Then he extended his arms and, after yawning luxuriously, interlaced his fingers and placed his hands behind his head.

"My dear," he observed, "be reasonable." Katharine closed her eyes with an expression of unutterable contempt. "All this, just because I ventured to suggest that, if Beatrice had time to do it, she might take charge of my linen."

"Have you ever heard of meiosis?" said Mrs. Festival. "It means the opposite of exaggeration."

"I repeat," said Giles, "that that was the humble suggestion at which you took offence. I mayn't have put it in those words, but——"

"You didn't," said Katharine. "You put it much more vividly. You said that the condition of your wardrobe was enough to make a beachcomber burst into tears——"

"So it is."

"—and that, if I hadn't got the moral courage to order 'a lazy sweep of a lady's maid to pull up her rotten socks,' I could 'blinkin' well finance her' myself. You added that you'd given up a valet, so that I could have more money 'to blow upon my back,' and that my interpretation of my marriage vows was funny without being vulgar."

Her husband swallowed.

"I was referring," he said doggedly, "to your promise to cherish me."

"You promised the same."

"Yes, but I keep it, Kate. I do cherish you. I'm always cherishing you. Only yesterday afternoon—seventeen blinkin' quid for a hat worth eighteen pence . . . and not a murmur."

Katharine inspired audibly, raising her eyes to heaven.

"When," she rejoined, "when you start recounting your virtues, I want to break something. Doesn't it ever occur to you that that's my job?"

"Frequently," said Giles. "But you never do it."

"You never give me a chance."

With a supreme effort her husband controlled his voice.

"Look here," he said fiercely. "Do you think it was—er—decent of me to give you that hat, or not?"

"Oh, you can have the beastly hat," said Katharine.

"Wouldn't suit me," said Giles mournfully. "Do you think——"

"I'll never wear it," declared his wife. "Never. I—I hate it."

"Well, let's take it back. They might allow us eighteen——"

"And why should I be overcome with gratitude just because——"

"The golden rule of blessed argument," said Captain Festival uncertainly, "is to keep to the blessed point. Let's try, will you? ... No answer. I referred to my short-sighted generosity solely to refute your suggestion that I was failing to cherish you. You deliberately pervert the reference into an attempt to magnify myself. What could be better?"

"Oh, that's easy," said Katharine. "You could get up half an hour earlier and put your rotten things in order yourself."

"On the *lucus a non lucendo* principle? If you want your cake, pay someone else to eat it, and then give it away? Thanks very much. Unhappily, my education was neglected. I cannot sew. Secondly, if it's either of our jobs, it's yours. Thirdly, why should I? If this house was more like a home and less like an Employment Exchange, these questions wouldn't arise. Fourthly, I'm fed up."

"How funny," said Katharine silkily. "So'm I. Yet you slept well. I heard you."

In majestic silence her husband rose from his bed and entered an orange-coloured dressing-gown.

"Have my bed put in the next room, will you?" he said coldly. "If you don't like to trouble the servants, tell me and I'll get the commissionaire from the Club."

Here he trod upon a collar-stud, screamed, swore, limped to a window and then launched the offender into Berkeley Square.

"That'll learn it," observed Mrs. Festival.

Giles regarded her with speechless indignation.

Then he swept into the bathroom stormily.

After, perhaps, five minutes he reappeared.

"I say," he said quietly, "it isn't much good going on like this, is it?"

Katharine shrugged her white shoulders.

"Is it?" repeated her husband.

His wife averted her head.

"The blessed answer," she said, "is in the blessed negative."

Giles set his teeth.

"Good. Well, let's separate. I take it you've tried. I know I have. I suppose we oughtn't to have married."

"As—as you please," said Katharine slowly.

"We'd better go down and see Forsyth—to-day, if we can." He hesitated. Then, "There's no reason why there should be any unpleasantness about it."

"None whatever."

"Only, don't let's be lured into backing out of it. It's perfectly manifest, to my mind, that it's the only thing to do. Already we've come to the brink of it half a dozen times, and then Sentiment's always chipped in and pulled us back." Katharine nodded. "Well, that's silly. We needn't scrap, but *don't let's be pulled back again*. It's—it's not good enough. Let's go through with it, this time, and—and see what happens."

"Right," said Katharine brightly.

Giles turned away slowly.

In the doorway he hesitated.

Then he spoke, looking down.

"You—you see what I mean?" he faltered. "I'd like us to—to part friends."

Katharine nodded.

When he was out of sight, she buried her face in her pillow and lay like the dead.

If the votes of Mayfair had been taken to elect the most popular married couple living, moving and having its being in Society, there is little doubt that Captain and Mrs. Giles Festival would have headed the poll.

The lady was twenty-five and of great beauty. She was very fair, and the light in her grave, blue eyes was a lovely thing. Her face might have been her fortune—easily. So might her figure. This was the dressmakers' joy. If Katharine liked fine feathers, she knew how to put them on. Dancing, bathing, riding—always she filled the eye. But if she was refreshing to look at, her fellowship lifted up the heart. I can think of no company which she did not adorn. Someone once called her 'Champagne': certainly she went to the head. That she had so few enemies is the best evidence of her remarkable charm. Women liked her—as often as not against their will. Her nature would, I think, have disarmed a Sycorax. Caliban would certainly have eaten out of her hand.

Giles was thirty, and looked a young twenty-six. Tall, fair, handsome, lazy-eyed, he did everything well. The way in which he made war brought him a V.C. The way in which he made love won him his wife. At the Marlborough he was universally liked. In certain cabmen's shelters he was adored. He had, I suppose, the secret of adaptability. His laugh was infectious; his turn-out, above reproach. His manners would have made any man.

Both had a keen sense of humour, and neither was ever dull. They went everywhere, and everywhere their coming was awaited and their going deplored. They had been individually invaluable: as a combination they were unique. What made them so excellent was their mutual devotion. Of this they offered no evidence, but it was obvious as the day. Had Society paraded in the Park, by common consent Giles and Katharine would have been led at the head of the column, like regimental goats. For the second year in succession they were the Season's pets.

But now an east wind had arisen out of a clear sky. Though no one else knew it, it had cursed the twain steadily for more than three months. The two peace-loving hearts found themselves constantly at war. Worse. The very qualities which should have pacified seemed monstrously to provoke. The position had become unbearable.

An hour had gone by.

As Katharine entered the dining-room, her husband looked up from his eggs.

"Forsyth," he said, "will see us at twelve o'clock. Meanwhile"—he tapped a volume—"this little Know All says that we ought to have trustees."

"What of?" said his wife.

"Heaven knows," said Giles. "As far as I can gather, they'ld be a sort of bufferee. Supposing you wanted to come and scratch me—well, you'ld have to scratch the trustee first. And if I found you were pledging my credit——"

"But I shall," said Katharine. "Why shouldn't I? I'm your wife."

"Only for necessaries, dear heart. No more eighteen-penny hats."

"Is that the law?" said Mrs. Festival blankly.

"Approximately. But don't worry. You'll have plenty to pay for them with. I can't endow you with all my worldly goods, but you shall have a fair two-thirds."

"Half," said Katharine, crossing to the sideboard. "Fair do's, old fellow. And you must have half mine."

Captain Festival frowned.

"My dear," he said shortly, "don't dither. I buy a dress-suit a year and don't pay for it. If I did, it'ld be about a pony." He paused significantly. "If an eighteen-penny hat and a half costs the same as a gent's dress-suit, how many evening frocks go to the Season?"

Abstractedly Katharine helped herself to kedjeree.

As she returned to the table—

"I don't care," she said slowly; "I won't take more than my share. What shall we do about the house?"

"Well, if you don't mind," said Giles, "you'd better stay on. It'll save a lot of trouble. If you don't—I can't very well live here, and the house'ld be going spare. That means we'ld have to let, which'ld send us both mad. The rooms'ld have to be done up, we should be done down, our effects would be done in and our finer feelings would be outraged. The idea of some sticky stranger wallowing in our private bathroom sends the blood to my head."

Mrs. Festival shuddered.

Then—

"But what will you do, Gill? Of course, I should pay you a rent. The house and furniture's yours, and——"

"I shall live at the Club. As to rent—considering that you'll be better than any caretaker, I shall be up on the deal."

Katharine digested this.

"I could only consent," she said, "on the understanding that, if ever you changed your mind, you let me know. And, of course, you'ld keep a key and use it whenever you liked."

"My darling," said Giles, rising, "I look forward to dining at this table at least once a week. Of course, I shan't come unasked. That would be molestation. Your trustee would be most rude. But if I behave myself. . . . Possibly, some afternoon when you were out, you might arrange for me to have a bath here. On my birthday, for instance. It'ld tickle me to death."

Katharine flung him a bewitching smile.

"If," she said, "you don't tell anyone, you shall use my sponge."

"Kate," said her husband, "I perceive that we are off. This separation stunt is going to work wonders."

He was perfectly right.

Galbraith Forsyth, solicitor, was an honest man. Also he knew his world and could tell the sheep from the goats. He could be stern, and he could be most gentle. To those whom he trusted, who trusted him, he gave a service which money cannot buy. His judgment alone was invaluable. The sheep liked him, immensely. The goats hated him. But both respected him with a whole heart. If he had any pet lambs, the Festivals were among them.

He received the two pleasedly, bade them sit down, and drew the lady's attention to a bunch of daffodils.

"Posies are seldom seen in Lincoln's Inn Fields. But when I knew you were coming, I felt that something must be done. I didn't want you to feel lonely."

"Now, isn't that charming?" said Giles. "If I could say things like that, we shouldn't be here to-day."

Forsyth looked at him sharply.

"You see, Mr. Forsyth," said Katharine, "we've made a hopeless mistake. We thought we'd be happy, though married: and we were wrong. We can't hit it off. We've tried like blazes, but it's not the slightest good. In fact, the only thing we've agreed about for something like three months is that the sooner we part, the better for Giles and me."

"D'you mean this?" said Forsyth. "Or are you—er—pulling my leg?"

"We mean it all right," said Giles. "It sounds like a comic dream, but it's the grisly truth. For no apparent reason, Katharine annoys me. For no apparent reason, I get her goat. If we started to discuss those flowerlets, in five minutes we should be slinging books at each other. She's witty, you know, and I'm a bit of a wag. We've always fenced, for fun—always. But now we can't stop, and—the buttons are off the foils."

"He's perfectly right," said Katharine. "I'm ashamed to say it, but we lead a cat and dog life. And now we're both agreed that it isn't good enough. Don't suggest change, because we've tried that. He went away for a week. The night he came back I threw a glass at him."

"An empty one," said Giles. "Missed me by yards. But it's the—the principle."

"Exactly," said Katharine. "Besides, the glass was a good one, and now it leaks."

Forsyth, who felt the sting beneath the banter, was genuinely dismayed.

He smiled politely.

"It seems a pity," he said. "When I say that, I'm putting it very low. A pity. You mustn't be impatient, because, though I'm the keeper of your legal conscience, at heart I'm an ordinary man—with eyes in his head. I think you're playing with fire. Life's very uncertain, you know. If anything happened after you'd gone apart—the other would grieve, I'm afraid . . . have something to remember they'd give a lot to forget . . . grudge the bit of their life they'd deliberately sworn away. . . . One never thinks of Remorse, until it touches you on the shoulder. I don't suppose I should, only I've seen it . . . at work."

There was a long silence.

Then—

"Thank you," said Giles quietly. "Now, whatever else we regret, we shall never regret having come to see you this morning." He paused. "Setting aside Sentiment, the answer is this. We should like to be able to forget the last three months. As we can't, we think it better to prevent their becoming six."

Forsyth inclined his head.

"Very good. Am I to draw up a deed? A deed of separation?"

"Please."

"What about trustees?"

"Are they a necessary evil? We don't mind you. In fact, you come under godsends. But the idea of inducting others into our private confessional is peculiarly repugnant."

"It's worse than that," said Katharine. "We three are familiar. If I think Mr. Forsyth a brute, I can ring up and tell him so. I couldn't do that to a trustee. In fact, the whole arrangement would become stiff, reinforced—like putting bones in a belt."

"You couldn't, for instance," said her husband, "employ that simile. For your information, Forsyth, that's not a proverb. Below the surface female woman wears a sort of comic cummerbund, four sizes too small. The idea is to displace the vitals. If she wants to shorten her life, she lines it with strips of whalebone, running the wrong way. Thus with the minimum of motion she gets the maximum of pain."

"That," said Forsyth uncertainly, "is not admittedly the function of trustees. Still, there are times when they are inconvenient. They certainly tend to cramp the style. Nevertheless . . . I'll tell you what," he added suddenly. "If you like, I'll be your trustee."

The two raised their eyes to heaven ecstatically.

"A little more," said Katharine, "and you shall use our bathroom."

"That," explained Giles, "is a kind of Garter—the highest honour it's in our power to bestow."

Forsyth picked up a pen.

"Tell me," he said, "what sort of an arrangement you want."

"Well, we're going shares," said Giles. "Once a month, I'll send her two-thirds of all the dividends and rents I've had."

"Of course it's grotesque," said Katharine, "but I'll do the same."

"Yes? What about the house?"

"She's going to caretake for me, and keep the servants on. I shall pay half her expenses."

"Oh, rot!" said Mrs. Festival.

"My dear," said Giles, "the bed of my mind is made up. Don't rumple it."

"I think that's fair," said Forsyth, wondering what the Law Society would say. "Next?"

"He'll take the Rolls," said Katharine, "and I'll have the coupé."

Giles hesitated.

"I had thought——" he began.

"Don't be Quixotic," said his wife. "You worship that car. Last time I drove her, you said——"

"Not before the child," said Giles. "I withdraw. Besides, I never meant it. I was all worked up, I was. You worked me."

"That all?" said Forsyth hastily.

"Well, I shall take my sponge," said Giles. "She's very kindly promised to let me use hers, if—er . . ."

By a superhuman effort Forsyth maintained his gravity.

"That sort of thing's understood," he said shortly. "I'll put in the usual covenants not to molest, pledge credit—er—er—etc., and myself as trustee. I suppose you want it at once?"

"As soon as you can," said Giles. "If we could have it to-night, we could go over it together, sign it, and I could push off to-morrow morning."

"I'll try. When you've signed it, return it to me. I'll send you copies to keep in a day or two's time. By the way, what's your address?" Captain Festival mentioned a club. "Right." The lawyer rose to his feet and preceded the two to the door. "I'm sorry, you know, but I'm glad you came to me. Come again whenever you please. I'll show no fear nor favour—I promise you that. Let three be company, even if two's none."

They shook hands silently.

By one consent, Captain and Mrs. Festival drove straight to Bond Street and selected a gold cigarette-case. This was presently engraved and then delivered to an address in Lincoln's Inn Fields.

The inscription was simple.

G

.

G.K.F

.

F

<hr size=20 width="30%" align=center>

The news of the separation spread slowly.

This was because it was wholly disbelieved. Everyone immediately assumed that Giles and Katharine Festival were being humorous.

The former was lectured upon 'cruelty' at the Club.

The latter was mocked over the telephone.

"Is that you, Katharine? ... I say, how many 'l's' are there in 'alimony'? ... What? ... Oh, but how sweet! ... Never mind. Put a fiver on Decree Nisi for luck. ..."

It was intolerable.

On the third day Katharine left Town—destination unknown.

On the fourth day Giles fled to Evian, leaving a note for his wife, to be delivered after he had gone.

On the fifth day they met on the shore of the lake of Geneva.

"Hullo, Gill," said Katharine. "How on earth did you know?"

"Know?" faltered Giles. "Go—go away. This is molestation."

"It looks rather like it," said Mrs. Festival. "Still, if you've got some possible cigarettes, I'll let that go. Oh, and you might take that, will you?" She gave him a letter bearing his name and address. "It'll save my posting it."

It seemed ridiculous not to dine together. ...

On the eighth day the papers announced:—

Captain and Mrs. Giles Festival have arrived at Evian-les-Bains.

This was misleading.

By the time the paragraph appeared, Giles was in Scotland. ...

For the time, however, the *suggestio falsi* effectually throttled any inkling of the truth.

Indeed, it was not until the end of May that people began to appreciate that what they had regarded as a fiction was a stubborn *fait accompli*.

That such an estrangement should create a profound sensation was natural enough. People could hardly believe their eyes or ears. Friends and acquaintances stared at the astounding truth, like stuck pigs. The projected divorce of an archbishop would not have occasioned one quarter of such amazement.

Again, it was natural enough that, having recovered her breath, Mayfair should prepare to let out a perfect squeal of dismay. Her sparrow was dead. The bear was robbed of its whelps.

The bellow, however, died on Society's lips.

Having rammed home the punch, Giles and Katharine proceeded to apply the healing balm.

In the first place, the linen they were washing in public was spotlessly clean. Secondly, the two laundered comfortably, without the slightest embarrassment. Thirdly, their cheerful disregard of the traditions of Separation turned the tragedy into *opéra bouffe*.

The general feeling of disappointment was still-born, to be immediately succeeded by a sense of bewildered relief.

Captain and Mrs. Festival became more popular than ever.

Isolated efforts to brand them died an inglorious death.

Mrs. Soulsden Clutch, who faithfully attended Divine Service at St. Paul's, Knightsbridge, and had nagged and bullied her husband into another world, announced that words failed her, and then spoke long and authoritatively upon the advertisement of indecency and of contempt for marriage vows.

Mrs. Busby Shawl, surnamed 'The Comforter,' went further and cut the two in the Park, afterwards broadcasting her achievement with the innocent air of one who, blinded with integrity, has shamed the Devil and is now uncertain whether it was a Christian thing to do.

But the findings of such censors of morality were coldly received: and, after exchanging malice for the inside of a week, the latter reviled one another and elbowed and fought their way into what they had lately described as 'the House of Rimmon.'

The fun became fast and furious.

Joint invitations which had been jointly declined were re-issued severally and severally accepted. Invitations which had not been sent were hastily extended. The dates of parties, dances, week-ends became actually contingent upon the Festivals' ability to attend.

The pets had become lion-cubs.

Katharine gave a dance.

Giles was invited, and gave a dinner beforehand, taking his guests on. He danced twice with his hostess, enjoyed champagne he had chosen, sat out in his own library.

Giles gave a luncheon, inviting eleven guests. Of these his wife made one, and, taking her proper precedence, sat on her husband's left. Afterwards, the Rolls being there, he dropped her at Sloane Street and was deliciously thanked.

That night they met at a ball in Belgrave Square, and the next week-end in Hampshire, as two of the Pleydells' guests.

On five days out of seven they junketed side by side.

On Derby Day they went to the Daneboroughs' dance—a brilliant affair, which blazed till nearly five on the following day. Its remembrance was slightly marred by Mrs. Festival's omission to take her latchkey and subsequent inability to 'make her servants hear.' Necessity knows no law. Giles, who had left early, was roused from a refreshing slumber by the night-porter of his Club and apprised of the facts. . . . There was only one thing to be done. He did it gallantly, with a suit over his pyjamas and pumps on his naked feet. The aggravated assault which he presently committed upon his own front door was audibly condemned by several infuriated residents in Berkeley Square. His butler, who had just got to sleep again, also condemned it with great savagery, but, after hoping against hope that the reinforcement his mistress had unearthed would also lose heart, himself at last succumbed to Captain Festival's importunity. . . . His work over, the latter returned to his Club, wondering whether he could with decency suggest that a duplicate latchkey should be kept at the nearest police station. He need not have troubled his head. The following day, a gong the size of a soup-plate was installed beneath the butler's bedstead. Upon observing its dimensions, the butler was greatly moved, but, while declaring in the servants' hall that Katharine was no lady, he was forced to admit to himself that his mistress was no fool.

Out of the flood of their engagements, the two were careful to save one evening a week, upon which they dined together at their own house. Afterwards they sat in the library until eleven o'clock. Then Giles would get up, and Katharine come to the door to see him out. Arrived at the threshold, her husband would kiss her fingers.

"Good night, sweetheart. Sleep well."

And the lady would answer gravely—

"Till next week, Gill. Good-bye."

One Thursday, half-way through June, such a meeting took place.

When coffee had been served, and the two were left to themselves,

"My dear," observed Giles, "let me thank you for a most toothsome repast."

"It isn't my fault," said his wife. "'Better is a dinner of herbs where love is.'"

"Oh, 'Cries of "Shame,"'" said Giles. "'Cries of "Shame" and "Withdraw."' 'Dinner of herbs'! Why, each of those tournedos was a stalled ox in itself. And no hatred, neither. That sole, too!" He sighed memorially, raising thankful eyes. "You know, we've beaten the sword into a fish-slice and the proverb into a cocked hat. Seriously, Kate, we've shown considerable skill."

"In reverting to the rank of private?"

Giles nodded.

"After being temporarily attached."

His wife regarded the tip of her cigarette.

"Ducks take to water," she said.

"And men take to drink," said Giles, "if they happen to be born thirsty. The point is——"

"Have another glass of port," said Katharine.

"No, thanks," said Giles. "Not that it isn't excellent. It's—it's not of this world. Uncle Fulke left it me. But let that pass. The point is, you and I are naturally gregarious. Our instinct is to flock. I like someone to talk to while I'm getting up. You like someone to obstruct while dressing for dinner. Don't think I'm being rude. The way in which you used to call me to give you your towel, is among my most treasured memories. Now, the curse of solitude has fallen upon our toilets." He spread out eloquent hands. "Yet, our personalities survive. The first two or three days, while shaving, the bath seemed a bit empty, but——"

"They do more than survive," said Katharine, tilting an exquisite chin. "To judge from the quantity and quality of our invitations, we cut more ice than before. In fact, Fate's been properly stung. By rights, we ought to be outcastes. As it is . . ."

She let the sentence go and inhaled luxuriously.

"Exactly," said Giles. "It's because we sink our feelings. Instead of bleating——"

"Are you sure we're gregarious?" said Katharine.

"Of course we are," said Giles. "We bleated because we were alone. We heard each other bleating, and—and forgathered. We were lonely, and hated the state. We were and are gregarious. I repeat that the way in which we have harked back to celibacy does us infinite credit."

"Honour to whom honour is due," said Mrs. Festival. "I'm not gregarious. I thought I was. I thought I would like a confidant—someone to cry my thoughts to without having to think what I said, someone who'd give me my towel and—and generally understand."

"In fact, a blinkin' soul-mate?"

"And towel-horse combined. Exactly. Well, *I was wrong.*"

"But you bleated," protested Giles. "I heard you. You advertised for a soul-mate, and I applied for the place. A waster by nature, I presently let you down, but that's irrelevant."

"It's also untrue," said his wife. "And you know it. You never let anyone down. Never mind. Gill, I'm afraid I married in much the same frame of mind as I try a new scent." The other started. "I've always used *Baladeuse*, and always shall. But now and again I go mad and waste your substance on a bottle of something else. Then, when I've used it twice, I give it to Beatrice."

Considerably taken by surprise, her husband regarded his ash-tray with an offensive stare. Presently he sighed.

"At least," he murmured, "I escaped that odious depository...." Katharine began to shake with laughter. "I see. Not to put too fine an edge upon it, you married out of pure curiosity. In a mad moment you ventured out of spinsterhood just to see what coverture was like. And I was under the impression that—— Never mind. It's a pretty simile. Perfume. I suppose I was a sixpenny flask of *'Ard an' Bright*.... Oh, *très intéressant*." Releasing the ash-tray, he shifted his gaze to the ceiling and, drawing at his cigarette, meditatively expelled the smoke. "Supposing," he added slowly, "supposing—to preserve the parable—you had another—er—*lapsus cordis* . . . got momentarily sick of *Baladeuse* and, forgetful of jolly old *'Ard an' Bright*, felt impelled to try *What are the Wild Oats Saying*, or some other frankincense?"

Katharine shot her husband a lightning glance.

Then she raised her sweet eyebrows.

"And you?" she said. "Supposing you hear someone bleating . . . and . . . and the flocking instinct once more asserts itself?"

Deliberately, Giles extinguished his cigarette.

"I shall put up a fight," he said coolly, "the deuce of a fight. I shall stick in my elegant toes and put up a fight."

Katharine leaned forward.

"And I," she said slowly, with a dazzling smile, "shall do precisely the same."

For a moment the two looked into each other's eyes.

Then—

"I—I hope you'll win," said Giles uneasily. "I mean—I should like to think that *'Ard an' Bright* was the only serious rival *Baladeuse* ever had. Besides . . . I'm sure *I* shall win," he added confidently. "You can bet your little boots about that. You know. The patent-leather ones I used to pull off after breakfast."

Katharine rose to her feet.

"I'm going," she said, "to the library. Remember me to the port and then follow me in." Her husband stepped to the door and held it open. As she was passing, she stopped and laid a hand upon his arm. "Promise me one thing, Gill."

"Of course," said Giles gallantly.

"Listen. If ever you hear someone bleat, don't come and dine here with me until—until the fight's over."

Her husband drew himself up.

"My darling," he said, "I give you my precious word." He hesitated. "And—and you'd put me off, wouldn't you, if—if anything looked like displacing *Baladeuse*?"

Katharine nodded.

Five crowded weeks had slipped by.

The Courts were over: Ascot had come and gone: another shining Henley had floated into the past.

People were beginning to collect their wraps. The carnival was nearly done.

Of late, the Festivals had not met nearly so much.

The reason for this is illuminating.

Each was declining a number of invitations.

Since, however, they never discussed their engagements, Katharine imagined that Giles was still 'going strong,' while the latter, lying wakeful in bed, pictured his wife dancing night after night into the dawn.

Fantasy did not stop there.

They had made two of the house-party gathered at Castle Charing a fortnight before. The weather had been inviting, and Katharine and Pat Lafone had been inseparable. When they were not playing golf, they were out in the car. On two out of three evenings they had been badly late for dinner, arriving at the table breathless and simultaneously. And Pat was twenty-seven and full of life. He was also most attractive in looks and deeds. . . . Then the party had dispersed, and two days later Giles had passed the pair, riding together in the Row. . . . His wife had waved, and Pat had shouted joyfully, but Festival had winced.

There is an old superiority of horse over foot which, other things being equal, may make itself felt. It is, I suppose, traditional. The knight went mounted. It may, of course, be merely a matter of inches. The ability of the equestrian to look down upon such as go walking is not to be denied. His is a commanding position—of which the pedestrian may be ridiculously conscious.

Wishing very much that he had been riding, Giles told himself not to be a fool and, on reaching the Club, rang up Madrigal Chicele and asked her to lunch. Afterwards, he drove her to Hurlingham, passing Katharine upon the road.

Madrigal had been very civil at Castle Charing. Her husband had been killed in the War, after a month of wedlock. That was six years ago, and if Mrs. Chicele yet mourned, she mourned in secret. She was extremely good-looking and had a delightful laugh. . . .

The next day, the four met in Bond Street—with two open taxis between them. They exchanged appropriate banter. Katharine's and Giles' contributions were suspiciously bright.

The following Thursday morning Captain and Mrs. Festival received two several communications by the same post.

> *Wednesday Evening.*
>
> DEAR GILL,
>
> *I'm awfully sorry, but I'm afraid I must put you off to-morrow. I've had so many late nights lately that one more or less has come to matter quite a lot.*
>
> *I'm sure you'll understand.*
>
> *Yours,*
>
> KATE.

Though she did not say so, Mrs. Festival had spoiled three sheets of notepaper phrasing that note.

> *Wednesday.*
>
> DEAR KATE,
>
> *Will you forgive me if I don't come to-morrow? Jonah wants me to play at Roehampton against the Red Hats, and they're sure to want me to dine and talk shop. You know.*
>
> *Yours,*
>
> GILL.

That was Captain Festival's third attempt.

Their reception of their respective bow-strings was anything but cordial.

Staring at the familiar handwriting, Katharine went very white.

"So," she said quietly. "Well, I've only myself to thank. I've whipped off the finest husband that ever a woman had—with the most natural result.... He's turning elsewhere. Madrigal, of course."

She bit her lip savagely.

Suddenly she remembered the letter she had written the night before.

"My God!" she cried, and clapped her hand to her mouth. "He'll think I meant it, of course. *I meant him to, and he will.* It'll drive him into her arms! I've cleared his way! He'll have no compunction *now.*..."

She flung herself down on the bed and buried her face.

"Why did I write?" she wailed. "Why did I ever write? If only I'd waited . . . if only . . ."

She began to weep passionately.

Giles, fresh from his bath, stared at his letter as at a death-warrant.

He read it through twice, carefully.

Then he sat down on his bed, sweating, and read it again.

Then he lowered the document to his knee and sat staring at his wardrobe with eyes that saw nothing.

Finally, he gave a short laugh and, getting upon his feet, proceeded to brush his hair, whistling softly. . . .

Half-way through the operation, he started violently.

"My God!" he cried. "*That blasted letter of mine.* . . ."

Brushes in hand, he gazed at his reflection in the glass.

"Oh, you poisonous fool!" he hissed. "You blundering, blunt-nosed idiot, you've put the burning lid on and screwed it down. You've torn it—bent it irreparably. Of course, she'll think I meant it. *I meant her to.* . . . And now—I've put myself out of Court. I've told her to run away and play. I've pushed her off!"

He closed his eyes and leaned heavily against the wall.

"Oh, Kate, Kate, Kate! . . . What have I done, my sweet? What have I done?"

Two hours had gone labouring, the second of which Captain Festival had spent perambulating Lincoln's Inn Fields and consulting his watch. His nervous demeanour was such that by ten o'clock he was being observed by the police. On the stroke of the hour, however, the suspect disappeared. . . .

As the door closed behind him—

"Forsyth," gasped Giles, "she's turned me down."

"No?"—incredulously.

"It's a shell-proof fact. And I've just tied it up, nailed it down and sunk it in the bright, blue sea. I warn you, I ought to be removed. I'm a public danger." He began to search his pockets with nervous inefficacy. "Where's that blinkin' letter gone?"

"Sit down," said Forsyth, indicating a chair. "And please begin at the beginning. I've another appointment in——"

"Now, don't rush me," said Giles. "I'm all of a doohah, I am. And if you rush me, I shall burst into tears." He mopped his brow feverishly. "About six weeks ago . . ."

The tale came pelting.

The lawyer, who had given a frenzied Katharine an appointment for half-past ten, began to see daylight.

"And there you are," concluded Giles violently. "That letter means she's attracted to Pat Lafone. I'll bet it cost her a hell of a lot to write it, because—well, it's a pretty thick thing to tell your husband, isn't it? And now she's had *my* letter, which tells her in so many words to count me out and go full blast ahead."

Forsyth fingered his chin.

"What did you write it for?"

"Ask the fowls of the air," said Giles wearily. "They might be able to tell you. I can't. I suppose I had some rotten, weak-kneed idea of frightening her back into my arms. Of course, it was a hopeless thing to do. But when you're desperate you do do hopeless things."

"Why 'desperate'?" said Forsyth.

"Because I can't stand it," shouted his client. "I'm not a graven image. For nearly three blinkin' months I've stood and watched all London swarming about my wife: I've smirked and bowed and scraped and pretended I didn't care: I've sat up and begged, like the rest, for a dance or a smile: and once a blistering week I've met her across our own table and made imitation back-chat and done the grateful guest. . . . And the last three times I went there she gave me grocer's port." He raised his eyes to heaven and clenched his teeth. "If ever I get a chance, I'll break that butler's back. I believe that's half the reason I wrote that blasted note."

Here the telephone bell intervened.

"Excuse me," said Forsyth. "Yes? . . . Very well. Mr. Maple's out, isn't he? . . . Then show them into his room and ask them to wait."

As he replaced the receiver—

"What the devil am I to do?" said Captain Festival.

"Nothing," said Forsyth.

"*Nothing?*"

"Nothing."

"Oh, the man's mad," wailed Giles. "I've infected him."

"As you and your wife's trustee, I say that you can do nothing. You've covenanted not to molest. Your hands are tied. And now. . . ."

He rose to his feet.

"Forsyth," said Giles, "be human. D'you mean to say I've got to sit still and watch my wife push off with another man?"

"When you came here," said the lawyer, "seeking a deed of separation, I warned you both that you were playing with fire. You thanked me handsomely—and then deliberately instructed me to sow the wind." He shrugged his shoulders. "And now I must see this fellow. You sit here and smoke. I shan't be long."

He left the room swiftly.

As he passed into Maple's room, Katharine rose at him.

"Mr. Forsyth, I've bought it. Giles has found somebody else. I never dreamed it was serious, but I got his letter this morning."

She thrust the mischievous document into his hand.

Forsyth read it carefully.

Ere he could open his mouth—

"He wrote that last night," said Katharine. "That means he's got off with Madrigal Chicele. And——"

"He doesn't say so," said Forsyth, turning the letter about.

"I know. But it does. You can take it from me. Listen. Giles doesn't love her, really. Not yet, at any rate. He still loves me. But now that he thinks I don't care, she—she'll just romp home."

"Why should he think that?"

"I told him I didn't," cried Katharine. "In so many words."

Forsyth put a hand to his head.

"But if you do care, why did you——"

"Because I cared so much that I couldn't go on."

"Sit down, won't you?" said Forsyth, indicating a chair. "I can't give you long, for I've got someone waiting upstairs. But——"

"For God's sake," wailed Katharine, "don't rush me. As it is, I'm beside myself. And if you——"

"Now, please go quietly," said Forsyth. "I'm going to state the facts. Correct me if I go wrong. Little dreaming that your husband had written this letter to you, you gave him to understand that, so far as you were concerned, he was free to place his affections where he pleased."

"Quite right."

"That you did in the hope of bringing him to your feet."

"Yes. It sounds insane, but women are funny like that."

"Your immediate fear is that, in view of the attachment which you say his letter discloses, your rash communication will have the opposite effect and drive him into a certain lady's arms."

"Exactly," said Katharine. "You've got a magician's brain, but let that pass. What, in Heaven's name, Mr. Forsyth, am I to do?"

"I think you must wait," said Forsyth.

"*Wait?*"

The lawyer nodded.

"You must wait for him to move."

"But he's *moving*," screamed Katharine. "He's moving into her arms. It's more than a million to one he's with her now."

"I hardly think——"

"Of course he is. And yet you tell me to wait!" Mrs. Festival threw back her head and pressed her hands to her eyes. "What d'you think I've been doing for the last three months? I'll tell you. I've been waiting. Waiting, waiting, waiting for Giles to come back. Waiting, with a jest on my tongue and a picture-postcard smile. Watching other women rushing after my husband, biting and scratching and lying to catch his eye, cadging seats in his car, eating out of his hand. . . . Once a week he's come to our house as a guest. Once a week we've met across our own table and been polite—*polite*! The last two or three times I thought his manner seemed strained, as if he was upset about something. But I never dreamed. . . ." Her lips were trembling, and she stopped. The next moment she had herself in hand. "I tell you," she cried, "I've stood up and grinned and borne it, till I can't endure any more. I wrote that wretched note in desperation. I thought . . . I hoped. . . . And now you tell me to wait!"

"As you and your husband's trustee," said Forsyth faithfully, "I say that you can do nothing. You've covenanted not to molest."

"Oh, blow what I covenanted. I'm not going to be bound by any rotten papers. Besides, I never read it."

"You signed it," said Forsyth mercilessly, getting upon his feet.

"Mr. Forsyth," said Katharine, "you told me to come to you if I was in trouble. Don't send me empty away."

"I must see these people," said Forsyth. "You stay where you are. I'm sorry I had no time to get any flowers, but you were rather precipitate. I'll tell you what," he added, as if voicing an afterthought. "Would you like to speak to your husband while I'm upstairs? You know. Just ring up casually, by way of clearing the air?"

"He's sure to be out," said Katharine. "With Mad——"

"We can but try," said Forsyth. "Of course, if you'd rather not . . ."

"I'd love to," said Katharine. "I don't know what on earth I can say, but——"

"The time will provide the words," said Forsyth, and left the room. . . .

He found Giles pacing the floor like a caged beast.

"While I've been away," he said quickly, "I've had an idea."

"Go on," said Giles, moistening his lips. "Go on."

"Would you like to ring your wife up?"

Captain Festival reflected.

Then—

"She won't be there," he said. "She's with Pat, for a monkey."

The lawyer shrugged his shoulders.

"You can try," he said. "Don't, if you don't want to, but I don't think a telephone call is molestation, and, at least, you'd be in touch."

"All right," said Giles. "I don't know what to say, but——"

"I'll tell them to get you on," said Forsyth, opening the door.

"Here! Don't leave me," said Giles. "Don't go away. Supposing she's in?"

"Well, it's not much good if she isn't, is it?"

"D'you mind saying that again?" said Giles weakly. "I—I wasn't ready. Besides, you can't say 'isn't is it.' It's not euphonious. I—I say . . ."

But the lawyer was gone.

Outside his own door, Forsyth leaned against the wall and bowed before a paroxysm of laughter as a reed before the gale. Then he pulled himself together and sought the switchboard.

"Put my room through to Mr. Maple's and ring them both up. Then plug me in. I want to overhear."

"Very good, sir."

After a moment's interval—

"Er—er—hullo," said Giles, wiping the sweat from his face. "Hullo."

"Is—is that you, Gill?" said Katharine tremulously.

"Er—yes, dear. How—how are you?"

"Oh, all right, thanks. How—how are you?"

"Oh, full of beans, thanks . . ."

There was a dreadful silence.

Forsyth began to shake with laughter.

"Are you there, Gill?"—anxiously.

"Yes, dear."

"That's right. I was afraid we'd been cut off."

"No, I'm here, all right. . . . How—how are you? Oh, I've said that, haven't I? I mean——"

"Are you sure you're all right, Gill?"

"Right as rain, dear, right as rain. Why?"

"I don't know," said Katharine. "I thought you sounded—er—not quite yourself."

"Well, I'm not really. I—I had a dream last night."

"Did you? What did you dream?"

"I—I forget now," stammered Giles. "But—you know. It's sort of unsettled me."

"Well, do be careful, dear. It worries me to hear you so—so unlike yourself."

"Does it? I mean—am I?"

Forsyth writhed.

"Gill, what *is* the matter?"

There was another silence.

Then—

"I say, Kate," said Giles.

"Yes?"

"I—I got your letter."

"Did you?" said Katharine. "So did I. I mean——"

"Yes?"

"What?" said Katharine disconcertingly.

"I only said 'Yes,'" said Giles. "You know. *Pour encourager.* Go on, dear."

His wife braced herself.

"Gill."

"Yes, dear?"

"I rang you up to——"

"Did you?" said Giles. "When?"

"*Now.*"

"Now? Oh, I see. I suppose they said I was out. Never mind."

"But why should they say you were out?"

"Well, mainly because," said Giles, "I don't happen to be in."

"Gill," cried his wife, "what on earth d'you mean?"

"Don't ask me," said Giles desperately. "I'm that badgered and bewildered, I can't think straight. As I was saying, I rang you up to——"

"When?" said Katharine.

A choking noise was succeeded by another silence.

With his eyes closed and tears running down his cheeks, Forsyth clung to his receiver helplessly.

At length—

"Kate," said Captain Festival in a hollow voice.

"Yes?"—faintly.

"Don't think I'm blaming you, darling, but I rather gather you're thinking of displacing *Baladeuse*."

"I'm *not!*" shrieked Katharine. "I'm *not!* It's—it's all a terrible mistake. I know you've heard someone bleating, but don't think——"

"I haven't!" yelled Giles. "It's false! No one's bleated for yiles—I mean mears. Not since you did. An' no one'll ever blinkin' well bleat again. . . . There! I'll make you a present of that. I've wanted to say it for months, but I didn't know how." Hurriedly Forsyth replaced his receiver. "And, as for *Baladeuse*—well, I'm thankful she's still on top—thankful, my darling. D'you hear? Thankful. . . . Of course, if at any time, in a mad moment, you felt like another dart at jolly old *'Ard an' Bright* . . ."

For a second his wife hesitated.

Then she bent to the mouthpiece.

"*Ma-a-a.*"

The noise Captain Festival made, descending the stairs, brought Katharine and Forsyth pell-mell into the hall.

Husband and wife stared at each other open-mouthed. . . .

The lawyer watched them in silence, one hand to his lips, the other behind his back.

Presently their gaze shifted and fell upon Forsyth.

"But what a man!" said Giles, laying his hands upon the lawyer's left arm.

"What a friend!" said Katharine, laying hers upon his right.

"What a trustee!" said Forsyth, raising his eyes to heaven.

"He's going to dine with us to-night," said Giles.

"Yes," said Katharine. "And we'll show him our bathroom."

"Two's company," said Forsyth, shaking his head.

"Thanks to you," said Giles, shaking his arm.

"So's three," said Katharine, shaking the other.

"That's over," said Forsyth, and sighed. "Here's the Deed."

"Oh, we're tired of that," said Katharine.

"Yes," said Giles. "We're going to give it to Beatrice."

SPRING

WILLOUGHBY GRAY BAGOT, gentleman, sat back in his chair.

From where he was, he could look conveniently out of the broad windows, across the shadowy lawns, and on to the stately timber of the sheltered park. He did so thoughtfully, tapping his teeth with his pen. Presently he frowned and, leaning forward, set a sheet of notepaper before him and proceeded to write.

> DEAR SIRS,—
>
> I believe your advice to be good.
>
> I will therefore accept Mr. Harp's offer and sell him Chancery—park, residence and furniture, as it stands, for forty-five thousand pounds, on one condition.
>
> The condition is this.
>
> The purchaser shall take into his service an individual whom I will indicate, to perform the duties of Groom of the Chambers at Chancery, at a wage of fifty pounds a year. This man shall receive no board, but shall be permitted to occupy the lodge at the West gate of the park, rent-free. So long as he behaves himself and faithfully discharges his office, Mr. Harp shall retain him in his service.
>
> I appreciate that this is an unusual request, but the man knows the house and its contents as I know them myself and is deeply attached to them. The service he will give will be worth having.
>
> Yours faithfully,
>
> WILLOUGHBY GRAY BAGOT.
>
> Messrs. Matthew & Scarlet,
>
> Solicitors,
>
> Serjeant's Inn, London, E.C.

Bagot read over his letter with tightened lips. Then he copied it carefully and, slipping the original into an envelope, sealed, stamped and addressed this forthwith. As he turned it about, the crest on the back caught his eye—a rose in a mailed fist. For a moment he stared at it: then he turned and glanced at the same emblem cut in the stone of the aged mantelpiece....

Presently he sighed.

"*Sic transit*," he said shortly, and, clapping a hat on his head, rose and passed out of the room.

It was true.

The glory was passing. Very soon it would have passed.

There had been a Gray Bagot at Chancery since Harry Plantagenet's day. In fact, that terrible king had given a Bagot the estate in return for valour. That it was not his to give is beside the point. Men took what they could get in those days, as they do now. And now, Mr. Albert Harp was taking Chancery.

Like the original Bagot, Mr. Harp owed his good fortune to his prowess in time of War. But, while Gray Bagot had won Chancery at the cost of an eye, an arm and a slash on the thigh, which only the bone stopped, Mr. Harp's succession was due to a judicious administration of his business, which was that of a purveyor of pork.

Sic transit . . .

Willoughby had done what he could. But when he came back from the War, things were in evil case.

A cold rain of demands beat upon his diminished income; the stream of outgoings was like to burst its banks: over all, the cloud of a heavy mortgage, once no bigger than a man's hand, was blotting out the heaven.

Of his passionate love for Chancery, Willoughby took his capital and gambled upon the Exchange. The franc was bound to appreciate....

Mr. Harp's offer was a bad one, as offers go. Chancery was a show place. Charles the First had stayed there, and Cromwell too. The latter had crossed the body of a Gray Bagot to gain admittance. Some of Chancery's furniture had stood in the same corners for more than three hundred years. The library had been collected by a Bagot in the reign of Queen Anne. Mr. Harp's offer was absurd. Still ... Offers were hard to come by nowadays. Mr. Harp's was the first that had been made in seven months.

When all that had to be paid had been discharged, of the forty-five thousand there would remain five thousand pounds. This, safely invested, would bring in two hundred a year. And a man could live on that—even one who had been a Captain in His Majesty's Household Brigade.

Sic transit . . .

Willoughby posted his letter and then walked round the park, and in by the western gate. He passed about the lodge, marking its bulwarks. After a final look, he turned slowly away.

"What a thought," he said. "Two hundred and fifty a year and rent-free. If it comes off, I shall be on *panne* velvet."

Two months had gone by, and Mr. and Mrs. Harp were beginning to grow accustomed to the thrilling reflection that Chancery was theirs. Their possession of the place was peaceful; their enjoyment of it quiet. But their unconcealed delight in their acquisition was almost childish. For days together they never went outside the gates. . . . After a week or two of private revelry in their surroundings, they pressed invitations upon a pack of friends and relatives, whose company they did not desire, because their pride of ownership simply had to be served. This was clamouring for the meat and drink of stares and ejaculations and bated breath. Their precious toy had to be admired. As for the Groom of the Chambers, not to advertise their employment of such a paragon would have been tantamount to suppressing the Kohinoor. He was the light of their eyes.

They had, of course, no idea that John Worcester, tall, quiet, respectful, constantly about the reception rooms, dusting, ordering, cleaning, polishing this old bureau, rehanging that picture, was Willoughby Gray Bagot.

There was no reason why they should have perceived the masquerade. They certainly recognized that Worcester was no ordinary servant, but the mystery stifled curiosity, as mysteries may. One never could tell. Revelation might cost them his service, and—the best was good enough for them. They had never set eyes upon the vendor before the sale, and Willoughby had spread it abroad that he was bound for New Zealand. At the lodge he lived quietly enough, his only servant being an old groom who kept his own counsel. In the village, two miles away, he had been scarcely known by sight. Such letters as he received went first to a Bank, where they were redirected to 'Mr. Worcester.' Captain Bagot had covered his tracks.

It must be admitted that the Harps' estimate was just. Willoughby gave their home a care which money cannot buy, and themselves a service which they had never dreamed of. He was the last word.

So far as the other servants were concerned, Mr. Worcester and all his works were naturally regarded with a profound disgust. This was not expressed, mainly because the staff profited so handsomely by his labour. But the scorn and indignation which his faithful maintenance of the reception rooms provoked, were largely responsible for the concord which ruled the Servants' Hall.

It was, indeed, as much the unpleasant personality of the butler as the virtues of the Groom of the Chambers that in June determined his patrons to attempt an important change. In a few days their guests would arrive. If only they could induce Worcester to take the butler's place, they would be spared the humiliation of being treated like dirt before their visitors, while their star servitor, instead of flitting in the background, would be agreeably conspicuous.

They approached him delicately, without success. The Groom of the Chambers was respectful, but resolute. He declined the offer gently, but definitely and without hesitation. Then he excused himself and withdrew to continue his revision of the library's catalogue.

As the door closed—

"□'Ell," said Mr. Harp, subjecting his nose to violence.

"Me too," said his wife miserably. "I'd set me 'eart on that, I 'ad. 'E'ld look so lovely in a dress-soot, too. An' now . . ."

A fat tear of disappointment made its appearance, and, after poising for an instant upon the brow of her cheek, fell heavily into the broad valley of her lap.

Mr. Harp rose to the occasion and crossed to her side.

"There, there, me dear," he said kindly, "don' take on. We can't 'ave everything. Bowler's very tryin', in course, but——"

"I 'ate the brute," sobbed his wife. "Anyone would. Nasty, 'ulkin' wretch. Laughin' and sneerin' at us 'cos we ain't gentry; and takin' our money and food, 'and over fist. An' hall the rest as bad, and that impudent, no one would never believe. An' the honly one wot is hones' and respec'ful as good as in 'idin'—goes out o' the room when we comes in, comes in when we goes out, 'ides. . . . It's too crool, 'Arp, and that's the truth. Worcester's a walkin' treat. 'E puts a thousan' pound on the 'ouse—easy. An' 'alf the blighters comin' 'll never know 'e's 'ere."

"I'll see they know," said Mr. Harp violently. "I'll fix that. Besides, they'll 'appen acrost 'im in the course of 'is dooties—boun' to."

"'Snot the same," cried his wife. "You know it ain't. We're buryin' a talent, we are. Other folk 'as fine 'ouses, but there ain't a mansion in London wot's got a servant like 'im. 'E tones the whole show up. We ain't stylish, and as for Bowler and the rest of them rotten sneaks, they'd let a doss-'ouse down: but Worcester's a peach. . . . An' we're *buryin' 'im*."

Her husband stamped to the window and regarded his smiling acres with a dismal stare. Mrs. Harp had a knack of reciting unpleasant facts with a pitiless clarity which paralysed consolation.

Presently, he took a cigar from his waistcoat-pocket and, after savaging the butt, thrust his quarry reflectively between his teeth. As he felt for a match, the idea flashed into his mind.

Trembling with excitement, he snatched the cigar from his lips, and swung round, mouthing.

"Jane, I've got it! Got it in one, I 'ave! Oh, lovely! Listen 'ere. Worcester's Groom of the Chambers, ain't he? Good. 'E shall 'ave a show as'll beat the ragtime band—'e, an' the 'ouse and us, the 'ole year round. 'Old me, someone: I'm that excited and wrought, I can't talk straight. Listen 'ere. Chancery's a show place, ain't it? Figures in the 'istories and guides—used to be shown, once. Well *we'll show it again—throw it open to visitors daily, from two to four.* The visitors won' worry us—I'll love to see 'em. *An' Worcester 'll show 'em round.* . . ."

With a seraphic smile, Mrs. Harp got upon her feet and began to dance. . . .

A few days later it was announced that, by the direction of the owner, Chancery, one of the most exquisite examples of a mediæval manor-house, had been thrown open to the public and could be visited until further notice any weekday between the hours of two and four o'clock.

The four Americans passed slowly round the broad, flagged walk and, turning a corner of the house, found themselves once more before the main doorway. Their tour of the apartments had lasted half an hour.

One of the men took out a note-case, but the girl touched his arm and shook her head.

"No, no," she whispered.

The man hesitated, pointing to the back of their guide.

"Put it away," said the girl shortly.

Her squire obeyed, staring.

Willoughby Bagot turned.

The moment he always dreaded had arrived.

He was about to be offered payment which he could not in decency refuse.

He always gave his tips to the butler, and was thought a prize fool for his pains, but his patrons could not know that.

"That is all that is shown, madam."

The two women inclined their heads.

"Thank you very much," said the elder pleasantly. "We've enjoyed it immensely."

Willoughby bowed.

For a reason which they could never satisfactorily explain, the two male visitors raised their hats, and the party turned towards the car, which was glittering before the lodge, two furlongs away.

Willoughby felt very grateful. . . .

From a window he watched the quartette making their way along the avenue. He had liked them, and they had made his task easy. Besides, throughout the tour, he had been used as a gentleman.

The girl, especially, seemed to have understood. He was faintly surprised that she had not added her thanks to those of her—her aunt, probably.

Suddenly the former turned and came pelting back.

The men, who were walking ahead, did not observe her movement. Her elderly companion proceeded more leisurely.

Willoughby left the window and returned to the door.

As she arrived, he opened this readily.

"I think I've left my bag in one of the chambers. I fancy I put it down in the picture-gallery."

Willoughby led her to the staircase and she passed up. He followed pleasedly, marking her as she went.

She was tall and slight, and moved with an easy grace. The slim, bare hand, resting upon the banisters, was small and firm and shapely. Its trim nails shone. Her straight back, the even poise of her head, her beautiful ankles, would have delighted a sculptor. Her plain tussore dress and pert little hat suited her perfectly. As for her white silk stockings . . .

At the top of the staircase my lady turned to the right.

"I know my way, you see," she flashed over her shoulder.

Willoughby smiled.

Her face was glowing. Its fine colour and the big brown eyes, the small nose and the proud curve of the lips reminded the man of a picture he once had seen. As for her friendliness, little wonder that it entered into his soul.

The bag lay in an alcove—a little, delicate business of powder-blue and gold. Its beads were so fine, they might have been stitches of silk.

The girl picked it up and turned to the man.

"I left this here on purpose," she said quietly. "I wanted to speak to you when the others were gone. You don't remember me, but I met you in Philadelphia, before the War. I had my hair down then. Why are you doing this?"

"I was staying with the Stacks," said Bagot, knitting his brows.

"That's right. In 1914. But I tell you, my hair was down, so you wouldn't remember. Besides . . . What are you doing here? You were in the Blues."

"That's over," said Willoughby slowly. "Now, I'm in service. This was my home."

"This?"

He nodded.

"I lost my money, you see, and the place had to go. They're very nice people, luckily. They've no idea who I am, and—and it serves my turn. I live at the second lodge."

"How can you bear it?" said the girl.

"Easily enough," said Bagot simply. "I couldn't let the place down."

"You speak as if it were a friend."

"It's been my people's home for nearly eight hundred years."

The girl turned to the door.

"You're faithful," she said.

Willoughby shrugged his shoulders.

"Time ties up the affections," he said. Then, "I'm so glad you came back. If I were still the owner, I should ask you to tea."

"And, if I was not a companion, I should accept." Willoughby stared. "As it is, my mistress'll light into me for being so long. You see," she continued, smiling, "we're fellow bondsmen." She put out a little hand. "And now good-bye. I think she likes this part, and, if I can persuade her to stay at Holy Brush, I'll call at your lodge one evening and ask for some tea. You're a Bagot, of course."

"I was," corrected Willoughby. "But that—that's over, like the rest. I'm known as Worcester now."

"And I," said the girl quickly, "am known as Spring. No 'Miss,' or anything. Just Spring."

Before he could answer, she was at the head of the stairs.

As he opened the great front-door—

"Good-bye, Spring," said Willoughby.

My lady flung him a bewitching smile.

"Good-bye, Captain Bagot. D'you think you'll know me next time?"

"Yes," said Willoughby. "Even if you have your hair down."

He watched her rejoin her companions, triumphantly waving her bag.

"The Stacks had a daughter," he murmured. "But she used to wear blue glasses because of her sight. Besides, you don't find paid companions worth seven million pounds."

This was quite true. Moreover, his memory was at fault. Mr. and Mrs. Stack had died childless. The whole of their fortune had been left to a beloved niece.

It was natural enough that for the next ten days the Groom of the Chambers at Chancery should reconstruct Spring's visit with a grateful heart. Her precious figure preceded him up the stairs, set a slight knee on this settle, stooped to observe those volumes: her laughter rang in the gallery, her voice fluted in the hall, her smile flashed in that doorway: her sympathy, grace, charm were lighting his memory with a glow which he found very valuable. In a word, the lady had wrought havoc. She had shown Willoughby Bagot something from which, for the last lean years, he had rigidly averted his gaze—the loneliness of his existence. With her little, firm hands she had rammed the truth down his throat. Had her mouth been less scarlet, had her throat been less white, her form less beautiful, the light in her eyes less tender, had the maid been less startlingly attractive in word and look and deed, it might have gone less hard with the Groom of the Chambers. Bagot could steel his heart with most men. His job was to cherish Chancery, at any cost. It had not been pleasant to play the servant in his own home; at the best, it had been a bitter-sweet business. Still, keeping his eyes upon the ground, he had become used to his monkhood—perceiving many things for which he had come to thank God. And now . . .

They had walked in Chancery together, he and she, walked and talked familiarly in his own home. It was no more his home, in point of fact, than it was hers. And yet—it might have been his and hers, if she pleased, too, but for ill fortune. That way lay madness, of course. Yet—the place suited her. Chancery was so immemorial that it had become natural: its furniture, tapestries, casements seemed to have grown where they hung: labelling age had stolen upon it, as lichen steals upon old tiles, till the spirit of the artifice that garnished had disappeared, and the house ranked with the oaks Gray Bagot had planted ere Richard was king. And Spring was natural. For all her badges of modernity—bead bag, silk stockings, nail polish, she was as refreshingly natural as Pomona herself. She fitted into Chancery as had no maid or man—except his father—whom Willoughby had ever seen treading those stairs.

When, therefore, some ten days later, the Groom of the Chambers approached his lodge at a quarter to five o'clock of a July afternoon, to see Spring seated upon the turf beneath his window, hatless, smoking a cigarette and talking earnestly with the old groom, he could have burst into song.

Spring picked up her hat and waved, and, when he came up, stretched out her little hands to be helped to her feet.

"I said I should come," she said simply. "You shouldn't have asked me."

"If I remember," said Willoughby, "I didn't so far presume."

Spring raised her brown eyes to heaven.

"Which means I've come uninvited?"

Willoughby bowed.

"Queens are not asked for favours," he said. "Yet they bestow them."

"Of course, you're wasted," said Spring, turning to the miniature porch. "You ought to be in some Embassy, flattering secretive dowagers. You know. Duels of polished wit and sleight of tongue. Never mind. I've got a great idea. I'll tell it you over the tea I've let you in for."

Bagot put his head on one side.

"Yet she looks generous," he said. "Of course, it's a proud mouth."

"It's a thirsty one," said Spring, passing inside.

Old William served them devotedly, hissing a little with excitement from time to time. He had not waited on a lady for many a year. Besides, that his master should have company at the lodge delighted his heart. Willoughby's monkhood went against the groom's grain.

"And so," said Bagot, frowning at the weather-beaten cup, which the proud mouth was using, "you managed to get to Holy Brush."

Spring nodded.

"Tact," she said. "I ought to be at an Embassy, too. I was most skilful. What I was really up against was that there's only one bathroom at *The Jade*: but I said that that was a custom which was rapidly dying out and that one day we should be proud to say that we'd used a common bath, just as some people boast of remembering inns where everybody sat around the same big dish, spoon in hand."

"Do they? I mean, shall you?"

"I hope so. Any way, it did the trick, and now she's perfectly delighted. She's bought two 'gate' tables already, and I left her on the bowling-green, telling the landlord the history of his church."

"I congratulate myself. If only a certain custom wasn't already dead—that of living and letting live—I'd put myself at your service."

"Which," said Spring thoughtfully, "brings us to my idea. If you want Chancery back, I think you may have it."

"How?"

"Go to America," said Spring. "You had a good time there before."

"I should think I did," said Bagot. "Your people are wonderfully kind."

"Well, go. Don't call yourself Worcester, you know. And use your—your sleight of tongue. With ordinary care you ought to marry an heiress within six months." She paused to take another piece of toast. "It's been done before," she added carelessly.

There was a long silence.

At length—

"I'm afraid I'm a bad business man," said Willoughby quietly.

"Perhaps," said Spring. "In fact, it's fairly obvious that, commercially, the Gray Bagots weren't in it with the Harps. But why be foolish? You needn't marry the first one that comes along. They're not all Harps, you know. Some of our psalteries are quite passable."

"Would you do a thing like that?"

"I don't know. But then, I'm a fool."

"Exactly," said Willoughby. "So'm I."

Spring frowned.

"Think," she said. "Think of sitting in your own library, with servants falling over one another to answer the bell when you rang, and hunters in the stables and four cars, and Royalty coming to stay with you, and money to burn, and 'The Wife of Willoughby Bagot,

Esquire' the picture of the year, and Chancery smiling in its sleep because a Gray Bagot was up in the saddle again."

"□'And hatred therewith,'□" said Willoughby, producing a pipe. "Nothing doing, you witch. I'm sorry to disappoint you, but I'm much too foolish. Quite idiotic, in fact. It's hereditary. After all, I've much to be thankful for. At the moment, I'm thankful for your dimple. I suppose it always comes when you're trying not to laugh."

Spring covered her face and shook with merriment.

Presently she sat up soberly.

"We don't do so badly, we servants, do we?" she said. "I guess our respective employers aren't laughing like that. I suppose you won't let me wash up?"

"Certainly not," said Bagot. "That's William's affair."

"Yes, but as often as not he does it with cold water. He told me so just now. And that's all wrong, you know."

"I can't help that," said Bagot, lighting her cigarette. "I like my guests to do as they feel inclined, but there's a limit to my hospitality. And now shall we go outside and sit on the grass? I want to see you against a background of box."

It was a brilliant afternoon, and the shadow of the lodge turned the recess between the grey and green walls into a little arbour, the mouth of which gave on to Chancery, slumbering warm in the sunshine, a quarter of a mile away. What traffic used the road, pounded or whirred about its business behind the close box-screen, alike blind and invisible, but lending the little bay an air of privileged privacy like that of a family pew.

"My summer parlour," said Bagot, ushering his guest.

"Hereafter the Servants' Hall," said Spring, taking her seat upon the turf. "Well, now I'm here, how do I look against the box?"

"You kill the poor thing," said Bagot. "Your eyes are too bright. Never mind. I'll have it watered before you come next time."

"I can't come unasked again. I mean, there's a limit to hospitality, isn't there?"

"You wicked girl," said Willoughby. "You——"

"Why did you want to see me against the box?"

"Because good pictures should be put into good frames. I didn't choose the paper on my sitting-room walls, you know, but I never noticed how very distressing it was until this afternoon."

Spring looked up, smiling.

"Keep something for the heiress," she said.

A car slid out of the distance, crept past the gates and stopped by the side of the hedge, three paces away.

"We're not far off," said a man's voice. "I know this property here, but these corkscrew lanes of yours have tied me up. I can't remember which side the village lies. Maybe there's a porter here. . . ."

A door was opened and someone descended into the road.

Before he could reach the gate, Bagot was out of his garden and in the drive.

"Can I help you, sir?"

As he spoke he recognized one of the two Americans who had completed Spring's party the week before.

And Spring was sitting in the arbour, with blazing eyes and her under-lip caught in her white teeth, straining her ears. . . .

The way to Holy Brush was asked and told.

The motorist re-entered his Rolls and, when this had purred into the distance, Willoughby returned to the arbour with his eyes upon the ground.

The look upon his face told Spring two things.

The first was that Bagot knew what was taking her compatriot to Holy Brush. The second, that he found the knowledge acutely distasteful.

"I must go," she said abruptly, getting upon her feet. "What are you thinking about?"

"I was wishing," said Bagot slowly, "that I was back at Chancery." He looked up suddenly. "And you?"

Spring looked away over the exquisite landscape.

"I was thinking that it's very refreshing to discover another fool."

For the next four days, when Willoughby returned to his lodge, Spring was seated upon the turf, hatless and at her ease, awaiting his coming. The man always assumed that she had just arrived. The assumption was wrong. On the last three days my lady had been there two hours before he came, ironing his washing and delicately mending his clothes. The care of linen was not old William's strong point. She also instructed the groom how to wash up and, shocked by his replies to an examination upon elementary cooking, gave him a written statement of the procedure for roasting meat. Moreover, she taught him to deceive so cunningly, that, when later, he volunteered that he had bought an old iron for sixpence and had been trying his hand, his master wholly believed him and praised his discretion. William's ears burned.

On the fifth day, Spring did not come.

When Willoughby, approaching the lodge, could see no sign of the lady, for an instant his heart stood still. Ridiculously enough, he had come to expect to find her beneath his window. Hoping against hope, he quickened his pace. . . .

Except for William, setting the table for tea, the lodge was empty.

Willoughby tried to believe that Spring was late. He washed and changed and made a dozen excuses for not taking tea. He gave her half an hour—three-quarters, while he smoked in the little garden or strolled in the road. Finally, tea was served at six o'clock. Long after that he listened to every footfall: not until half-past eleven did he retire to rest. And all the time he knew that she was not coming, that he would not see her that day.

Thinking things over in his bed, he became frightened. He would see her again, of course—he hoped, many times. But a day had to come—already it was set in Fate's diary—when he would see her no more, when their idyll would be definitely finished, to be presently bound in Memory and go up to the shelf of Time. The thought shocked him. Till now, he had never realized how pleasant she was. Her company, her ways, had become a necessity to him. Not in four days, of course. That was absurd. Custom is not so rapidly delivered. It was not a question of custom. Spring had become a necessity in half an hour. The gap she filled had been yawning for months and years, but, until it was filled, he never had known it was there. And now he did know, and its emptiness would gape upon him. Could he have quitted the place, changed his way of living, flung himself into some pursuit, had he but gone to her and she not come to him—it would have been different. As it was, so long as he cared for Chancery, dwelt at the lodge, always between five and six he would miss her excellence, turning his lonely parlour into a gallery of dreams.

For Willoughby, there lay her magic. She was his dream-lady. She had come to him as dreams do come. Their instant understanding, their immediate intimacy, their full-grown fellowship—things which should have been impossible and yet were natural as the day—were stuff that dreams are made of. . . .

Finding his legend good, he took it further, recklessly. He made her mistress of Chancery, loaded her with presents, taught her to ride. . . . The hopelessness of such fantasy did not matter at all, because it was founded on fact—a breathing, sweet-smelling fact, that sat beside him on the turf, all apple-green frock and white silk stocking and tiny tennis-shoes. With her perfume in his nostrils, he could afford to be extravagant—with her perfume in his nostrils. . . . And now . . .

Sic transit gloria mundi.

My lady's absence was deliberate. Spring was as wise as she was fair. She wished to discover whether Gray Bagot's steady eyes counted with her as much as she thought they did, whether she was losing her head instead of her heart. She was not expecting for an instant to be able to read her own soul, but she was more than hopeful of extracting a valuable hint.

Her hope was realized.

By the time her aunt and she had dined she had become so *distraite* as to provoke that usually imperturbable lady's indignation, while, retiring at ten o'clock, she remained awake for one hour, immersed in the distasteful reflections that Time can in no wise be recalled and that they who fling opportunities in Fortune's face can hardly be surprised if their future relations with the lady are rather strained.

At last, picturing Willoughby, she fell asleep.

Let us use her heavy brown eyes, as the delicate ranks of lashes are closing up.

Tall, spare, soldierly, the descendant of the old Gray Bagot was good to see. His hair was fair and close cut; his complexion clear and fresh; his nose aquiline. His mouth was well shaped; his voice pleasant; his grey eyes, set far apart. It was, indeed, his steady, grave gaze which was so notable. He always looked you in the face and expected to be so regarded. He liked to see, and was perfectly content to be seen. If you did as he expected, you had your reward. His character, his various emotions were spread before you in such print as a child could read. If he liked you, you saw it in his eyes, and there was a friendship made in a second of time. If he disliked you, you saw it, and that was that. But he never disliked anyone without just cause. As a matter of fact, he was generous to a fault. He looked his best, I fancy, upon a horse, but so does many a man. He had a fine, upright carriage, and his shoulders were broad. Honest, unassuming, dignified, he did his blood credit. That Chancery suited him is indisputable: his looks, his bearing, his ways agreed with her: and Chancery was a show place.

Willoughby tried not to hasten upon the sixth afternoon. His working hours were from seven till four o'clock, but, since the measure he gave was always good, he seldom left the apartments till nearer five. To-day, however, there had come no visitors to interrupt his labours, and by a quarter-past four there was no more to be conveniently done.

It follows that he reached the lodge rather before he was expected—in fact, in comfortable time to witness the delivery of a pair of pyjamas, four soft shirts and six handkerchiefs to his valet by his *repasseuse*.

"Hullo," said Spring cheerfully. "I guess you never dreamed I could iron." She turned to the groom, who was standing upon one leg. "That's all to-day, William. The other two need mending, so I'll do them to-morrow."

"Very good, m'm."

With an apologetic look at his master, William made good his escape.

"You will do nothing of the sort," said Willoughby. "If I'd had the faintest idea——"

"Live and let live," said Spring. "It amuses me and it doesn't hurt you, so why deprive a poor servant of her innocent fun?" She slid a cool arm through his. "And now take me into the garden and give me a match. By the time you've changed, William will have brought us some tea."

Willoughby did as he was bid.

It was when the meal was over that Spring put her elbows on the table and knitted her brows.

"I want your advice."

"That's very easy," said Bagot. "Let sleeping suits lie, and Grooms of the Chambers do their own dirty work."

The red lips tightened.

"Thanks very much," said Spring. "Perhaps I ought to have said that the advice I want is upon a matter upon which I value your opinion."

Willoughby considered his finger-nails.

"I've got an awfully good answer to that," he said. "A regular winner."

"What?" suspiciously.

"Can't think of it for the moment," said Willoughby, "but——"

"Oh, but you will before I go. We shan't go before next Friday. In fact I can't. You see, I only get off in the afternoons, and William says there's a waistcoat——"

"I capitulate," said Willoughby quietly. "Friday? In three days' time? Is Mrs.—er—Mrs.——".

"Le Fevre."

"—Le Fevre weary of Holy Brush?"

"Not that I know of," said Spring. "I want your advice."

"Yes?" said Willoughby.

"I have been offered another situation."

"As companion?"

"Yes."

Bagot took out tobacco and started to fill a pipe.

"First of all," he said slowly, "are you happy with Mrs. Le Fevre?"

"Very. She's awfully sweet."

"Then I take it the new situation would be an improvement financially?"

"Yes," said Spring shortly, "it would."

"D'you think that you'ld have as much freedom?"

"I know that I shouldn't."

"You might be happier."

"I might," said Spring. "I'm not at all sure; but I might."

Willoughby frowned. Then—

"Might you be less happy, Spring?"

"Easily."

The man slid his pouch into a pocket and rose to his feet.

"My dear," he said, "unless the increase in salary is too big to be ignored, my advice is to stay where you are."

There was a pause.

At length—

"I think I ought to say," said Spring slowly, "that the offer was made by a man."

Willoughby's heart gave one bound.

For a second he hesitated. Then—

"That alters everything," he said.

"Why?"

"Because companions, like Grooms of the Chambers, do not figure in the table of relative precedence, whereas. . . ."

Spring stared out of the window and into the park.

"You've seen him," she said. "Twice. But then you knew that."

Willoughby nodded.

"I should say," he said quietly, "that he was one of the best."

"In fact, if I don't accept, I shall be selling a bed of roses for the second 'o' in smoke?"

Willoughby set his teeth.

"Dear Spring," he said, "I can't advise your heart—only your head. But I'm bound to say that, placed as you are, you should do what your head tells you, if you possibly can. Think of the future."

"I do," said Spring. "That's what worries me so."

"Supposing Mrs. Le Fevre were to die and you to fall sick."

"Supposing my husband treated me like a dog."

"I'm quite sure he wouldn't," said Bagot.

"He wouldn't do it twice," said Spring sweetly.

"The point is," said Willoughby, swallowing, "that companions can be given notice, but wives can't."

"Wives can't give notice, either."

"I've heard of its being done."

"Then you advise me to take my precious offer and thank my stars."

"How can I? But I can point out that a girl in your present position is up against it. You can't get away from that. Think. You depend for the bread you eat upon somebody else's whim. I bet you've never saved. You haven't had time. And so, you see, it's vital that, if you can improve your position—scramble on to firmer ground—you should. Well, you've got a roaring chance. He's rich, of course, and a white man—two pretty good points, you know. I don't suggest that, if you were not a companion, you couldn't have half London at your feet; but, as it is, my lady, you don't get a show. So that this chance that's come your way may never come by again. If you were rich, I should tell you to please your heart. As it is, you don't dislike him, you've no reason to think he won't do you slap up—I'm perfectly certain he will—and so I simply suggest you should please your head."

"Which do you do?" said Spring.

"I'm a man."

"Exactly, and you jolly well please your heart."

"Not at all," said Bagot, "I——"

"I imagine you could do better than serve the Harps. I mean, you weren't born or bred to fix parlours, but, because you're mad about Chancery, you just do."

This was unanswerable.

After a moment's reflection—

"A male man," said Willoughby, "can shift for himself. If he likes to buy trouble, he can. He can always get through."

"And what," said Spring, ignoring his careful evasion, "what about my suggestion that you should marry a wife? You wiped the floor with it. But the instant the position is reversed, I must swallow my feelings and follow my head. What if you are a man? Men aren't immune from sickness. Don't say that you've got William, or I shall scream. If William's as good a nurse as he is a seamstress, you wouldn't live twenty-four hours. And look at the women there are who are up against it. They don't go under because they're not on concrete."

"I don't suggest that you would. But some of the roads of Life are pretty bad. If one can avoid the roughest, it's—it's just as well. Spares the frame, you know."

"Don't I look strong?"

"You do. I'm sure you're as hard as nails, but nobody's any the better for being hammered."

"And so, although the sun's shining, I'm to dive into the subway of marriage, in case one day it may rain."

"At least there's a station here," said Bagot doggedly.

"In other words, I mayn't get another chance. Go on. Say it right out. You've been hanging around, trying to hand me the statement for a quarter of an hour."

Willoughby gasped.

"You wicked, ungrateful child." He raised his eyes to heaven. "For sheer, bare-faced perversion, that breaks the tape. Never mind. I'm through, I am. I've done my best and I'm through. As some poetaster has said, 'You can lead a girl to the altar, but you can't make her think.' Or is that out of *Paradise Lost*?"

With that, he seated himself upon the table and felt for a match. He was really ridiculously relieved.

Spring gave a little laugh.

"My dear," she said, with her eyes upon his face, "I was only playing you up. I think your advice is sound and provident, and you've perfectly satisfied me that if I don't take it, I shall be a brass-bound fool."

The punch was unexpected, but, to Bagot's eternal credit, the hand that was holding a flaming match to his pipe never wavered. The man knew how to lose.

As for Spring, she was so proud of him that she had much ado not to burst into tears.

Before she had time, Willoughby had laid down his pipe and picked up her hand.

"That's right," he said, smiling. "For your sake I'm awfully glad and I believe you'll be very happy." He kissed the cool fingers, and turned away. "And, now that's settled, let's go into the Servants' Hall."

He had, to my mind, done well, had this Groom of the Chambers. He was, of course, desperately in love with Spring. More. By taking the office he held, he had made himself outcaste. He never could marry, because he could never allow any woman to forfeit her own degree by becoming his wife. The possibility of finding a woman whom he could love, who also was outcaste, had been too ridiculously remote to be considered. And now, this very thing had come about. Exquisite, dazzling Spring was within his reach. Whether she would have married him is beside the point, which is that he could have wooed her with a clear conscience. Yet, because of her chance of marrying one who was not outcaste, his wonderful, shining occasion must be renounced.... Willoughby renounced as he loved—with all his might. The man was resolute. No passing flash of pity must be permitted to affect the case, no tear of sympathy for him fall into the trembling scale. For Spring to suspect that he loved her would have been unearthly sweet. That it would actually embarrass her was most unlikely. What was a broken-down Bagot, haunting the home of his fathers like a seedy ghost—what was such a man to her? Still, the slight risk must not be taken. If she could possibly do it, she must marry her wealthy swain. To Bagot, Spring's happiness was everything. His own did not count.

To my mind, such love was worth having.

And Spring thought likewise.

"I must be going," she said.

Willoughby bowed.

In silence they passed through the garden and out into the drive.

As he opened the wicket-gate—

"Tell me one thing," she said. "Why did you say you were sure he was one of the best?"

"Because I knew that, if he was not, you wouldn't have considered his proposal."

"But I didn't," said Spring, with a positively blinding smile. "I turned him down last night."

"You turned him down?" shouted Bagot.

Spring smiled very sweetly.

"I thought I told you," she said, "that I was a fool."

She left him staring, and pelted down the road.

Spring came the next afternoon, but was gone before four o'clock.

Then came Thursday.

Willoughby found her framed in the little porch.

"Change quickly," she said. "I mustn't stay long to-day."

"Packing?" said Willoughby quietly.

"Yes."

They ate their tea without laughter. The spirit of parting was hovering over the meal.

Afterwards they sat by the window, for, though the sun was shining, it had rained a lot that morning, and the world was wet.

Spring sat like a child, perched on the deep sill, smoking a cigarette and peering at Chancery out of the leaded panes.

"You will remember it all?" said the Groom of the Chambers.

"Yes—all."

"It's like a tale, don't you think? A slice of a fairy tale. In the distance, the shining castle, and here, on the fringe of its domain, the little cot."

"Where the poor boy dwelt who was really the rightful heir, with one old retainer to whom he was still the lord."

"And one day a Princess came, with hair as dark as night, and eyes that were unfair, they were so big, and—and silk stockings, and all. And she recognized the poor boy (*sic*) and, because she had a nice, soft heart, she came and had tea with him, instead of visiting the castle."

"And the silly part of it was," said Spring, "that she wasn't a Princess at all, but an ordinary, poor girl, who was——"

"She was a Princess," said Bagot. "She hadn't got the riches or the Court she should have had, but—oh, anyone could see she was a Princess."

"Any way, the boy treated her like one, which was very nice for her, and, when the time came for her to go——"

"The boy lost his wits," said Bagot steadily, "and made a fool of himself." Spring turned and looked at him. "You'll never guess what he did. He forgot that he was no longer lord of the castle. It wasn't altogether his fault, because the presence of the Princess had made his cottage all glorious. Be that as it may, he thought how wonderful it would be if only—the—Princess—didn't—go. . . . And when he came to his senses and saw what a madman he'd been, the idea was so precious, that he couldn't get it out of his head. You see, she'd seen what his life was, and she seemed to understand, and she did like Chancery, and he had two hundred a year, as well as his wages, and he could be home by half-past four every day, and there was a bathroom upstairs, and——" He stopped short there, and clapped his hands to his temples. Then he burst out tempestuously. "Oh, Spring, darling, why did you ever come to dazzle my wretched eyes? You couldn't stick it, I know. It's absurd, grotesque, comic. The clothes you're wearing are worth more than I earn in a year. I'm mad—raving." He sank his head upon his chest and put out his hand. "Give me your blessed fingers to kiss before you go, and then—go as you came, my sweet, like a breath of air, like a perfume out of the night. I'll try and think it's been a dream—a wonderful, golden dream, which the good gods sent me, to make my memory rich. You know. When first you wake, you could weep to think it isn't true; but, after a while, you're grateful for just the dream."

Spring put down her face and kissed his hand.

Then she slid off the sill and put her arms round his neck.

"Why d'you think I came back that day? Why d'you think I left my bag in the gallery? Why d'you think I've come here? Because I love you, Willoughby—loved you before you loved me. I don't care what you've got, or what you haven't. I only want to share your life."

"My wonderful darling," said Bagot, and kissed her mouth.

Miss Consuelo Spring Lindley became Mrs. Willoughby Bagot ere August was old. The wedding took place one morning at Holy Brush and was extremely quiet.

Mr. Worcester obtained one day's leave without arousing suspicion, and the quick congregation consisted of a tearful Mrs. Le Fevre, that lady's solicitor, who gave the bride away, and William, the groom. For the dead I cannot answer, but if polished brass and marble may be believed, eleven Gray Bagots slept through the simple service beneath the cold, white flags.

The following morning, Benedict was back at his work.

This, however, was destined to be disturbed.

Shortly before ten o'clock, his employer summoned him to the library, and bade him close the door.

"Worcester," said Mr. Harp, "I 'ave some very queer noos. In fac', I'm all of a shake—never 'ad such a night in me life, wakin' up all of a sweat and tossin' and tryin' to think, till me brain rebelled against me." He sighed heavily, holding a hand to his head. "As for Mrs. 'Arp, she's that struck and bewildered, she's stayin' in bed."

Willoughby regarded his employer and then fixed his eyes upon the floor.

"Yes, sir?" he said steadily.

"Yesterday afternoon I 'ad an offer for the 'ouse." The Groom of the Chambers started and then went very pale. "Lock, stock and barrel—just as I bought it meself." Mr. Harp paused as if seeking for appropriate words. Suddenly he smote upon the table and let out a cry. "They might've offered me twice—free times what I gave and I'd 'ave 'ad 'em shown out wiv a flea in their ear. Forty-five thousan' I paid, as p'r'aps you know. Well—I can't 'ardly believe it, *but they offered me ten times that.*"

"Four hundred and fifty thousand!"

"Four 'undred and fifty thousan'," said Mr. Harp. He slapped his breast. "I've a bankers' draft in 'ere for a quarter of that—'undred an' twelve thou—five. I 'ave to keep takin' it out to believe it's true."

"You took the offer, sir?" ventured Bagot.

"Why man alive," screamed his master, "wot else could I do? You can't turn away money like that. You 'aven't the right. I tell you straight, I'm dotty about this place, but 'Business First' 's my motter, an'—an' it's pretty nigh 'arf a million," he concluded absently.

For a moment, blinking, he scribbled figures upon the blotting-pad, his lips moving, his eyes fixed. Then he sat back in his seat and covered his face.

"Two o'clock they come, and give me till four to decide. Immediate possession, in course. I 'ad to take it or leave it by four o'clock. I never 'ad two such hours in all me life. One thing I said. I asked if the buyer was British, for I couldn't 'ave sold to a foreigner, come wot might. 'Yes,' they says, 'British.' So I signed her away at this table wiv tears in me eyes. I s'pose we'll 'ave free seats now an' do the grand, but shan't be never so 'appy as we've bin 'ere."

There was a long silence.

"When am I to go, sir?" said Bagot.

"I mentioned you," said his master. "I didn't forget. I said as I 'oped you'd stay with me and Mrs. 'Arp, but if you didn't do that, maybe you'd like to stay 'ere. I said you was a Groom in a million an' did the work o' five, an' that wot you didn't know about the place could be counted out. The fellow listened and took a note o' your name, but 'e said that he 'ad no authority to promise to take you on. 'Owever, the purchaser's comin' this afternoon at free. You'll show 'im round, in course, and it's Lombard Street to a norange 'e'll jump at the chance. Mrs. 'Arp and me'll be out. There ain't no call for us to stay, an'—an' we'ld rather not. The deal's to go through nex' Monday at twelve o'clock."

There was nothing more to be said.

Chancery had passed.

Five hours and a half had gone dragging by and Bagot was in the gallery, oiling an aged hinge, and wondering how to word his *communiqué* to Spring.

Suddenly the throb of a bell came to his vigilant ears.

The can went into a locker, and the Groom of the Chambers descended into the hall.

He tried his best to be calm, but his nerves were taut. A good deal depended upon this interview—their tiny home, their living, their . . .

With his hand on the mighty latch, Willoughby moistened his lips. . . .

Spring was standing alone on the broad flags, very smartly dressed, looking ridiculously girlish, and inspecting her thin gold ring with her head on one side.

Behind her, in the hot sunshine, was gleaming the grey and silver of a magnificent *coupé*.

Husband and wife regarded each other with beating hearts.

Then—

"Please may I see over the house?" said Spring. "It—it belongs to my husband."

Willoughby put a hand to his head.

"F-four hundred and fifty thousand," he stammered. "Then——"

"Yes, dear," said Spring, entering and closing the door. "We might've got it for less, but I didn't want to take any risks. You see," she added, setting her back against the oak, "in spite of all your protests, you took my advice. In fact, you married the first one that came along."

Willoughby tried to speak, but no words would come.

Suddenly he began to tremble.

In an instant, Spring's arms were about him and her cheek against his.

"Willoughby, my darling, my darling!"

So she comforted him.

Presently he picked her up as one picks up a baby child.

"I never dreamed," he said slowly. "I never dreamed. . . . I didn't know how to tell you, and I was going to ask the people if they could see their way to keep the Groom of the Chambers on." A shy smile came playing into his face. "Do you think you could—madam?"

Gravely, his sweet regarded him.

Then—

"You must ask my husband," she said.

ELIZABETH

THOSE who dine at the Richelieu sit over their cups. It is the custom. A dinner at the quiet Duke Street restaurant is never a prelude to an entertainment. It is the entertainment itself. People go there to dine and talk leisurely. The kitchen and the cellar are probably the best in London; the service and the atmosphere are certainly the best in the world. There is an unseen orchestra, which plays so softly that you are just aware of melody while you converse. There is no light but that shed by table-lamps, so that it is more easy to identify the dish your neighbour is tasting than your neighbour herself. You may be sitting by Royalty; often enough you are. And if you ring up to take a table you will be told that they are all booked—unless the clerk at the bureau knows and respects your name. It is the custom.

Upon the ninth evening of December the elements seemed to have conspired to enhance the Richelieu's charm. Without, a gale was raging. Squall after tearing squall flung down the dripping streets, fuming at every obstacle, blustering at every corner, lashing the pitiless rain into a very fury. The latter fell steadily and, with the wind behind it, drove and beat passionately upon a miserable world, harrying, chilling and stinging till such as might gave in and pelted for shelter, while such as might not fought their way through the *mêlée* with tightened lips.

Behind the curtained double-windows of the restaurant only the wilder squalls obtained an audience, but those who sat there had proved the night while they came, and the muffled stutter of the rain and the dull growl of the wind about the casements vividly remembered the malice of the streets.

Little wonder that the comfort of the room entered into the soul.

Lady Elizabeth Crecy set down her glass.

"Degeneration," she announced. "That's my trouble. I'm degenerate. I worship luxury—silks, furs, perfume, shaded lights, deep carpets, shining bathrooms, electric broughams and the rest."

Her host pulled his moustache.

"I've seen you stick it," he said. "I remember a day with the Cottesmore when——"

"Perhaps. But all hunts lead up to a bath. If there was no hot water, I should never get up on a horse."

"Neither would stacks of people: but that doesn't mean they're degenerate. Cleanliness may be next to Insanity, but it's well meant."

Elizabeth laughed.

"You can get clean with cold water."

"It 'as been done," said Pembury. "I've done it myself. But you can bet your life it wasn't my fault. I bathed in a fountain once—one January day." My lady shuddered. "Exactly. I admit I got clean, but it put me off water for weeks."

"Perhaps," said his guest. "The point is, Dick, that you did it, while I——"

"So would you," said Dick stoutly. "I mean, other things being equal, of course. One or two screens, for instance. You're no more degenerate than I am. The best's good enough for you, of course. And quite right too. We're all of us out for the very best we can get."

"I've got it to-night, any way."

Thoughtfully the man regarded her beautiful fingers. He may be forgiven. The fierce light of the little table-lamp could find no fault in them.

"Thank you, Dot," he said quietly. Then he gave a light laugh. "But that's because you oughtn't to be here."

"But I ought," said my lady. "It's most appropriate. *Après vous*—the deluge. To-morrow I take the plunge. I'm dining with you for support—ginger. You're my Best Man. If the truth were known, my future husband is probably seeking inspiration at the hands of his best girl."

"I'll bet you've told no one."

"I didn't inform the Press, if that's what you mean. All's fish that comes to Scandal's net. Though why I mayn't dine with you to-night and announce my engagement to Hilton to-morrow morning I fail to see."

"Degeneration," said Pembury. "That's the answer. Not ours—the world's. The blinkin' age is degenerate. People would immediately assume there was something wrong. 'Engaged to one cove,' they'ld wheeze, 'an' dinin' out with another? Hul-*lo*!' And they'ld wink an' wag their heads an' lick their thick lips ... Oh, it makes me tired, Dot. It's made me tired for years. We're not hot stuff, you and I. Then why should we be branded? But we should. If we were charged with stealing, people'ld shriek with laughter. They know we're honest and they'ld know there'd been a mistake. But just hint that we've been forgathering, and our respective reputations'ld be blown inside out."

My lady regarded the end of her cigarette.

"Yes," she said slowly, "they would. It's bitterly unfair, but they would. But was there an age when they wouldn't?"

"There must have been," said her host. "Besides, things usedn't to be so bad. Everyone's got a muck-rake nowadays. They almost sell 'em at the Stores."

"You haven't," said Lady Elizabeth.

"Neither have you," said the man.

"Perhaps that's why we get on."

Pembury raised his eyebrows.

"It's a tie, certainly," he said. "Still, you and I hit it off before we thought about muck-rakes. I imagine it's bigger than that—a question of taste. We've always had the same tastes. We've always loathed golf——"

"Don't mention the game," wailed Elizabeth. "Hilton's determined to teach me—says the great thing is to learn while you're young."

"—an' loved hunting. We both hate claret and love beer."

"A vulgar taste," said my lady. "Hilton would have a fit. When I can't bear it any more, you must send me a bottle of Bass by parcel post."

"We're both of us fools about dogs, if we must see a show we like music with a small 'm,' we're both left-handed, we don't know what it is to be seasick——"

"I trust Hilton doesn't. Otherwise, the yacht . . ."

Pembury frowned.

"You called me your Best Man just now. Did you mean that, Dot?"

"I did. Why?"

"It gives me a right to say what I'm going to say." Lady Elizabeth stared. "You're not to gird at Hilton before me again. I know you'd never do it before anyone else: and we're such very old friends—we've always discussed everyone—that it's easy enough to forget. But you———"

"Forget what?"

"That we're on a new footing now. Hilton's up on the daïs, and I've stepped down."

The girl's eyes narrowed.

"Upon my soul," she said, "I think that beats it. First, you set out to teach me manners: then, you calmly announce that Hilton has usurped your place."

"Hang it, Dot, I never——"

"When you said I oughtn't to have come, you were perfectly right. I oughtn't. I ought never to have come here with you. I thought you could stand corn, and I find you can't. I thought you understood, and I find I was wrong. I tell you now you were never 'up on the daïs'— never within miles of it. Because I gave you my friendship, I suppose you thought I cared."

"I did," said Pembury quietly. "It was very presumptuous, but I did. And if I'd had enough to keep you, I'd 've made certain. . . . And now that you know, old lady, have a heart. Forgive me for being clumsy and call it 'Nerves.' I'm like a spoilt child this evening. You've spoiled me by being so nice. And now I know that it's over, I'm kicking against the pricks."

There was a long silence.

At length—

"What's over?" said Lady Elizabeth.

"Act One," said her host shortly. "The spoiling process. My—er—tastes being what they are, I must retire. If you want another reason, Hilton hasn't much use for me. I don't know that I blame him, but that's neither here nor there. He hasn't. And since he hasn't, neither must you. Incidentally, you haven't, any way. I said it first."

"You know I have, Dick. You know I have. I'm sorry I burst out just now. You're perfectly right, of course. You always are. To laugh about Hilton to you was shocking form. To turn and rend you because you told me so was painfully cheap. I was wild, because I was guilty. I was guilty, because I was wild."

"Dot, don't——"

"Listen. You say I've spoiled you. What rot! What blazing rot! Why, all my life you've spoiled me. You're spoiling me now. And I'm wild because I know that it ends to-night. 'Nerves'? Yes, if you like. Call it 'Nerves.'□" With a queer, dry laugh, she glanced at the watch on her wrist. "I'll have to be going, my dear. Have you got the car?"

"She's in St. James's Square."

"Good." They rose to their feet. "See how I bank on your goodwill. If I were a man, I wouldn't drive a girl home when she'd just told me off across my own table."

"I think you would," said Dick.

John Richard Shere, Viscount Pembury, was thirty-two. He had looked thirty-two for years and was likely to look thirty-two when he was forty. And there you have the man—steady, conservative, faithful. With it all, he was never dull. He was gay, eager, brilliant—could have taken his place anywhere: and his place was high. The tragedy of it was that access to his place was denied him. If his ways were charming, his means were unhappily of no account. What was worse, they would never be anything else. The collapse of Russia had finished the House of Shere. His father had sunk to an annuity and dwelled at a Club. His mother was dead—mercifully. He had sought employment, of course, but his style was against him. Besides, he had been bred to be an earl. He was certainly offered six hundred a year to show motor-cars, but had declined the honour. He was ready to sell his labour, but not his name. His greatest regret was that he would never hunt hounds. Tall, slight, dark, gentle-eyed, he was a man to look twice at. If you did so, you saw the strength of his pleasant mouth and the firm set of his chin. At Oxford, where he had been President of Vincent's, he was known as 'The Velvet Glove.'

Lady Elizabeth Crecy was twenty-nine, dark and grey-eyed. She could, I suppose, have married anyone. Her beauty, her wisdom, her excellence in all she did made three distinct, forcible appeals. I do not think the man lives who, had she pleased, could have resisted successfully so dazzling a combination. That she did not please made little enough difference. The result was the same. Men fell in love at first sight—and Sir Hilton Shutter among them. People said he had proposed six times.

Shutter believed in living and indulged his belief. He did himself very well—on thirty-five thousand a year. His ocean-going yacht was the last word. He was forty-six years old and had been handsome. He was also the second baronet and had been High Sheriff of Berkshire, in which county his name was respected almost as highly as he respected it himself. He was well known in London and believed in writing to *The Times*. A letter above his signature appeared about once a month.

Lady Elizabeth Crecy had, in her own right, three hundred and fifty a year.

The wind had died and a fine rain was falling when Pembury turned into King Street in quest of his car. The wet did not stop him from looking the old Rolls over to see that she had taken no hurt. Besides, he feared that rain might have forced an entrance.... But the coupé had been built by men who knew their business. Cushions and floor were bone dry. He started the engine and left for the Richelieu at once.

Elizabeth was waiting in the hall—all great fur coat and soft, dark hair and little shining feet—as she had waited before, so many times. As he came into the hall, their eyes met and she smiled—as she had smiled before, so many times. As she stepped into the coupé, an exquisite stocking flashed—as it had flashed before, so many times. . . .

A moment later they were heading west.

"Slippery night," said Pembury. "Oughtn't to be, but it is."

"That's the way of the world," said Elizabeth. "It's an irrational age. And Nature's catching the disease."

Neither spoke again, till the last turn had been taken and Pembury had berthed the coupé under the shelter of some trees. My lady's home lay farther, by twenty paces.

The girl stared.

"Why have you stopped, Dick?"

The other smiled.

"Would you like a drink, Dot?"

Elizabeth caught his arm.

"Not my favourite beverage? I can't bear it."

"The same," laughed Pembury. "In the pocket by your side is an imperial pint of beer——"

"Dick, you darling!"

"—and here"—he produced a silk handkerchief—"is a perfectly good glass. I brought it as a sort of stirrup-cup, just—just to show there's no ill feeling. You know. Wash out the good old times an' wash in the new. Come on, old lady. Forward with the bay rum."

In silence the bottle passed. . . .

"Here's your best, Dick," said the girl uncertainly.

She emptied the glass, and Pembury filled it again.

Elizabeth put it aside.

"You drink that, Dick."

"I brought it for you."

"I know. I accept it and give it back. Drink it and wish me luck."

Pembury raised the glass.

"Your best—now and for ever," he said quietly.

He drank, laughed, slid bottle and glass into a pocket and set his foot upon the clutch. . . .

An instant later they were before the broad steps.

At the top of the flight Elizabeth lifted her head.

"You see I'm crying, Dick."

"Yes."

"You've never seen that before."

"Nerves, dear, nerves."

My lady shook her head.

"And it's not the beer, either," she said shakily.

Pembury took off his hat and picked up her hand.

"Good night, Dot," he said, and kissed the slight fingers.

These were very cold.

Then he opened her door, and she passed in. . . .

Pembury's rooms were in Brook Street. Thither he drove mechanically, gazing out of the windscreen with a strained, fixed stare.

As he was flying up Park Lane, a taxi shot out of South Street across his path. . . .

Instinctively, he clapped on the brakes, and the Rolls skidded to glory.

Two buses were coming. He could see them.

By a violent effort he straightened the great car up.

Then she skidded again—the opposite way.

He accelerated—tried to get through....

Then a taxi pulled out from behind the second bus.... A woman screamed....

With a soft crash, the Rolls came to rest against the taxi's off side.

As collisions go, it was a slight one—a matter of running-boards and wings.

The buses stopped, and their two conductors appeared. In blasphemous terms, the cab-driver called the world to witness that it was not his fault. His fares alighted indignantly. A crowd began to collect....

Then the police came up.

"Were you drunk?" said the Earl shortly.

"I was not, sir. But just now the police have got drunkenness on the brain."

"What evidence have you?"

"None."

"Who did you dine with?"

"I can't say, sir."

"You mean, you can't drag her in?"

"Exactly."

"For her sake, or ours?"

"Hers."

Lord Larch pointed to a table.

"Give me pen and paper," he said.

Pembury did as he was bid, and the Earl lay back on his pillows and wrote a note.

MR. FORSYTH,

>   Be good enough to attend to this matter. Lord Pembury was not drunk and so should not be convicted. Call me if you think it advisable.

LARCH.

"Take that to Forsyth," he said. "And dine with me here to-night."

"Thank you, sir."

Father and son understood each other perfectly.

The latter went his way and duly surrendered to his bail at eleven o'clock.

Evidence of arrest was given, and then, at Forsyth's request, the case was adjourned.

Some evening papers gave much prominence to the affair. So did some morning papers of the following day. Down in Somerset, with the Fairies, Lady Elizabeth Crecy never saw the reports. Out of regard for her, none of the house-party drew her attention to them. It was known that she and Pembury were very old friends.

As for Pembury himself, the man prayed hourly that, ere the news reached her, the case would be over and done. She was not a reader of news-sheets: she was well out of Town; that anyone would inform her was most unlikely. Of course, she would know one day, but, with luck, not until it was . . . too late . . . with luck. . . .

Mr. Quaritch, of Treasury Counsel, removed his pince-nez.

"The police contend that you were drunk. Three things, they say, corroborate their contention. First, Lord Pembury, you collided with another vehicle. Secondly, you smelt of liquor. Thirdly, a bottle and glass, both of which had recently contained beer, were found in a pocket of your car. Very good. Our answer to the first is that the collision was due to a skid, which was itself due directly to the fact that a taxi shot without warning across your path and indirectly to the fact that you were admittedly driving rather faster than the condition of the streets was warranting. Am I right?"

"Perfectly," said the delinquent.

The lawyer inclined his head.

"Our reply to the second is that, very shortly before the accident happened, you had consumed one half of a small bottle of beer."

"I had."

"Very good. What is our answer to the third?"

Pembury shrugged his shoulders.

"I've no explanation to give. Finding a bottle and glass doesn't prove I was blind."

"It's pretty strong evidence of drinking. Mind you, I *know* you weren't drunk. But we've got to satisfy the Court. What construction will the Court put upon the discovery of that bottle and glass? Assuming the Magistrate is reasonable, he will consider it peculiar. Even if they're addicted to drink, people of your position do not as a rule go about with a glass and a bottle of beer. So, finding the discovery peculiar, the Magistrate will expect an explanation. If you don't give him one, he will very naturally put the worst construction upon those unfortunate utensils."

"What'll he think?"

The lawyer raised his eyebrows. "I don't know what he'll think. He'll certainly assume that your explanation is not forthcoming because you know very well that it wouldn't assist your case. And if he thinks any further, I suppose he'll class you with the thirsty and prudent undesirable who carries a flask in his pocket wherever he goes."

"And he'll send me down?"

"Wait. The time is late in the evening—ten-twenty-five. That is the hour when those who do get drunk may be most easily encountered. You have a smash—which ought to have been avoided. You smell of liquor. Real evidence of liquor, recently consumed, is found. The police say you were drunk. If you were on the Bench, would you accept the accused's unsupported statement that he was sober?"

"Frankly, I don't think I should."

"Add to all this two scandalously irrelevant facts, which, because the Magistrate is human, will be constantly present to his mind. One is that of late the crater of public indignation upon the subject of drunken drivers has been in violent eruption: the other is that at the present moment there are hundreds of thousands of people who are simply living for an opportunity of demonstrating that there is one law for the poor and another for the rich."

"And he'll send me down?"

"I think he will have no alternative."

Lord Pembury laced his fingers and put them behind his head.

"Can't be helped," he said. "I've nothing to say."

Forsyth put in his oar.

"Look here," he said. "The most formidable position we're faced with is that which is erected upon that bottle and glass. If we can reduce that position, the moral effect upon the Magistrate's mind will be precisely as powerful as the position was formidable. You always get most credit for doing what seems to be the hardest thing to do. If you won't explain the presence of those infernal vessels, it's not the slightest good insisting that all you had recently consumed was half a small bottle of beer."

"Well, there's the blinkin' bottle to bear me out. I tell you, I shared it with a friend."

"Then produce the friend."

"I can't," said Pembury.

"'Can't'?" said Forsyth. "Or 'won't'?"

"Won't."

Forsyth threw up his hands.

Quaritch leaned forward.

"You do see the point, Lord Pembury? The introduction of the friend makes it a shade more palatable, but it doesn't eliminate that distressing element of eccentricity. Is it your practice to—er—sport a bottle of beer? Of course not. Then why did you do it? From hospitable motives? For a wager? Why?"

"I'm not going to say any more," said Viscount Pembury. "I'm sorry to be so graceless. I know you're trying to help me and I'm carefully crampin' your style. But there you are. Please do what you can with what you've got."

There was a long silence.

"He mayn't ... mayn't be content with a fine, you know," said Forsyth.

"I know. It can't be helped."

Counsel folded his Brief and rose to his feet.

The conference was at an end.

As the door closed behind Pembury—

"Who the devil is he shielding?" said Quaritch.

"I wish to God I knew," said Forsyth bitterly.

Sir Hilton Shutter was thoroughly pleased with life. For one thing, he was standing with his back to a roaring fire: for another, he was a guest at Castle Charing, a pleasant residence to which he had long hoped to be invited: for another, his future wife, seated on a sofa before him, was looking particularly lovely in a frock of powder-blue and gold: finally, from the solemn, almost subdued demeanour of his host and hostess, he perceived that his discourse was creating a profound impression.

A booming note slid into his voice.

"Leadership. To-day, more than ever before, people require a lead. Point them the way, and they'll move. But you must point it definitely. Your indication must be downright, courageous." He paused to flick his cigar ash into the grate. "I wrote to *The Times* to-day," he continued, frowning.

"Did you?" said his hostess pleasantly. "What about?"

"This question of drunken motorists," was the reply.

Mrs. Fairie started, and her husband's hand flew to his moustache.

"It's more than a public scandal," continued Shutter. "It's a national disgrace. I don't mean——"

"I know," said Fairie nervously. "There's been a lot of agitation about it, but——"

"I agree. But the evil remains."

"Oh, they'll stamp it out," said Fairie. "Trust them. People are beginning to see it's not good enough. By the way——"

"By 'national disgrace,' " said Shutter, "I mean that the failure of the authorities to observe the will of those who appoint and pay them to do their will is a state of affairs which would not be tolerated in any other country in the world."

"I agree," said his host heartily. "It's wicked."

"Monstrous," said Mrs. Fairie. "What about some Bridge?"

"One minute," said Lady Elizabeth. "What's monstrous?"

"This drunkenness stunt," said Fairie. "Let's——"

"No, no, no," cried Shutter. "I thought you didn't quite follow me. My point is that, outrageous as is the offence, the failure of those whose signal duty it is to eradicate it is still more infamous."

"That's the word I was trying to think of," said Fairie. " 'Infamous.' So it is. What about roping in the others an' havin' a quiet game of——"

"As I said in my letter to-day," said Sir Hilton, frowning, "the community no longer asks for protection—it demands the abolition of these pests: and that, by the infliction in every case, without fear or favour, of a penalty—imprisonment, of course—so harsh as, once for all, to frighten would-be offenders back into the path of decency."

"You are fierce," said Elizabeth. "Why——"

"Yes, isn't he?" cried Mrs. Fairie. "Never mind. Let's——"

"Isn't it time someone was?" demanded Sir Hilton. "Look at the latest——"

"*Ouch!*" squealed Fairie, leaping to his feet.

"Whatever's the matter?" cried Elizabeth, considerably startled.

"Must've sat on a pin or something," said Fairie desperately. "What about that poker? It's much——"

"As I was saying," boomed Shutter, "look at the latest case. There's a man with all the advantages which birth and education can offer——"

"Excuse me, Sir Hilton," blurted Fairie, "but—I know you'll forgive my saying so, but the fellow in question's rather a friend of mine, and——"

"Pembury is?"

"WHO?"

Elizabeth was on her feet, flushed, blazing-eyed.

"*Who?*" she repeated.

Fairie sank into his seat with a groan.

"Pembury, Elizabeth," said Shutter. "Young Pembury. Haven't you seen the papers?"

"No," said Elizabeth, "I haven't. What do the papers say . . . about . . . Lord Pembury?"

The broad shoulders were shrugged.

"Oh, he's the latest instance of the drunken driver. That's all. I'm not particularly surprised, but——"

"Hang it, man," cried Fairie, "you've no right to——"

"Why aren't you surprised?" said Lady Elizabeth.

Her fiancé stared. Then he gave a short laugh.

"Oh, I don't know. But don't let's pursue it. Didn't you hear Fairie say that he's——"

"Does it occur to you that Lord Pembury's a friend of mine?"

"I know he was," said Sir Hilton.

"Is," said Elizabeth. "Is. And always will be. Never mind. Who says he was drunk?"

"The police, dear," said Mrs. Fairie, putting an arm about her waist. "He ran into something—a taxi, on Sunday night—— *What is it, darling?*"

Elizabeth was trembling violently.

"Nothing," she said. "Nothing. Let me sit down. 'On Sunday night,' you were saying. Yes?"

"On Sunday night, in Park Lane. He wasn't hurt. And the police—you know what they are—immediately jumped to the conclusion——"

"Be just, Mrs. Fairie," said Shutter. "It wasn't a question of jumping to any conclusion. Finding him drunk, they——"

"If you'll forgive my saying so," said Fairie, setting a brandy and soda in Elizabeth's hand, "whether they found him drunk or sober has yet to be decided. At present he's merely charged with being drunk."

"Of course," said Shutter, "if you like to split hairs——"

"It isn't a question of hair-splitting," said his host. "It's a question of cold facts. If the charge is dismissed—as it will be—he could sue you for slander for this, and just waltz home."

Elizabeth was speaking.

"Will somebody please tell me exactly what's happened?"

"I will," said her host. "Dick had a smash late on Sunday night. Nobody was hurt. He was arrested and charged. They say he smelt of liquor and a bottle was found in the car. He appeared on Monday morning and pleaded 'Not guilty.' Evidence of arrest was given and the case was adjourned for a week."

"What's to-day?" said Elizabeth.

"Friday."

"Thank you. Go on."

"That's all, dear," said Mrs. Fairie. "We didn't tell you, because——"

"You did, though, didn't you?" said Elizabeth, looking Sir Hilton in the face.

"I naturally assumed——"

"Quite a hobby of yours, isn't it? Recreations—golf, yachting, assumption. You assumed that he was drunk. You assumed that I knew about it. I suppose you assumed that, in view of my knowledge, I should relish your recent conversation, including the fact that you had written to *The Times*, urging 'the infliction of penalties—imprisonment, of course—so harsh . . .'" She stopped dead there. Then her voice rang out. "*Why did you write that letter?*"

Sir Hilton started.

"'Why?'"

"Yes. Why?"

"Well—er—because, I suppose, I felt——"

"Was it in the hope that it would appear on the day Dick's case came on?"

"Good Heavens, Elizabeth! What——"

"Cut it out," said the girl, quietly. "I know. And so do Madge and Harry. We all three know. And so do you. And I'll tell you another thing we know—we three. We know Dick wasn't drunk."

"Right!" cried the Fairies in a breath.

"And so do you," said Elizabeth, rising.

"Don't be ridiculous," said Shutter. "If I like to——"

The girl stretched out her hand.

"Just hold my drink for a minute, will you?" she said.

Mechanically, Sir Hilton received the glass.

Elizabeth took off her pearls and slid an enormous emerald off her finger. She pitched the gems together at Shutter's feet. Then she looked into his eyes.

"How I came to make such a mistake, I can't conceive. I think I must have been mad. To be perfectly honest, I liked the idea of being rich. As far as you're concerned, I'm not so terribly to blame, because, when you asked me to marry you, you dangled your rotten wealth before my eyes. You prayed it in aid of your suit. And I thought it was good enough, I did. . . . Well, I find I was wrong."

"But, Elizabeth——"

"My good sir, *I wouldn't be seen dead with you.*" She stretched out her hand. "Thank you."

She took the glass from his fingers and flung the liquor in his face.

Sir Hilton recoiled and Madge Fairie started to her feet. Lady Elizabeth and Fairie stood perfectly still.

Floating from behind closed doors, the lilt of the latest fox-trot disputed possession of the silence with the pleasant flare and crackle of the logs in the grate.

"What's Mr. Forsyth want?"

"I don't know at all, my lord. He simply told me to find you, wherever you were, and bring you back in a cab to Lincoln's Inn Fields."

Pembury, who was at his tailor's, adjusted his tie.

"All right," he said slowly. "If you'll get a cab, I'll be ready in two minutes' time."

The clerk bowed and withdrew.

Pembury wondered, frowning, what was afoot.

Had Forsyth got hold of something? Had he been making inquiries and come on the truth? Had the Richelieu been talking? Had . . . Forsyth had found out something. Not a doubt of it. Something about Sunday night. And Forsyth was going to try to force his hand. He was going to threaten to put Elizabeth wise. . . .

Pembury smiled a grim smile.

As he entered the lawyer's room—

"Good morning, Dick," said Elizabeth. "Where did they pick you up? I told them to try——"

"Forsyth," said Pembury sternly, "I don't remember instructing you——"

"One minute," cried Forsyth. "One minute. My hands are clean. I haven't moved in the matter. I never found the lady. She found me."

"But——"

"It's perfectly true," said Elizabeth. "I only heard last night. Of course, it's my own fault. I really must read the papers: but they're so frightfully dull—usually."

"Who told you?" said Pembury.

"Hilton, of course. But observe how astute I am. A fool would have rushed to you. The woman of the world goes to a lawyer."

"Why does she do that?"

"Because," said Elizabeth, "it's Saturday, and lawyers are closed at one. By the time I'd had it out with you, the lawyers would have been closed. As it is, we're in just nice time. My statement's being typed now."

"I won't have you called," said Pembury.

"Quite sure?" said Lady Elizabeth.

"Positive. That's flat. You can't be called without my consent, and, short of pressin' me to death, you won't get that."

"But, Dick——"

"My dear, it's no earthly. I'm absolutely resolved. I not only won't call you, but I won't have you near the Court."

He flung himself into a chair and crossed his legs.

"Now, Dick, just listen. Put yourself in my place. Supposing I was charged with something I hadn't done. And everything——"

"Dot," said Pembury, "it's not the slightest good. You know as well as I do that it's a question of sex. What's sauce for the goose may be sauce for the gander—but it can't always be served. For people to know that we were dining 'ld be bad enough, but what about the beer?"

"Well, what about it?" said Dot. "What's the matter with the truth? Remembering my affection for the beverage, you were considerate enough——"

"My dear girl," said Pembury, "it's out of the question. You can't parade intimate nursery incidents in a Court of Law. Possibly, if we were brother and sister——"

"We are, practically. As I was telling Mr. Forsyth——"

"Well, it's not the moment to advertise it. Forsyth knows that as well as I do. Of course, he's out to pull me out of the muck, but I'm not takin' any. Either I get out myself, or I stay where I am. *I won't have you called.* More. Unless you give me your word not only to hold your tongue but not to come within a mile of the Joy Shop till it's all over, I'll—I'll plead 'Guilty.'"

Forsyth shifted in his chair.

Lady Elizabeth raised her delicate eyebrows.

"Well, there you are," she said. "If you will cut your own little throat, I can't stop you. Only, I can't marry a man who's been convicted of drunkenness." Pembury leaped to his feet. "I can't, really. You see, I'm funny like that. It's—it's against my principles."

"Dot!" shouted Pembury. "Dot! What on earth d'you mean? You're engaged to——"

"Finish, my dear, finish. I've turned him down. You'll see it in *The Times* on Monday. I just couldn't stick the swine. If we could have lived apart, I might have managed it. But together—no thanks. Charing opened my eyes. I was happy enough there, until he came.

Then everything crashed. Better is a cold tub, where love is, than a tiled bathroom and hatred therewith. Don't you agree, Mr. Forsyth?"

"Dot! Dot, my darling, is this a have?"

Pembury had her hands and was gazing into her eyes. The man was transfigured, blazing.

"No," said Elizabeth. "It isn't. It's ordinary, natural love. Don't go, Mr. Forsyth. I'd rather like you to stay. I say it's ordinary love. I've loved you for years, Dick. But when you never spoke, at last I came to the conclusion that you didn't care for me—that way. And so—I turned elsewhere. Not to another man, because there was no other man and never could be. So I turned to money, instead. I told you I was degenerate.... And then, when on Sunday night you showed your hand—the hand you'd never played, the hand I'd been waiting for you to play for such a long, long time—I didn't know what to do. You see, things had gone rather far.... And then—Sir Hilton Shutter very kindly showed me the way."

A door closed. Forsyth had disobeyed.

"But, Dot, my darling, we'll be awfully poor."

"D'you think I care? I only worshipped riches because I hadn't got you. Luxury was the god I set up in your place. I tried to drown my love in a butt of Malmsey. But, you see, it couldn't be done. Malmsey's sickening stuff. I'd much sooner drink beer. And now about this old trial. I'm to be in attendance, in case——"

"Oh, damn the trial," said Pembury, taking her in his arms. "I haven't kissed your blessed mouth since——"

"August the seventh, 1914," said Elizabeth. "I've got it down in a diary. 'He kissed my lips.' □"

"My sweet, my sweet...."

The girl just clung to him.

After a moment or two she lifted a radiant face.

"I think I shall have to marry you, whether you're convicted or not. You see, you're not only my Best Man—you're so much the very best man I ever saw."

On Monday, those sections of the Press which had been hoping to be able to announce *Sensational Developments* under the heading WELL-KNOWN VISCOUNT CHARGED were more than satisfied.

Before the case was called on, the Magistrate left the Bench, and Quaritch and his opponent were summoned behind the scenes. This was unusual. By the time the three reappeared excitement was running high.

The Magistrate's clerk nodded, and the case was called on.

Pembury stepped into the dock, and the Magistrate cleared his throat.

"Mr. Shorthorn," he said. The Solicitor to the Police rose to his feet and bowed. "I have decided, before proceeding with this case, to tell you that I have formed a very definite opinion.

"The position in which I stand is one of peculiar difficulty. If the charge was less grave, if the social position of the defendant was less considerable, if all the circumstances did not combine, rightly or wrongly, to attract to this case a good deal of attention, my path would be plain and easy to follow. As it is, I have thought proper to consult the Chief Magistrate and I may say that he agrees with me that the course which I am about to take is the only one which is at once convenient and just.

"By the merest accident, I am in possession of information which has a direct and powerful bearing upon this charge. That information would become evidence, if I could be put into the box."

He paused.

Except for the noise of breathing and the flick of a reporter's page, the Court, which was crammed with people, was still as death.

In a retired waiting-room Lady Elizabeth sat fretfully straining her ears, continually crossing and recrossing two sweet pretty legs and striving desperately to possess a mutinous spirit.

The Magistrate proceeded.

"In view of what I have said, Mr. Shorthorn, would you prefer that another Magistrate should deal with this case?"

"I am more than content, sir, that you should deal with it."

Mr. Shorthorn resumed his seat.

"And you, Mr. Quaritch?"

Treasury Counsel smiled whimsically.

"The best, sir," he said, "is good enough for me."

An attempt at applause, which succeeded the roar of laughter, was instantly suppressed.

"Very well, then. On the evening of the defendant's arrest I was dining out. Though he is probably unaware of the fact, I patronized the same restaurant as he did and, what is more, I sat at the next table." Everyone's gaze shifted to the accused. The latter stood like a rock. "And I observed—if I may say so, with surprise—that he drank nothing but water."

A nervous ripple of laughter ran through the Court.

"I see that my words were equivocal. I should say that my surprise was provoked not by his personal failure to drink wine—for I do not know his habits and I never set eyes on him before—but by the spectacle of anyone of his age who to-day considers water fit for internal use."

The Court laughed tremulously.

"The results of my observation do not end there. We are told that the collision occurred at ten-twenty-five. As luck will have it, I saw the defendant leave. I did not notice the time, for there was, of course, no reason at all why I should: but, recalling my own movements, I am satisfied that he finally left that restaurant not earlier than ten-fifteen. He was then unquestionably sober.

"The opinion I have formed is that in no circumstances is it possible for a man who is sober at ten-fifteen, who for the last two hours has touched no alcohol, to be drunk at ten-twenty-five."

That upon the evening in question the learned Magistrate's watch was ten minutes fast was not his fault. The man was scrupulous.

The case for the prosecution died there and then.

The prosecution was withdrawn, apologies were offered, the defendant left the dock, applause was suppressed.

Mr. Quaritch knew his job.

He rose to his feet.

"If, sir, I may complete the solution of this matter by disclosing what happened in the ten minutes of time during which my client was under observation neither by the judiciary nor the executive, I must confess that he seized the opportunity to consume a small glass of beer."

The Court roared its merriment.

"Possibly, the discovery of a small bottle of Bass—grim relic of some picnic—was responsible for his lapse from grace. Upon that point I have no instructions. It follows that at the time of the collision he indubitably smelt of liquor, and, while personally I should become uneasy if to smell of liquor were to be regarded as the peculiar privilege of drunkards, it was presumably his indignant recognition of that mocking perfume which provoked the constable, whose name, I observe, is Worthington, to . . ."

The rest of the sentence was lost in an explosion of delight—which the defendant missed.

In a retired waiting-room, cheek against cheek, Pembury and Lady Elizabeth let the world slip. . . .

And, as I have said, certain sections of the Press were perfectly satisfied. Could they have perused one document, reposing in Counsel's Brief, I imagine their satisfaction would have melted like snow upon the hearth. The very first words would have fused it—*THE LADY ELIZABETH CRECY will say*. . . . As it was, they were perfectly satisfied. And, when they were able to announce the lady's engagement to *the hero of a recent cause célèbre*, they could have thrown up their hats.

It was generally admitted that Lady Elizabeth was to marry by far the best man. Harry Fairie, of Castle Charing, put it much more strongly.

JO

I
JANUARY 7TH, 1926

I AM writing this down because Jo says I must—dear, beautiful Jo, with the great grey eyes and the maddening mouth. I tell her it is ridiculous—that in a short month the miracle will have sunk to a coincidence, the marvel to a curiosity. But she will have none of it: and, since she is leaning over my shoulder and has set her blessed cheek against mine, for what the business is worth down it shall go.

Last night we dined with the Meurices. Not of choice, but we agreed it was politic. A refusal might have been thought bilious. It is hard to see how, but it might. After all, I have been perfectly frank about my resignation. Now that I am married, I cannot stay on if I am not to be paid two-thirds of what I can earn elsewhere. And 'The Office' has been equally frank and, while expressing its deepest regret, has said that fifteen hundred for a spy is as much as it may afford. However, the Meurices being, so to speak, brass hats, might have misconstrued our refusal. So we went. We did not enjoy it. I cannot keep pace with these diplomats. No doubt they're good at their job, and all their ice-and-brandy ways are probably part of the game. But I am a regimental officer and I am not at ease hobnobbing with the gilded staff. I don't suppose they'd 've been at their ease drinking with the shunters at Carlsruhe. . . . But there you are. *Chacun à son goût.*

Well, after dinner a girl—one Roach—was induced to tell our fortunes by dealing cards from a pack. 'Induced' is misleading. Lady Meurice said, "Sarah, you've had a good dinner: now tell us some lies." And Sarah replied, "☐'And me the seaweed, Lulu, and I'll tell you where Arthur wore the dog-bite." The next minute she was off.

I've heard some junk in my time . . .

Presently my turn came, and I took my seat at the table and shuffled the pack. Only pausing to take my cigarette from my mouth, use it to light her own and then replace it between my lips, Miss Roach picked up the cards and began the rites of prophecy.

What first she said I forget, but it was thin enough stuff. As a matter of fact, she seemed puzzled: something—some combination, she said, kept turning up. Finally she dropped the cards and took hold of my hand, holding it flat on the table, palm up, and blinking at it through the smoke of her cigarette.

"You're on the eve of meeting someone," she said: "someone who'll influence your life to an amazing extent. They'll affect your outlook more violently than anything else in your life. They'll alter all your plans. The queer thing is they'll do it indirectly. You'll hardly see them at all."

"Will they do me good or harm?"

"I can't say. But, whichever it is, they'll do it through somebody else. It's a terrific influence."

"In fact, I shall be swept off my feet?"

She frowned.

"Not exactly. Your existence will be changed. What's so remarkable is that you retaliate. You're going to influence their life even more strongly still. Only, your influence will be direct and—and concrete."

"Concrete?" said I.

"Physical. Theirs on you will be mental. They'll get off first. After they've influenced you, you start in on them. I should think——"

Mercifully at that moment Berwick Perowne was announced. As he was straight from Moscow, the conjuring went by the board. I was rather interested to see him—I'd heard so much. He'd certainly do any staff credit—a dazzling A.D.C. The face of a careless angel, a tongue of silver, the impudence of the Fiend. His news left Jo and me gasping. He gave it as though he were describing a game of Bridge. After a while we made our excuses and left....

All the way home in the taxi Jo chattered about 'the prophecy,' till at last I told her that it meant that a nicer man than I was going to steal her away, and I was going to follow and break his back.... She put her arms round my neck.

Bugle was waiting for us when we got in: he's a good little dog: he's never really happy unless we're both of us there.

Sitting by the fire in the study, we discussed my resignation. Now that the War's past, I should have been at home a good deal—actually at home with Jo. But we really cannot throw away twelve hundred and fifty a year. Not that I shall have that yet—I start at fifteen hundred: but in a year or two ... with luck ... And it means so much. It means a car, frocks, flowers about the house.... Jo's eyes were like stars. I think she is the most beautiful thing I ever saw.

But I digress.

'The Office' rang up in the morning and wanted me down at once. I answered the telephone in my pyjamas. Jo was twittering with excitement. I found her, wrapped in a towel, hanging over the banisters, wild to know if it was 'the prophecy.' I tried to scold her, but she refused to be rebuked—as it happens, with good reason.

The prophecy, or some of it, has been fulfilled.

At 'The Office' I was introduced to Sir George ——, a nervous little man with a short leg. He used to be in the game, and came back to help at 'The Office' during the War. Shortly, it is his wish to be permitted to supplement my old pay so that it reaches my figure—two thousand seven fifty a year. He considers it would be a pity for 'The Office' to lose my services: he understands my position: and, provided I agree to remain, he will hand the Treasury sufficient War Stock to pay twelve fifty a year, such money to be paid to me quarterly while I do my job and, when I retire, to be added to my pension. ...

I tried my best to thank him, but I kept seeing the stars in Jo's dear eyes....

There. I have set out the miracle. As Sarah Roach said, so it has fallen out. I have met the person I was on the eve of meeting. By him my life is to be influenced to an amazing extent. My existence is to be changed. Instead of being a partner in a shipping firm, I shall go back to my own old job. My outlook has been switched from bills of lading to that exhilarating game of blind man's buff. Instead of lunching in the City and arranging about freights, I shall be studying men and the ways of men, peering into their brain-pans, searching their hearts, watching and waiting and coping with sudden issues, stalking the truth under strange heavens, trying to beat Delusion at her own game.... More. Sir George is doing it indirectly—through somebody else: and I shall hardly see him at all.

It remains to be seen how I am to influence him ... even more strongly ... directly ... physically.

Sufficient unto the day is the perfection thereof.

And now we are going out to look at a car fit for a queen to drive ... my queen ... my darling Jo. ...

II
NOVEMBER 22ND, 1926

The contrast is so ridiculous that I must set it down.

It is half-past nine, now, of a streaming night.

At this hour a week ago I was in Madrid.

Why I was there does not matter, but I was leaning back in a chair, just as I am leaning now, regarding the ugliest man I have ever seen. And he was regarding me with beady eyes. The room was filthy and bare and frightfully cold. And I was soaked to the skin. One naked electric lamp hung from the ceiling, shedding a harsh light. I was smoking a filthy cigar and from time to time I spat upon the boards. When I spoke, I spoke in vile Spanish, helping myself out with Russian words. I tried to speak the Russian very well. To be frank, I was very uneasy. I was keeping a certain appointment—an appointment with the ugly man. I had arrived early, an hour too soon. The appointment had been arranged for a quarter to ten. My early arrival hadn't mattered at all. In fact, he was quite nice about it—as nice as he was capable of being, this ugly man. And everything had gone very well. I gave him my news, and he gave me his. His, I may say, was the more valuable. I was extremely glad of it. I did not say so, of course. But I was—extremely glad. And now, having stayed with him nearly an hour, I was inclined to be gone. It was really rather important that I should bid him good-bye, because the appointment I had kept had been made for somebody else. And, as I had kept it without advising them, in the ordinary course of events they would keep it, too. Indeed, unless they were late, they would knock twice on the door at a quarter to ten. Possibly they might be early. . . . But one thing was certain. That was that, whenever they did arrive and they and the ugly man found out that a total stranger had been receiving his valuable news, they would both be most annoyed. . . . The trouble was that my host didn't mean me to go. . . .

I owe my life to the fact that my hearing is good—at any rate, better than that of my ugly friend.

I heard the step on the landing before he did.

So I broke the electric lamp, hit the ugly man on the nose with a bottle of wine, sang out in infamous Russian "Come in," adding a vocative which will send any Russian white to the lips, opened the door quietly, and when the other had entered, which he did with the rush of a bull, faded away, as they say, and left them to it.

That was a week ago.

And now once more I am leaning back in a chair, regarding my *vis-à-vis*. I am in London now. The room is warm and pleasant, and its walls are lined with books. Here and there hangs an etching. The windows are heavily curtained, and there is a fire of logs in the grate. The light is soft and grateful and filters through rose-coloured silk. The floor is of parquet, on which are spread Persian rugs. And I am in dress-clothes, dry and smoking a pipe. And my mind is at ease.

And, instead of the ugly man, I am regarding, I think, the loveliest woman I ever saw. She's wearing a flowered silk frock, and her arms lie like marble along the arms of her chair. Her knees are crossed, and the flames are lighting the sheen of a satin slipper and the pale silk stocking above. Her sweet chin is down on her chest, and her great grey eyes are looking upon my face. And when I look up a light comes into the eyes and a smile comes to play about the beautiful mouth. . . .

And as I wrote those last words she did a thing the ugly man never did and never will do—to me. She blew me a kiss.

I'm sorry I hit him so hard. He deserved it, I know. He deserved to be sawn in two. Still, he did give me a cigar. And, perhaps, if ever he'd known the love of a lady—if anyone ever had looked and smiled on him as sweetheart Jo is looking and smiling on me, he wouldn't have been so vile or kept such doubtful company.

III
MARCH 3RD, 1928

I am dazed ... stunned ... I keep thinking I am asleep and that any minute I shall wake and find it is a dream. I have picked at and felt the letter a score of times to see if it was real. I repeat, I am stunned. My brain is staggering, making fumbling efforts to grasp the frightful truth, getting hold of it—and then, because the truth sears it as an iron sears the flesh, dropping it and clutching fantasy with a wild, desperate clutch.... And fantasy grins and shakes it off and thrusts it back upon the scorching truth....

> *Oh, Richard, I don't know how to write. You've been so wonderful to me, and now—I'm letting you down. I can't help it, Richard. It's something stronger than me. If only I could have you both. But I can't. I've got to choose. And I must go to Berwick —Berwick Perowne. I've tried not to—indeed, I have. But now I can't fight any more....*
>
> *Try and forget me, dear. I'm not fit to be remembered. Try and forget the waster you treated so well. And don't think I'm ungrateful. Strange as it sounds, I'm not. I'm so ashamed, Richard, so terribly, bitterly ashamed, that I can hardly lift my head. But Berwick.... There's something, Richard, you and I never knew. I know it now. I've found it in Berwick Perowne. And I pray the time will come when you'll find it, dear, in someone better than me. And then, I think, you'll understand.*
>
> *Good-bye, Richard. I'm leaving a bit of me behind—a bit of my heart.*
>
> Jo.
>
> *I am so thankful Bugle will never know.*

There. I have copied it out, word for blinding word. Some of the writing is blurred, but it is beautifully plain and easy to read. I remember the first note she wrote me—how pleased I was to see what a good hand she had ... nothing bizarre, just simple, downright, strong. Nothing is slurred—nothing.

I perceive I am trying to gain time—to put off recording the truth. I never did that before, never shrank. If I had to report a failure, I always began with the worst. 'I regret I have failed to secure ...' I don't know why. I think it seemed easier that way. Certainly, putting it off makes it no easier. More difficult, I think.

Jo has left me.

I think I'll give that sentence a line to itself. Incidentally, I can't imagine why I'm writing this down. I don't write things down as a rule—not these sort of things. I suppose I am writing it down because my brain is plunging like a terrified horse and I am hoping to calm it by showing it exactly what it is up against, and so to be able to coax it under this frightful archway and into—into the hell beyond. I suppose, poor brute, it doesn't like the look of hell, and that's why it shies and jibs as if it had seen a ghost.

My good fool, you have seen no ghost, but a perfectly plain, crisp fact—the fact that Jo has gone. Those are her gloves on the table: they still smell of her perfume. If you look at the finger-tips, you will see the faint outline of her beautiful nails. And that is her photograph, there, in the silver frame. But the original has gone ... leaving behind this letter and—other things. Me, for instance. ...

For God's sake let's get down to facts—to see if there isn't some loophole, some flicker of hope.

I had to go to Scotland two days ago. I went by night. I promised Jo I'd be back to-night without fail. We dined without dressing that evening, and Jo seemed rather quiet. I thought it was because I was going away. And—God forgive a fool—I tried to cheer her up. I said that when I was back we'd go down to Bond Street and ask the price of that ring. And Jo put her head in my lap and burst into tears. ... Of course, I see now. At the time I thought ... I kissed her good-bye and went. At twenty to seven to-night I was at King's Cross, and I got the ring with about a minute to spare. That's it—in the box on the mantelpiece. Then I drove home. As I let myself in, Bugle and Mason appeared. As the latter was taking my coat—

"Where's her ladyship?" said I.

"Her ladyship's out, sir," said Mason. "I think she's been called out of Town."

I stared at the fellow blankly.

"'Called out of Town'?" said I.

"I—I believe so, sir. But she left a note, on your table, sir. I expect that'll say . . ."

I hurried into the study, wondering what on earth . . .

I see by my watch that that was four hours ago—four hours. And I am thirty-six and as hard as iron. In the ordinary course of things I shall live to at least sixty-five—another twenty-nine years. How many hours is that?

Well, there are the facts. And here is the letter she left. And here am I. I am the latest instance of that most common unfortunate—a man who has lost his wife.

Will nothing make me realize it? I write these things down—these ghastly, frightening facts. I say them over aloud—without result. They are ugly strings of words, but that is all. I know that any second I shall hear her key in the lock. And Bugle knows it, too. He is lying couched by the door, with his head between his paws. He has lain like that for three hours . . . waiting . . . waiting. . . . And he is losing his labour: because, though Jo has gone out, she will never come in . . . never. . . .

I think I am beginning to comprehend the truth. The sight of that little white dog lying there by the door seems to have—to have emphasized something . . . rammed home . . . something. I know. I know what it is. I realize his folly in lying there. I see that he is a fool—because he is waiting for something which never will come to pass. I don't lie there and wait, because I know better. And I know better because I can read . . . read Jo's letter . . . which says . . . that—she—is—not—coming—back . . . not—coming—back . . .

My beautiful, darling wife is not coming back any more.

That light step in the hall, that eager voice, that quick flutter in the doorway—are silent for ever. Bugle and I will never hear them again. For the last time Jo has leaned over my shoulder, sat by my side at meat, put her sweet arms about me and kissed my lips. She had a way, I remember, of holding her little hands—when she was specially interested, sharing some venture of mine. "Yes, Richard? Yes?" she'd cry, with her precious lips parted and a light in her blessed grey eyes that made me feel heroic and turned my twopenny tale into an exploit. It was always like that. Always her fresh, panting spirit lifted me up. Whatever the road, her footsteps made it shine. I'm not a dancer, but I could dance with Jo.

And now—finish . . . *finish*.

'Finish.' The word stares at me with a queer, crooked look. I never thought of it before, but what a funny-looking word it is. It looks as though it ought to have two n's. 'Finish.' Never mind. The point is that several things are over. My dancing days, for instance. And the light in Jo's grey eyes. And the little way she had of—*My God!* What shall I do? How shall I live and move? I'm like a man in the dark in a dangerous place. I don't know which way to turn. I'm left . . . left. Everything I did was with Jo, or for Jo, or because of Jo. I moved round her, as planets move round their sun. And now my sun's gone . . . my sun . . . my glorious sun. . . .

I must pull myself together. I've done it before. I mustn't gibber and crouch. I must stand up and look Fate in the eyes. I've done that before, too. And she shrank back, as she shall shrink back now.

Jo, my wife, has gone to another man. What of it? I shall be lonely, of course. The little house'll seem strange, I shall go more to the Club, as I used to do—before I was married. I shall have to order the meals and keep the servants more or less up to the mark. And the evenings will seem a bit long. And when I go—to Scotland, there won't be any occasion to hurry back. And that—that's about all.

I think I'll keep her things just as they are. I mustn't get maudlin, but I think that I can do that. Just keep them out and about. It'll seem more natural. And after a while they can gradually be put away . . . after a while. . . .

And now I must go to bed.

I must go to 'The Office' to-morrow and, before I go, I must get out a short report. I meant to have done it to-night, but it's too late now.

She was so exquisite, Jo was . . . so beautiful, gay, sweet . . . so proud to all the world, so tender to me . . . I'd 've said I was too old for her, only she lifted me up and made me a child.

Berwick Perowne. I hardly know the man, except by name. I've only met him twice. Once that night at the Meurices' and once again at the Ritz. I wonder where——

I must go to bed. I must let old Bugle out and go to bed. The great thing is not to think. If Jo were here, I should——

I must go to—*God! My God! I can't.* . . .

I think I shall sleep here to-night. There's nothing the matter with the Chesterfield, and I can get some rugs from the hall.

And I don't think I shall go to 'The Office' to-morrow. If I do, they're bound to act. Whereas, if I hold my hand for another day, S. will have had his money and cut his own throat. And, instead of a bad ten minutes, he'll be broken on the wheel. After all, why shouldn't he be broken? Others are.

IV

FEBRUARY 20TH, 1929

At half-past nine last night I was sitting in the study with Bugle with only the fire for light, when I heard the front-door open and someone come in. Now that Jo's gone, no one but I has a key, so Bugle and I got up and went to the door.

It was Jo.

Before I could speak her arms were round my neck.

Her cheek, her lips were red-hot: her breath coming in spurts.

"Sorry I'm late, my darling, but Daphne's going away and she simply made me——"

The sentence lost itself in a savage cough.

I watched her sway to the sofa as if I was in a dream. . . .

Then I closed the door and switched on the lights.

Something was wrong, of course.

Jo was seriously ill: her skin was burning like fire. Besides, she was talking nonsense. At least . . . For one thing only, I knew that Daphne Pleydell was in the South of France.

Bugle, poor fellow, was almost out of his mind. He was all over Jo, scrambling and whining and pawing and licking her face. For an instant only Jo held him up in her arms. Her sleeves fell back, and I saw how wasted they were. Then—

"You're getting heavy," she laughed, and the poor thin arms gave way and Bugle was in her lap.

Sitting there, flushed, on the sofa, Jo talked and coughed and talked, while Bugle kept whimpering with pleasure and I stood watching and noting and thinking what I must do.

She was wet, very wet, sopping—I could smell the reek of cloth—and very, very shabby. I knew the dress she was wearing—a blue coat and skirt. We chose it together at Bradley's . . . ages ago. Her little hat was a ruin, and her toes were thrusting out of the wreck of a shoe. Her gloves were awful. One tress of her lovely hair was half-way down, and her face was pinched and peaked with two splashes of dusky red about her cheekbones.

I rang for Mason and told him to send a maid to warm my bed and light a fire in the room: after that, to summon a doctor. Then I picked up Jo, still talking, and carried her up the stairs. . . .

All that I did she suffered, just as one suffers the barber to cut one's hair. She took no notice at all of anything, except that now and again she caught my cheek to hers. But she coughed and chattered—nonsense, without a break.

By the time the doctor was there, I'd got her out of the bath and into bed.

He said that she had pneumonia and sent for nurses and drugs.

By eleven o'clock the women had taken over, and all that treatment can do was being done. . . .

Till a quarter past seven this morning I hardly left her side.

At half-past eleven the medicine took some effect, and from then for nearly an hour she never spoke. Then she started again—not chattering any longer, but speaking sterner stuff. The scene had changed.

She talked in a low voice, off and on, right through the night. The cough interfered and her breathing troubled her sorely, but she would talk.

And this, pieced fairly together, is what she said.

"What will I do? I'll tell you. I'll go back to my husband. Perhaps he'll turn me down; perhaps he won't. But, whichever he does, he'll be kind to me, Berwick Perowne. He'd never kick a woman when she was down. I imagine I was bewitched when I turned to you. . . . You 'willed' me, you say? Well, I don't quite know what that means, but I don't see why you should laugh. It's not very generous, considering that you won—while I lost all I had. It broke my heart to leave Richard. You know it did. The first thing I said, when I saw you that awful evening, was that I couldn't go. And you—you begged and argued until you'd made me late—too late to get back and get my letter before he came. . . . Yes, I know. Oh, you acted well. I never dreamed you were doing it on purpose. I never would have, if you hadn't told me so. . . . Why do you laugh so, Berwick? It's so—so unkind. . . . 'Can't go back'? '*Can't*'? What do you mean? It shows you don't know Richard. I tell you . . . What? Well, what if I did? I shouldn't have told you, of course. It was a secret thing. Richard told me, because I was his wife. I don't know what he'd say if he knew that I'd told you, but—why do you laugh like that? I haven't said anything funny. It's very serious. I don't think you realize how serious it is. If you repeated that secret—if you were to tell anyone that Richard had left for Scotland *and never gone there*, that he'd been at Chatham nearly the whole of the time, that he'd only left for Scotland because he knew he was watched and he wanted to make certain people believe he was out of the way—if you were to mention *that*, why, don't you see you'd be doing a frightful thing? You'd be betraying Richard and 'The Office,' too: while, as for me, you'd be stamping me as a traitress in Richard's eyes. He thinks ill of me, of course. I've done him an awful wrong. But, short of absolute proof, he'd *know* that I never was that ... not treacherous.... I've got so little left. I've chucked so much away. But what I've still got I treasure—oh, more than life, far more ... a little shred of honour, very shabby and worn, but clean.... And you see, if you talked, you'd be tearing that shred away. It'd come to Richard's ears in twenty-four hours. He knows everything. He's got to. And, as I was the only soul in all the world he told, he'd know it was me. So you see how terribly important it is that you shouldn't breathe a—— Why do you smile like that? What have I said? Can't you see how ... You can? Then why do you laugh? ... 'Because I've put it so well'? What do you mean? Put what so well? ... 'Your case'? It isn't your case. It's mine. I don't understand. I said I'd go back to Richard, and so I will. For all the wrong I've done him, he'll still be kind. He'd never jeer at a woman because she cried. And he never struck a woman in all his life.... 'Can't go back'? Why? What do you mean? ... 'I've told you myself—just now'? *'Told* you'? I don't understand. How have I told you I can't go back to Richard? ... *My God!* You wouldn't! You couldn't do such a thing. Only a fiend ... You know I shouldn't have told you; but you—you pressed me so hard. And that was between you and me. You can't use an indiscretion to force my hand. You can say you'll tell people this or tell people that, but you can't give away a secret that wasn't mine to tell.... 'Can'? Well, 'won't,' then. You won't do a thing like that! Think what it means to Richard and means to me. Think ... You *will* ... if—I—go—back? You—*will?* Give Richard away ... and 'The Office' ... tear up my shred of honour ... blacken me in Richard's eyes ... ? *Oh—my—God* ... All right.... Yes, I'm beaten.... I—I give you best.... You've won. You've won again.... I see, I understand. I see that I—I can't go back.... Yes, I see why you laughed.... Yes, I suppose it was.... I do indeed, Berwick. I do, I do.... It was peculiarly humorous—my failure to perceive that I was stating your case.... No, don't make me say that.... I'd—I'd rather not. It sounds so hideous, so—— Oh, don't, Berwick! You're hurting! *A-ah!* All right. Let me go. I'll say it. 'Damning my chance of withdrawal out of my own pretty mouth.' . . . Yes, I do see. I've said so. I see that I—can't—go—back. . . ."

One more extract I'll give.

"I'm very sorry, Berwick. I think it's a little cold. . . . No, I promise I won't. You shan't know there's anything wrong. I think if I wear my fur. . . . All right. I won't wear it. I don't mind a bit—really. . . . You know I won't let you down. I shall be all right to-mor—to-night. I'm very strong. . . . Oh, I just felt shivery. . . . No, I promise I won't. . . . I know you hate anything sick. I know you do. I didn't think when I shivered. I won't again. . . . I know, but I won't to-night. I didn't know you heard me. . . . 'Why'? Oh, I don't know. I didn't sleep very well, and I suppose I felt like crying. Women do—sometimes. But I won't cry to-night. . . . I'm very sorry, Berwick. I promise I won't to-night. . . ."

And again one more.

"Only two hundred and fifty! Couldn't you give me more? It's a very good fur—worth two or three thousand francs. I don't expect that, of course, but—two hundred and fifty's not enough. I mean, I need four or five . . . I'm afraid I've nothing else. I'd let you have this umbrella, only it's raining so. Yes, it's a tortoise-shell top. . . . Couldn't you make it four hundred, or even five? You see, my ticket's expensive and. . . . Five hundred with the umbrella? All right. I must let it go. . . . Five hundred. Thanks very much. . . ."

It was almost six o'clock when the change took place.

Jo stopped talking and began to fight. Of course, she hadn't a chance: but she fought for an hour, like the Great Heart she always was. Again and again she rallied: time after time she tore Death's grip away. And I knelt by her side, while the nurses moved to and fro, ministering, whispering words of encouragement, like seconds plying their principal between the rounds.

As it was striking seven, Jo opened her great grey eyes.

For a moment they wandered over and round the room. Then they fell upon my face.

"I got here, then," she said gently. "I am so awfully glad. I wanted to tell you I loved you and—and other things.... Our dream was broken, I know. I broke it, of course. I never knew why. I think that man had some power—I don't know what. Never mind. I broke our dream. But I'd like you to know, my darling, it's the only dream I've had.... And I've kept the broken pieces as one keeps a sacred thing. I've worshipped—reverenced them. They've been my only star. There isn't a flinder missing: they're just as they were that day—sparkling and gay and perfect.... Only, they're pieces, Richard—broken bits and pieces of what was once our dream.... Such as they are, I give them back to you. You gave me the dream, and I broke it. But I've kept the pieces clean, and—here they are."

"I see no pieces, my sweet. You've given me back my dream."

"In pieces, Richard. I broke it."

"And now you've mended it, darling. You've given me back ... our dream."

The old wonderful light flung into those peerless eyes. The old exquisite smile came playing into her face.

"Oh, Richard," she whispered, as though I had made her a present she never had dared expect.

Then she closed her eyes, but the smile never left her face. And presently, with my cheek against hers, she fell asleep.

And that is all, except that I am going to kill Berwick Perowne.

V

MARCH 11TH, 1929

'The Office' gave me two months' leave—'for the purpose of attending to private affairs.' That was on February 25th. Upon the following day I disappeared: and forty-eight hours later I was in touch with Perowne. He had no idea, of course. But I was in touch ... waiting....

I found him at Barcelona, engaged on some Government job. What the job was I don't know, but it left him plenty of time—to take two people about in his great big car. They were French, these two, and pretty rich. The girl was young and handsome, with a dangerously short upper lip and masses of fine red hair. When Perowne took them out, she sat in front with him, her husband and the chauffeur sitting behind.... The husband stuck it until five days ago. Then they left for Valencia, they said, he and his wife ... going by road.

That night I took the lady's name in vain.

I wired from Pampeluna—I had a big car, too—suggesting Perowne should come. He came. I fancy his vanity was tickled. I may be wrong. But I think he liked the idea of the husband chuckling to think that he'd thrown him off the track, while the wife was giving him the tip that they'd taken another road.

A maid at Pampeluna did the rest. At least, she gave him a message, when all the rest of the staff denied the very existence of the lady with the short upper lip and the masses of fine red hair.

The message bade Perowne take the north-east road. This leads into the mountains and is but little travelled till April is old. He took the road the next day, and he took it alone. His chauffeur had supped with me the night before—holding a very short spoon....

I saw him coming when he was miles away, driving like fury along the elegant road that swept and curled and thrust like some stately serpent up and up into bleak places, where, even beneath the sunshine, spring seemed very distant and the monstrous silence of the depths on either hand turned the trickle of running water into the rush of a sluice.

When he was two miles off, I knocked out my pipe. Then I adjusted my goggles and entered my car.

I drove slowly to meet him on one of the bends. The corner was blind, but he cut it—I knew he would. He found me full in his path on my proper side. He tried to get through, but I squeezed him and crammed him into the ditch....

I let him talk for a minute, while I moved on and turned my wheels into a bank. Then I locked the switch and got out of the car.

As I came up he let out at me in French.

"How long have you been driving?"

I answered in English.

"Ten or twelve years," I said.

"Had many accidents?"

"None. And you?"

He stared.

"Let me give you a tip," he said. "When you're driving a car, don't stick too close to your rights. It's not much good to be able to shout 'You're wrong' when they're pickin' what's left of the wind screen out of your brain."

"That's a true enough saying," said I, "and here's another. If you shout for trouble, don't squeal when your prayer is heard," and, with that, I took out tobacco and started to fill a pipe.

For a moment he looked like thunder. Then he flung out a laugh.

"I see you're one of the Die-Hards. I confess I never drive with a Bible under my arm. But there you are." He rose and peered at the ditch. "Another two inches of your precious slice of the way, and I should have been all right."

"Four," said I, and pointed to a scar in the road. "That was your safety crease. With a wheel on that, I knew you were bound to go."

Perowne stared at the scar. It might have been cut with a punch. As a matter of fact, it had. Presently he looked at me. I pressed my tobacco home and stared at the sky.

Perowne got out of his car and looked at her tracks. Then he picked up a stick and did some measuring. . . .

"You're right," said he. "Right to an eighth of an inch."

"I know," said I. "I measured your car last night."

For a moment he never moved. Then he took out cigarettes, lighted one carefully and leaned against the door with a foot on the step.

"So I was wrong," he said softly. "You do know how to drive."

I shrugged my shoulders.

"Maybe," said I, watching his right arm move. "I took your pistol, too," I added carelessly.

For a moment or two he almost lost control. Then he took a deep breath.

"Well," he sighed, "you're thorough. I'll give you that. And my chauffeur? I suppose I owe his failure to the same virtue."

"You do," said I. "And the message."

"Dear, dear," said he. "Not the telegram, too?"

"The telegram, too," said I.

"Well, I'm damned," said he, crossing his legs. "You do work hard, don't you?" With half-closed eyes, he let the smoke make its way out of his mouth. "Glorious view from here. . . . That why you brought me?"

"In a way," said I. "It's quite a good place to—to see the sun go down."

Perowne shot me a glance.

"No doubt," he said shortly. "But—I'm afraid I can't wait so long. And now tell me your game, and I'll see if I care to play. Which is it—blackmail or murder?"

"It's not blackmail," said I, and took off my goggles.

"Hullo," said Perowne. "If it isn't old What's-his-name!"

The thrust was shrewd. Almost I lost my temper. To pretend that she'd meant so little that her name was out of his mind. . . .

Instead—

"Some names sting the tongue," I said quietly.

He lifted his head and looked at the cold blue sky.

"True," he said. "And the brush of some lips the mouth."

"I'll take your word for it," said I.

"Tell me," he said, frowning. "Did she go back to you?"

"She did," said I: "to die."

"I thought she would," said Perowne.

"Forgive me," said I. "You thought she wouldn't dare." He started. "You used her love for me to bind her feet. That's how you held her, you rotten loose-lipped thief... trading on her devotion to another man.... And then at the last, poor lady, she called her bully's bluff, stared Blackmail out of countenance, and came back."

The fellow's face was livid: his eyes like swords. For a moment he stood trembling, with fists clenched. Then he seemed to think better of his valour and, clapping his hands behind him, threw himself back with a jerk against the spare wheel.

"And now you're out for blood?" he burst out presently.

I knocked out my pipe.

"Some years ago," I said. "I was in Macedonia. Up in the mountains, I remember, there was an old churchyard, quite full of graves." I looked about me. "The place was not unlike this.... And every grave had been opened—to release the spirits of the dead. It was a local superstition. Now, what do you think lived *and grew fat*.... in that churchyard?"

There was a long silence.

At length I leaned forward.

"Snakes, Perowne, snakes. Snakes that traded on devotion ... turned piteous piety to their own ends ... used women's love for their husbands to fill their bellies ... battened upon the dead ... And you ask if I'm out for blood. What do you think?"

"Think?" said he. "Why, I think you're very confident."

"I confess it," said I. "I'm a poacher to-day. But you should watch your preserves."

He stared at the edge of the road and into the depths beyond. Then he tilted his chin and scanned the grandeur of Navarre—all mountains and sudden valleys and again mountains like footstools to mountains greater than they, so that the world seemed nothing but a black sea of breakers foam-crested, petrified.

"You're sore, of course," he mused. "It's a way relicts have.... But why have you left it so long?"

"I thought she was happy," I said. "It never occurred to me that the man was born who could treat such a lady ill. But it seems you struck her, Perowne."

He cried out at that, but the blood was in my head and I shouted him down.

"More," I raved, "more. You jeered at her grief ...... mocked at her misery ... twisted those delicate arms ... cursed her for weeping because it spoiled your sleep ... bullied my dying girl ... My God! My God!" I bowed my head and covered my eyes with my hands. "Don't think she told me," I muttered. "She never gave you away. But——"

As I lifted my head, the spare wheel caught me full in the face.

I went down like a log, with the wheel on the top of me. I never remember feeling so shaken up. I wasn't exactly unconscious but things were distorted—unreal.

I saw Perowne seize a kit-bag and drop it into the ditch. I saw him slip into the car and I heard her start. I saw her begin to move ... lurch ... pitch to and fro. I saw the pitches grow longer—more pronounced. I began to get quite interested, wondering at every failure whether he'd get her out at the next attempt. All the time his engine kept storming like an angry fiend....

Suddenly my brain cleared, and I realized that he was like to be gone and leave me sitting in the road with a wheel in my lap.

I heaved the wheel off my legs and leapt for the luggage-grid, as the car shot back. Its off hind wheel went over the spare with a couple of jerks that nearly threw me off. Then he clapped her into first, bumped over the spare wheel again and flung up the pass all out....

Perhaps for the very first time in all his life Perowne had lost his nerve. I thought he had, and the moment I saw him I knew. And the knowledge did me more good than the wind in my face. The man was not sitting: he was crouched—with his shoulders up to his ears. His one idea was to get away from that spot. The silence, perhaps....

He never saw me climb up over the hood or settle myself on the seat behind his back. But I did. As a matter of fact, I sat there a minute or two—to get my breath and recover—before I put him wise.

Strangely enough, my touch seemed to bring his confidence back.

He gave one whoop.... Then he threw back his head and laughed up into my eyes.

"You do work hard," he said. "I thought you were done."

The road was falling now for a long half-mile.

I stretched out a hand and switched his engine off.

He cursed me for that. Then he stamped on the clutch.

"I'll take you to find her in hell," he cried, and headed straight for the brink.

I clapped my hands on his and wrenched the wheel about.

For a second I thought we were over.... Then the car swung back to the crown of the road.

Again he swerved to the off, and I wrenched her back.

All the time the car was gathering speed.

I had the strength, but he had the position. We swayed and swung and swerved all over the road, fighting and raving like madmen to get the upper hand. Twice I went for the brake, but each time, before I could reach it, I had to catch at the wheel. I crushed his fingers, and he screamed and spat in my face.

We were doing fifty now, and a curve was coming. The man wasn't born that could take it without brakes. Perowne saw it, too, and laughed.

"Behold our spring-board," he said.

I seized his neck and jammed his face between the spokes of the wheel.

"Now turn it," said I.

Then I applied the brakes. . . .

When the car came to rest, I let him lift his head.

Then I put my hands under his chin and looked into his eyes.

"You'll never see her," I said. "She's up in heaven."

He smiled.

"With the rest of the *demi-monde*!"

I began to bend him back.

"Where there aren't any bullies," I said. "She had her hell upon earth."

"I devilish nearly won," said he.

"You did," said I. "But you made one bad mistake."

"Why, what was that?" said he.

"You lost your nerve."

He struggled at that, and I bent him back again.

"This won't help her," he blurted, panting.

"The more's the pity," said I. "But it'll help me and it'll make the world cleaner."

Again I bent him back, till his eyes were starting and his back curved like a bow.

"For God's sake, end it," he whimpered.

"Ask in her name," said I.

"For . . . her . . . sake."

I broke his back.

Then I turned the wheels to the edge and started the engine up. . . .

The car came to rest finally about six hundred feet below the road—a battered blazing wreck.

For a moment I watched her burn, and, being human and very much in love with my dead wife, felt better than I had felt for many a month.

That was three days ago.

To-morrow morning I shall report for duty.

VI
SEPTEMBER 5TH, 1929

I came up from Bristol to-day.

Just as the train was starting, the door of my carriage was opened, and a woman was hoisted in.

She stuck a glass in her eye and waved to her breathless squire.

"So long, Nosey," she said. "'Fraid I'm out of bananas, but here's an onion's heart."

She blew him a kiss and flung herself back in her seat.

I knew her at once: and I began to wonder if she'd remember me. She did. After a little reflection she opened her mouth.

"Didn't I meet you," she said, "at the Meurices'?"

"That's right," said I. "You told my fortune from my hand."

She looked at me sharply.

"I remember," she said. "Did—did it ever come true?"

"Half of it did. You said I should meet a man who'd have a terrific influence on my life—indirectly, through somebody else. Well, you were perfectly right."

"That all?" she said, looking at me very hard.

"Yes," I said. "That's all that's been fulfilled. So far as I know, I've had no influence on him. And I assume I should know. Mine was to be direct, if you remember."

"And physical," said Sarah Roach.

"And physical," said I, "whatever that may mean. If it's coming off, it'll have to come off quick. He's over seventy-four, and the papers say he's ill."

Miss Roach stared at me as if I was drunk.

"Seventy-four?" she snapped. "Who—what's his name?"

"That I can't tell you," said I. "But he's in Debrett. Why shouldn't he be seventy-four?"

"Oh, I don't know."

She picked up her papers then, and we said no more.

As the train was running into Paddington—

"I don't talk," she said, "but I study women and men and put two and two together rather as you do yourself. And when I've done my addition I like turning up the answer to see if I'm right."

"Well," said I, wondering what was afoot.

"Well, I've done a sum," she said, "and you've got the answer. If I tell you my result, will you tell me whether it's right?"

"It depends on the sum," said I. "I don't talk either, you know."

"It's nothing to do with your job. It's a purely personal matter."

"In that case I'll say 'Yes' or 'No.'"

"Right," said Sarah Roach, "and remember—I don't talk. Did you kill Berwick Perowne?"

"I had that pleasure," said I. "But how did you know?"

She laughed.

"Simple addition," she said. "Besides, I'm half a prophet."

Which is all she'll ever be, so far as I'm concerned. For I see from this morning's paper that Sir George —— is dead.

ATHALIA

"I FEEL," said Fairfax, "that I must marry you."

His partner threw back her head and laughed delightedly.

"I warn you," she flashed, "I'm very rich."

"Oh, but why 'warn'?" said Fairfax, swinging her off her feet and then subsiding abruptly into a step of which the progressive nature was almost imperceptible. "Besides, I knew it before. Besides, if you had been poor, I shouldn't have spoken."

"Are you seriously asking me to be your wife?"

"I am. So far as you're concerned, the advantages of such a course may not be obvious. To be perfectly frank, I can hardly see them myself. Still, you might do worse. At least, I'm clean, honest and sober."

"I'm not so sure about that," said Athalia Choate.

The man raised his eyebrows. Then he laid hold of the lady and started to dance.

It was a superb performance.

The floor was crowded, but, for all the notice of others that Fairfax seemed to take, it might have been empty. The two passed as one through the press, whirling, side-stepping, poising, translating every whim of the capricious measure into a masterpiece of motion. Athalia found herself treading as she had never trod before, yet making no mistake. The firm pressure upon her back became a powerful government, urging her to right or left, turning her, keeping her clear of collision, lifting her into the very spirit of the dance. The pace of the music grew hotter; the fury of the band, madcap. All about them people were labouring hilariously in a feverish endeavour to keep abreast of the rhythm. Fairfax's feet moved like quicksilver . . . the two swam the length of the ballroom with a clean rush . . . he was doing another step, and she was late . . . she was off her feet, and he was thrusting again into the very heart of the crowd . . . her head——

Then the music stopped, and she was released.

"Am I sober?" said Punch Fairfax.

Miss Choate took a deep breath.

"Indubitably," she said.

They made their way downstairs to a dim library, and Fairfax drew two chairs to the slow wood fire. Then he gave her a cigarette, lighted it, and took one himself.

"Will you do me a favour?" he said.

"Try me," said Miss Choate.

"Be perfectly honest with me for a quarter of an hour."

The lady knitted her brows.

"What do you mean?"

"That will appear," said Fairfax. "The best way to learn a game is to start playing it. Now then. Are you averse to wedlock?"

Miss Choate started.

"I—I never agreed to play," she said uneasily.

Punch pulled his moustache.

"It's a very good game," he said. "I have to answer, too—any question you ask."

Athalia subjected the toe of a ridiculously tiny slipper to a prolonged scrutiny. At length—

"The answer," she said, "is in the negative."

"Good," said Fairfax, marking the excellence of her instep. "I'm seven years older than you. As a matter of fact, I think that's just about right. Do you agree?"

"I don't disagree," said Miss Choate slowly. "Anything between five and ten years. . . . When do I start?"

"When you please," said Fairfax, comfortably exhaling smoke. "What a sweet pretty leg you've got! Do you like my style?"

Miss Choate swallowed.

"You are quick," she said. "Of course, I've never played this before, so——"

"Neither have I," said Punch. "I give you my word. Er, do you?"

The lady stared into the fire.

"Yes," she said, "I do. If I had been poor, you wouldn't have spoken, would you?"

"I should not."

"Why?"

"Because I haven't enough to keep you—us as we should be kept."

Athalia laughed.

"'I could not love thee, dear, so much,'" she quoted, "'loved I not *comfort* more.'"

"My dear," said Punch, "that was most admirably put. It exactly represents my point of view, your point of view and the point from which, furiously as they would deny the impeachment, every rational male and female in this edifice views the rich vale of matrimony."

Miss Choate raised her sweet eyebrows.

"We are a topping lot of wash-outs, aren't we?" she said.

Fairfax shook his head.

"Not at all. We're just wise. We have the sagacity to avoid the steep and narrow path which leads to heroism, because we blinkin' well know that we should never get there."

"But——"

"One moment. If Fortune puts us upon that path, as she may, that's another matter. We get to heroism then. But if we choose it of our own free will—never. Never. Because, sooner or later, we always regret our choice. And there ain't no admittance to 'eroism for gents wot regrets their choice."

"I seem to know that line," said Miss Choate. "Isn't it out of *His Sin against Her Love?*"

Fairfax appeared to wince.

"Tennyson, dear, Tennyson. Hiawatha's address to the Boy Scouts."

There was a pregnant silence.

As soon as she could trust her voice—

"Aren't you leaving love out of the question?" ventured Athalia.

"I don't think so. I know love jettisons fear, but I don't think it sandbags the instinct of self-preservation. I don't mean that if you tottered into a bear-pit I wouldn't go in to get you out. But if you dropped your lip-stick in—well, the bears could have it."

"Supposing it was the only lip-stick I had?"

"Nothing doing," said Fairfax.

"Supposing I said that if you got it out I'ld marry you?"

"Love doesn't——"

"Don't evade," said Miss Choate. "There's another ten minutes to go."

Fairfax looked at her.

Silhouetted against the black of an old bureau, the delicate features looked especially beautiful. The smooth brow, the straight clean-cut nose, the sweet droop of the mouth—from temples to pert chin my lady's face was a picture for men to kneel to.

Her squire covered his eyes.

"Rot it," he said shakily. "I—I believe I should have a dart."

Athalia permitted herself to smile.

"But if I was poor you wouldn't?"

"No. For both our sakes. . . . Yes—I'm honest. For both. We're earthy, you know. It'ld mean that we'ld have to come down—come down in the world. Well, I shouldn't like that—I'ld hate it. And so would you. And on the top of it all I should always know two things—first, that I'd brought you down, and then that you might have married a richer man."

"How would you bring me down if I was poor?"

"My dear, your face is your fortune—your face and your pretty ways. You might be poor as blazes, but as long as you stayed single you could dine and dance and sleep in half the ancestral homes of England."

"Sort of second Queen Elizabeth?" said Athalia. "I must be nice."

"Oh, but you are," said Punch. "Most—er—most nice."

"D'you mind speaking the truth?"

Fairfax moistened his lips.

"You are probably the most adorable woman in London to-day. I have never heard anything said of you which you would not have liked to hear. Finally, you are frequently indicated as a future Duchess: in fact, if you married me, I believe sterling would drop two stitches—I mean, points."

"I wish I was poor," said Miss Choate.

"What would you do?"

Again the lady smiled.

"I should probably marry you," she said.

"But I shouldn't 've asked——"

"I should waive that preliminary," said Miss Choate calmly.

So soon as he could speak—

"You forward girl," said Fairfax. "You wicked——"

"And you," continued Athalia, "not having had any say in the matter, would go up the steep and narrow path to heroism—touching the ground in spots. I should see to that," she added darkly.

Fairfax wiped his brow.

"Oh, the vixen," he said. "Listen at her."

"As it is," said his companion, "though my feet are of clay—'earthy,' I think, was your expression—the man who marries me must think them of fine gold."

Fairfax looked down his nose.

"There are plenty of coves," he said, "who'll tell you the tale. Besides, when I said you were earthy, I only meant 'human.' Hang it, Athalia, if I told you your little feet were golden, you'ld tell me to go straight home and sleep it off."

"Also," continued Miss Choate, "he must prefer my smile to any comfort that he has ever dreamed of."

"But I do," protested her swain. "Infinitely. They're not in the same street."

"Rot," said Athalia. "You love your comfort best every time. My smile doesn't come off with my pearls. If I was poor, my smile'ld still be there. But you wouldn't want it then."

"Of course I should. And if I was rich, I'd have it. It's not your money I want, but it *is* your money we need. I've been honest about it. 'Live and let live,' you know."

"Have you anything," said Athalia, "but what you earn?"

"Not a bean," was the cheerful reply. "I had sixty thousand, you know. But I've been through the lot."

"Good," said my lady. "Look here. Jobs tend to cramp the style——"

"They're a weariness of the flesh," sighed Punch.

"—and my husband's style must not be cramped. If you'll give up your job, I'll—I'll marry you."

Punch Fairfax sat up, open-mouthed.

"What an' keep me?"

"I'll settle two thousand a year on you. That's twice what you earn."

There was an electric silence.

Then Punch rose with a laugh.

"'Clean, honest and sober,'" he said quietly. "I see that I should have added 'respectable': but, to tell you the truth, I——"

"Sit down, Punch, me lad," said Athalia Choate. "Dismount and sit down. You've given the answer I wanted. Not that I really doubted, but—one likes to make sure."

Fairfax regarded her thoughtfully. Then—

"Talk about edgywedged tools," he said, resuming his seat. "Supposing I'd said 'D-d-done!'—all quick like, with bulging eyes...."

Athalia laughed.

"I should have found a way," she murmured. "And now go on—ask me. There's still five minutes to go."

"As you please," said Punch. "Why does one like to make sure?"

"Because, so far as I'm concerned, there are only two starters for the Athalia Stakes—and you're one of them."

"Athalia!"

"Wait. I'll be perfectly straight with you. I've had one or two proposals—most women have. But as yet I haven't had one from . . . the man I love." Her companion started. "That's often the way, you know. Perhaps I shall never have it. Many women don't. . . . But oh"—she laced her slight fingers, set them against her cheek and raised her eyes ecstatically—"oh, I hope I shall, Punch. If you knew what it meant to me! I'd be so awfully happy. . . ."

"Well, I—I hope you will, too," said Fairfax dismally. "I—I do really. . . . But what are you telling me this for?"

"Because you can help me. You see, he is such a dear, but, though we're quite good friends, the idea of falling in love with me doesn't seem to have entered his head. And, if he saw us together, I think it might make him think."

Fairfax laughed hysterically.

"Excuse my emotion," he said. "The—the humour of it's sort of dawning on me—that's all."

"'Humour'?" cried Athalia.

"Humour—'h' mute. Let me explain. Only two runners for the Stakes, of which I'm one and the other won't start. So I'm to show off my paces—play about on the course and generally show the other what fun running is, and then when it finally dawns on him that if he follows the rails they'll bring him to the post, I'm to—— Well, where *do* I come in? I suppose I get a lump of sugar and a dazzling smile."

"Perhaps," said Athalia dreamily, "the other'll never start."

Punch set his teeth.

"Does it occur——"

"Perhaps," continued Athalia, "when he does, you'll leave him standing." The man stared. "That's my trouble. I love him desperately now—possibly because he doesn't love me. But, once he's started, you may go right away."

Fairfax fingered his chin.

"D'you really think that likely?"

"It's quite on the cards. At the moment I like you and I love him. So I obviously can't marry you. If once he gets going, I shall see him in quite a new light. And then—why, I mayn't love him at all."

"Are you sure you've got it right?" said Punch. "I mean, these 'ere love-squalls are very tricky. Perhaps you don't really care about either of us. I'm sure you think you do, but perhaps you don't. I remember Dusty Bligh wobbling between Ray Darling, that was, and Monica Pump. Neither of the girls would have been seen dead with him, but that never entered his head. His trouble was that he couldn't decide which to have. It was like a billiard match. In the afternoon Monica'ld be leading, and in the evening Ray'ld get her eye in and fairly walk away. It might have been going on now, if a widow with three kids hadn't rolled up and pinched the prize."

"Serve him right," said Miss Choate. "But I'm not wobbling. Don't you believe it. If the man I love would only propose to-night, I'd fairly jump at him."

"The devil you would," said Fairfax.

"But he won't," said Athalia sadly. "Don't be afraid." A tender note slid into the fresh tones. "I think he's love-shy. He'll want a lot of leading. And then, as I've said, perhaps it won't be the same."

Punch frowned upon his finger-nails.

"You know, it's all damned fine," he said uneasily, "but in the course of this running-up stunt I may get fond of you." He hesitated. Then—"Not soppy, you know, but—but troubled . . . go off my feed and that sort of thing. At the present moment I'm sorry, and there you are; but if I saw a lot of you, as you seem to suggest I should—well, I might easily get distracted. And then if the other gent comes off I'm carted good and proper, I am."

Athalia shrugged her white shoulders.

"That's your look-out. On the other hand, I may get fond of you. It's a gamble, of course: but so are a lot of things. And I've told you the absolute truth. I needn't have. Not one woman in a million would have. They'd 've played you up all right without putting you wise. And you'd 've blessed or cursed them according as it fell out. But I agreed to be honest—for a quarter of an hour. . . . Incidentally, I see the time's up."

"Make it twenty minutes," said Fairfax hastily.

"Not for worlds," said Athalia, with a bewitching smile. She rose and, standing a-tiptoe, peered at herself in the mirror above the hearth. "And now, which is it to be?"

Thoughtfully Punch regarded her exquisite form.

Presently the girl turned her head and looked at him over her shoulder.

In silence their eyes met.

At length—

"I feel I'm asking for trouble," said the man, "but I may as well have a dart." He rose, stepped to her side and took her small hands in his. "I don't believe I've an earthly, Athalia dear, but, whatever happens, I'll have been with you a bit, won't I? And—when I'm hungry, I expect I'll be glad of those crumbs."

Miss Choate said nothing.

Fairfax kissed her cool fingers.

Six weeks had gone by, through which, so far as his secretaryship permitted, Punch had devoted his time to Athalia Choate. Three days out of five he saw her by hook or by crook. One night they danced together, another they dined. Twice, time being hard to come by, they had met before breakfast in the Row. On three out of seven Sundays they had spent the day in his car—a powerful grey two-seater, aged and greedy, but sound and good to look at. The comfort of its rubbed cushions stuck in the memory, like that of a glass of old port.

Such attention would not have been possible, but for the lady herself. Athalia's parents were dead, and, though she visited America every autumn, the great mansion in Philadelphia was rented year after year, and its girlish landlord spent nearly all her time within hail of a beloved aunt. The latter had married one of the King's Household. . . . The engagement-book of an exceptionally attractive heiress, so chaperoned, is apt to be full. But Athalia saw to it that Punch was not crowded out. More. True to the spirit of their contract, the girl never fobbed him off. Whenever he sought her company, she gave it with a quick smile. If his work made their meeting difficult, she helped him to find a way. If he bored her, she never showed it: if another should have stood in his shoes, she gave no sign. Only, though she had her own cars, she never used them once when Fairfax was there. Whatever the night, she came and went by taxi if Punch was to be her squire. And though two or three times he came to her uncle's house, it was always to big parties, where he was one of a crowd. If she entertained herself, Fairfax was never asked.

That this faintly surprised the latter, the following letter will show. He wrote it to his twin sister, Lady Defoe.

July 18th, 1923.

DEAR JUDY,

> The worst has happened. I knew it would. I'm off my feed. As gentle a brace of kidneys as ever you saw.... I give you my word, I had to cover them up—they stared so reproachfully. Well, it's my own fault. I walked slap into the cage—Athalia showed me round it: together we looked at the bars. And now I can't get out. I tell you I've got it bad. I've got to the mathematical stage—adding up how many hours before I see her again, subtracting so many for sleep and glaring at the balance as if it were a bad debt. Did you ever do that, Judy? And all the time I'm racking my rotten brain.... I'm sure it's Beringhampton. I'm positive. He knew her before, of course: but he never sat up and took notice until a month ago. And now—well, Mary's lamb isn't in it. He's always around somewhere—always. I happen to know he loathes racing, but the two days she was at Newmarket there he was. I must admit he's good-looking—I think he's the best-looking man I ever saw. But he's a queer-tempered cove. And I'm sorry if he's the man—as he surely is. You see, Judy, no one else fits. If you asked me to find a fellow who needed a lead, who didn't know his own mind, who'd keep on staring at a strawberry and thinking what a whopper it was without it entering his head that he might as well pick it—I should shout 'Beringhampton.' Everyone would. Oh, of course it's him. 'The man I love.' Aren't women funny? Of course I may be wrong. There's plenty of other lads all over Athalia; but they're not hard up for ideas. They don't need any pushing: most'ld look a bit better with four-wheel brakes. Again, it may be someone who hasn't stripped: but, if it is, they're lying devilish low. I tell you I've racked my brain.... But whoever it is has done me in all right—mucking about like this. Damn it, they must love her, unless they've got tea in their veins. You've only got to see her for that. Then what's their mouth for? And while they're boggling, I'm being broken up.... And there you are. If somebody said, 'All right: they shall speak to-night,' I'ld knock his face through his head. I love my tenterhooks. You know—the 'sweet sorrow' stunt. I tell you, Judy, I'm on the edge of poetry. I want the business finished and I don't want it finished. I don't know what I want. Yes, I do. **I want Athalia.** I want her as I never wanted anything before. I thought I wanted her six weeks ago. 'Want'? I didn't know what the word meant. I'm absolutely mad about her, Judy. I don't let her see it, you know, but when she appears I have to hold on to something or I'ld be jumping up and down. Her eyes, her hair, her blessed mouth—why, her little mouth'ld make most women, wouldn't it? You do like her, don't you?

Of course I know you do, but just say so in your next letter. Just make up something nice and shove it in. It'll be like a drink to me. . . . Well, I don't know what's to happen. We never fixed a time-limit, so this may go on for months. Sometimes I feel I can't bear it—only last night I damned near had it all out. But then, if I do and she thinks the other cove's warming up, everything'll be queered: I shall be fired on the spot and my precious little bubble'll become, as they say, disintegrated. Whereupon I shall seek the water under the earth. . . . At other times I'm afraid—terrified, Judy old girl, that the very next time I see her she's going to say, 'He's won,' and wring my hand and thank me for working Beringhampton up to the scratch. You see, she's no idea that she's shortening my life. She knows I'm out to marry her, but she doesn't dream that I'm nearly off my head. I hide it all right, you know. Most casual, I am. And when she isn't looking, I kiss her blessed gloves. . . .

She doesn't ask me to dinner. That shows how little she knows. Of course she'd ask me if she thought I'd care to come. It just doesn't occur to her, Judy. I admit she asks Beringhampton—at least, she did last time. . . .

I suppose you couldn't write and suggest that she came to Biarritz. Wrap it up, you know. Say the bathing's a treat, and it's the first time you've been warm since the War, and all that sort of wash. You see, I can get leave in August, and what more natural or pious than that I should come and see you? Incidentally, that'd show us whether Beringhampton means business. If he follows her to Biarritz, he simply must speak.

So long, Judy love,

PUNCH.

P.S.—Of course, it may be all over before August. I don't think *B.'s going strong, but, except for Sundays, I never see her by day. From ten to six he's got the course to himself. These cursed idle rich. . . . I tell you I'm seeing the Labour point of view.*

P.P.S.—What an histoire *this letter is! I've just been reading it through, and it's shaken me up.*

I'm coming unbuttoned, Judy. Poor old Punch is coming unbuttoned at last.

Seven days later Miss Choate confided to Fairfax that she had heard from Judy.

"Not my twin-sister?" said Punch, with a daring display of amazement.

"The same," said Athalia. "Why shouldn't I hear from her?"

"No reason at all," said Punch, "except that she never writes. I've had six letters from her since she was married—that's seven years ago. Mole says she's a vegetarian—thinks it cruel to use ink, but, speakin' as one who's known her all her life except the first twenty minutes, I incline, as they say, to the view that she's labour-shy. What does she say?"

"Suggests that I come to Biarritz. By way of inducement she adds: *The bathing's a treat, and it's the first time you've been warm since the War, and all that sort of wash.*"

Mentally, Fairfax consigned Lady Defoe to a resort where the warmth would be still more remarkable.

"Must be losing her mind," he said shortly. "What 'wash'?"

"Can't conceive," said Miss Choate innocently. "Never mind. The point is, shall I go?"

"Why not?" said Punch. "It's about the only place in Europe I know where you can bathe in comfort without a fleece-lined wet-off bathing-suit and a sealskin towel. I shouldn't faint with surprise if I rolled up there myself. I want to see Judy, and my leave starts on the sixth."

"I'm not sailing till the end of September," said Athalia musingly, "so I could put in a month. I must confess I'd rather like to get warm. When's your Bank Holiday?"

"Sixth of *août*," said Punch. "I should give that a miss."

"If I went on the fourth . . ." She sighed. "At least, it'll be a change. After all, Life's rather like a frock. If it's to be a success, you must see it from every angle. Besides, to tell you the truth, I think it'ld be a good move—my suddenly leaving the stage. Nature abhors a vacuum."

Fairfax' heart stood still.

After an awkward silence—

"Is—is he showing any signs of life?" he said uncertainly.

Athalia looked away.

"I—I think so," she whispered.

Upon being approached, Sir Charles Grist could see no reason at all why his secretary's leave should not commence at five on Sunday afternoon instead of at twelve o'clock on Sunday night.

It was therefore eight-thirty o'clock of a pleasant August evening when the old grey two-seater slid through the streets of Newhaven and down to the idle quay.

Two other cars were waiting to go aboard. One was a green cabriolet with red wire wheels.

Fairfax knew it at once—and stopped in his tracks.

It was an Hispano-Suiza, the property of a nobleman—that, in fact, of the Most Honourable the Marquess of Beringhampton.

For a moment or two Punch stared at the equipage. Then he took out his case and lighted a cigarette.

"They're off at last," he said. "After seven weeks at the gate, at last they're off.... If I wasn't a blinkin' fool, I should turn round and drive straight back. As it is ..." He shifted uneasily. "*Damn* it all, why shouldn't I have a run? Why shouldn't I have it out before he comes— get there and have it out? An' tell her he's coming an' then push gracefully off? I've nothing to lose, and I'd like her to know how much I really cared." He sat up suddenly. "By George, I will. When she knows he's really off, perhaps she won't——" He stopped short there, took off his hat and carefully wiped his face. Then he put on his hat, adjusted it carefully, thrust his cigarette between his lips, and folded his arms. "The art of Life," he announced, "is to keep one's bullet head. If I go, it's simply because I've got nothing to lose."

As the A.A. man came up—

"Last on the boat, first off—am I right?" said Fairfax.

"You are, sir."

"Then put me on last, please."

"I will, sir."

Punch handed over his papers and sought for a drink.

As he passed into the hotel, Beringhampton came out.

"Hullo," said Fairfax cheerfully. "Come and have another."

The other stared.

"Are you crossing?" he said.

"I am that," said Fairfax, "complete with automobile. Destination, B-B-B-Biarritz—where the rainbow ends."

"What are you going there for?"

"Pleasure," said Punch shortly. "And you?"

For a moment Beringhampton looked him in the face. Then the peer's eyes fell to the mat at his feet.

"I never talk," he said. "I never talk."

He spat the words rather than spoke them.

"All right," said Fairfax, laughing. "But come to the harbour bar and have a——"

"'S damned bad form to laugh," flashed Beringhampton, and went his way.

Fairfax looked after him.

"The man's mad," he murmured. "Staring mad. Face like a Greek god, an' a kink in his brain. . . . And to think she thinks she loves him!" He raised his eyes to heaven. "Oh, where's the bar?"

That night in his cabin Fairfax remade his plans.

Between Dieppe and Biarritz lay five hundred and twenty miles. He had intended to stay one night on the road and had chosen Tours as his lodging. From Dieppe to Tours the distance was two hundred miles. Thus, travelling at ease, he would have come to Biarritz on Tuesday afternoon.

His meeting with Beringhampton had altered everything.

Generally, it suggested that any avoidable delay should be avoided. Specially, it emphasized the desirability of extreme haste, first, because Beringhampton would naturally propose to reach Biarritz before the grey two-seater, and, secondly, because the Hispano-Suiza was far and away the faster car.

Punch knitted his brows.

The boat would reach Dieppe at 4 a.m.: with luck his car could have passed the Customs and be actually on the road at five o'clock; and then—five hundred and twenty miles. . . .

Rejecting travellers' tales in favour of the report of personal experience, Punch decided that if he could maintain an average of thirty-five miles an hour he would do extremely well. If he allowed two hours for meals and rest, that would bring him to Biarritz by ten o'clock. To shave, bathe, change and locate Athalia would take the best part of an hour. Eleven o'clock. Punch wrinkled his nose. Mercifully Miss Choate kept late hours . . . mercifully. . . . And this was assuming that he ran to time.

With a sigh, Fairfax took out tobacco and lighted a pipe.

By what hour the Hispano-Suiza could reach Biarritz he deliberately declined to calculate. The answer could do no good and would be discouraging. Given a car which can average fifty upon the open road, and a chauffeur to take the wheel when you feel tired. . . . But then who was to say that Beringhampton would go straight through? Besides . . .

Fairfax folded his map and took off his collar and shoes. Then he lay down on the seat and wished for the day.

This came in due season, fresh and cloudless: but other things first—the port of Dieppe, for instance, and shouts and clangings of the telegraph.

A press of miserable passengers, cold, heavy-laden, white-faced, squeezed and fought its way towards the steep gangway, stumbled up the rude slope, clattered over setts and metals and swarmed nervously into a grisly Custom House, there to protest despairingly that it had 'nothing to declare.' Blue-jerseyed porters, frantic with excitement, panted and screamed and staggered under stupendous loads. A steam crane swung to and fro about its business, responding with an uncanny intelligence to the medley of confused directions constantly hurled at its cab. Trucks, seemingly designed for uproar, bumped and rumbled and crashed from quay to platform, their governors bawling for '*Attention*' in a monotonous drawl. A man in charge of a refreshment-waggon was crying his wares: another shouted recurrently that the train would not depart for thirty minutes and urged the prudence of a meal at the buffet: a boy was dismally chanting the names of newspapers; a porter who had lost his patrons was howling "*Soixante-dix*": four Frenchmen were arguing explosively about 'summer time': a terrier was barking like a fiend: over all, the deafening roar of escaping steam strengthened the resemblance of the scene to the evacuation of hell. As if to clinch its identity, here and there stood the cloaked and hooded figures of Authority, motionless, silent, indifferent to the bustle and hubbub, smoking contemptuously, sinister, lynx-eyed. Their deliberate detachment from struggling humanity, their sullen observance and studied disregard of a thousand needs, were arguing a stony misanthropy, malicious, Satanic.

Fairfax watched and waited with an eye on the clock. So did Beringhampton. The latter's chauffeur had a very bad time. It was not, of course, his fault that the officials declared their intention of disembarking the cars as they came. Neither, indeed, was it his fault that, when the cars were ashore, a certain necessary officer was not forthcoming. Yet he paid for this, as did the A.A. man—generously. The idea of waiting till seven did not appeal to Beringhampton—nor, for the matter of that, to Punch, either. Still, the latter kept his temper and cursed with a smile on his lips. . . .

While Beringhampton stalked off the quay in search of a lodging, Fairfax took off his coat and went over his car. Not so the Marquess' chauffeur. After asking Punch if he could be of any assistance, the latter climbed into his charge and endeavoured to sleep. Injustice makes a bad servant. It also may do a rival a very good turn. It did—that Monday morning. Of the five cars to be cleared the grey two-seater was the first inspected and the Hispano-Suiza the fifth. Beringhampton raged. Then a tire was found flat, and the wheel had to be changed. . . .

While Punch was clear of Dieppe by seven-fifteen, it was half-past eight ere the other took the road.

A start of fifty miles was not to be sneezed at, but the ghastly delay of more than two hours had altered everything. Fairfax knew in his heart that his chances of reaching Biarritz upon the right side of midnight were very small. If he could average forty the whole of the way, well and very good. Otherwise, any interview he might have with Athalia would take place the following day. She kept late hours, certainly, but not so late as all that. On the other hand, barring accidents, there was no reason at all why a clear eye and a determined arm should not bring the Hispano-Suiza to Biarritz by nine o'clock. The devil of it was that Beringhampton must know that, if he but pleased to hurry, he could have the field to himself. The three hours lost would have been of no use to him. Had he arrived at six, by the time he had changed, Miss Choate would have gone to dress, and thence to dinner. Not till, say, half-past nine would he have had a look-in. And by then Fairfax might have come up to cramp his style. But now, if he pleased, he could have the field to himself. . . .

Punch swore beneath his breath and coaxed the grey two-seater to sixty-two.

He ran into Rouen as clocks were striking eight, and, meeting the river, followed it out of the town.

Past a quarry and up through the rising woods, over the glittering Seine, through Pont-de-l'Arche, by Louviers' precious church, into mitred Evreux, where the broad road splits into a delta of aged streets, up over the railway and on to the rolling plain the grey two-seater flung like a thing possessed.

The first real check came at old Dreux, where it was market day. Horses and cattle and carts lumbered and lurched and sprawled and backed over the pavement, thrusting and being thrust: lorries panted and stormed, insistently demanding passage and finding none: little groups of peasants stood in the fairway, absorbed in discourse, shifting mechanically as the raving traffic pushed its way by: gossiping eagerly, old women plunged and bundled from side to side, apparently oblivious alike of time and place until dragged from under cartwheels or overthrown by collision: urchins were baiting dogs, set to guard tail-boards: gentle-eyed calves stared over sides of gigs: chickens, pinioned and thrown, eyed the welter with indignant surprise.

Ere he had time to withdraw, Punch was engulfed, and ten precious minutes went by before he was out of the town.

Troubles are gregarious.

Ten miles from Chartres a tire burst.

Fairfax changed the wheel and then, looking over his engine, found that his fan-strap had gone.

It was past ten now and becoming immensely hot. Not to repair the defect there and then would be the act of a fool. Punch shook the sweat from his eyes and sought for a spare. . . .

The sight of Chartres' exquisite spires, rising like toy steeples out of the hazy plain, was comforting, but his relentless wrist-watch and the thought of a useless tire jabbed viciously at Fairfax' nerves. He could not make up his mind whether to stop at Chartres and fit a new tire or to take what risk there was and go his way. As he swept up the boulevards he decided to stop for water and nothing else.

He must pass the *Place des Epars*, and he knew a garage was there. . . . The next moment he saw its pump. He drew up to the gap in the kerb with a swift rush. . . .

While they were drawing water, he ran across the *Place* and purchased a pie. The *pâtés* of Chartres are famous and a meal in themselves. Then he bought two bottles of Evian and hurried back. He found the mechanic regarding the near fore wheel. There was a gash in the cover through which you could see the tube. . . .

It was a quarter to eleven by the time he was out of Chartres, and Beringhampton passed him five miles beyond Vendôme.

Punch marked his passage mutely, with stony eyes. Then he slid under some trees and took out the clutch. . . .

He broke his fast quickly and then lay down in the grass by the side of the road. He knew what it meant to feel sleepy over the wheel. For perhaps ten minutes he dozed. Then he rose, bathed his face and swung himself into the car. . . .

The road was wicked now—broken to bits. The grey two-seater leaped like a young ram. But Fairfax let her have it and went like the wind. He had nothing to lose. . . .

The broken road took its toll, and when he slid into Tours, one of his wings was flapping and his number-plate hanging by a thread.

He pushed up the *Rue Nationale*, to see Beringhampton's colours crawling ahead.

With a hammering heart, Fairfax drew very close. . . .

As he slipped by he glanced round.

The chauffeur saw him and smiled and touched his hat. Except for him at the wheel, the car was empty.

Punch pulled into the side, and the other slowed up.

"Where's his lordship?" said Fairfax.

The man's lips tightened.

"He's just taken the train, sir."

"Why?"

"We 'ad a very near shave, sir, a mile or two back." He passed his hand over his eyes. "As near to death as ever I want to be." He paused. Then he burst out. "I've given 'im notice, sir. I've only got one life. If they mark a bend over 'ere, you can bet it's a turn and a 'alf. I pointed 'im out the sign, but 'e didn't care. . . . An' a steam-roller waitin' the other side." He wiped his face. "I thought we was done, I did. . . . When we was through, I told 'im I'ld leave 'im at Tours. 'E asked me if I was afraid, an' I said, Yes, I was. 'Then drive,' says he. 'An' be cursed an' 'ounded,' says I, 'till I can't think straight? Not much, my lord,' I says. 'I'll leave at Tours.' When we got 'ere 'e drove to the station an' asked if there was a train.... Some train was there—movin' ... They 'auled 'im in and I pushed 'is dressing-case up. 'Deliver the car,' he cries, an' there you are."

"What filthy luck!" cried Punch, half to himself. "What filthy luck!"

The man looked at him curiously. Then he glanced at the car.

"You're coming to pieces, sir. Are you going far?"

"Biarritz," said Punch.

The fellow glanced at his clock.

"I suppose you'll be needin' your car, sir, or I—I could give you a lift."

Fairfax' heart leaped. Then he shook his head.

"I can't use his car," he said.

"It isn't 'is car," cried the man. "'E sold 'er a week ago—sold 'er to Mr. Fairie. 'E's at St. Johndylose. An' as 'e was goin' to Beeritz, 'is lordship made the offer to bring 'er out." He dived at a pocket. "Why, 'er papers an' all's in Mr. Fairie's name."

"Mr. Fairie of Castle Charing?"

"That's right, sir. Is he a friend of yours?"

"I should think he was," shouted Fairfax. "But I say—I want to move."

The chauffeur smiled.

"She'll move, sir. D'you know the way?"

"I do. D'you want any petrol?"

"I was just going to fill the tank, sir."

"I know a garage here. You follow me."

Ten minutes later the faithful grey two-seater had been worthily bestowed, the Hispano-Suiza's tank had been filled to the brim and Fairfax had taken his seat beside her driver.

As they moved off—

"She's better nor any train," said the latter shortly.

If the surface was none too good, at least the way was straight and the road open. The reaches became gigantic: after each bend you could see for miles ahead. The traffic, too, was negligible. It was, indeed, the exception not to have the road to yourself.

With the roar of a lion, the great car leapt at her prey....

Time and again the illusion of the frantic approach of things stationary was almost irresistibly real. Time and again, when the road rose and fell, the sensation of using a switchback was painfully acute. Time and again, as they passed another vehicle, the fierce cuff of uproar made Fairfax wince. Time and again pace dislocated sight and left the brain fumbling.

Villages sprang into being out of flat places: a huddle of distant dots shivered into a town: as for the eternal trees beside the road, they seemed no farther apart than a ladder's rungs.

The windscreen was open, and the warm air tore at their ears: the thunder of the engine became a stock background of resonance against which other sounds stood up as against silence: it seemed that hearing was going the way of sight.

Presently came Poitiers.

They skirted the ancient city and streaked up the Ruffec road.

Punch began to wonder what time Beringhampton would arrive. If it was the Spanish Express which he had caught, he might, he reckoned, reach Biarritz by seven o'clock. That meant that at eight o'clock he could take the field—not a very convenient hour, but better than nine. Oh, infinitely better than nine. And if Athalia could help, of course she would. He had only to send up a note and ask her to give him ten minutes before she dined....

Punch began to construct the interview with narrowed eyes, and presently, being very tired, he fell asleep.

The chauffeur roused him, to point to a fine old city piled up on a hill.

Fairfax could only stare.

It was Angoulême.

They swept the hem of her garment and on to the Bordeaux road.

It was during this lap most of all that the burden and heat of the day made themselves felt. The sun seemed to know that they were fighting with Time and to take up the cudgels upon his captain's behalf. The fury of light and heat punished them mercilessly, scorching their faces, keeping their eyes hooded and making the muscles of their eyelids ache hideously with the strain. But the chauffeur never complained or slackened speed. The man understood well enough that Fairfax and Beringhampton were riding some race, and the memory of the stripes which the latter had laid upon him made him strain every nerve to bring the former home. Punch was certainly well horsed. The fellow knew his engine inside out: besides, he had done some racing and remembered the tricks of the trade.

There were times when the car swept like a blast of the wind: at others she whizzed like a shell shot out of a gun: now she swooped and sailed like a ranging gull, and now she soared up a hill with the rush of a lift: and once, on a good piece of road, for three long minutes she seemed to be standing still, heaving gently like a ship riding at anchor, while five miles of the countryside slid into and out of sight.

They ran into Bordeaux at a quarter to six.

There they took in petrol and ate and drank. And Fairfax called for a time-table and studied it while he fed. He might have spared his labour. The table was two years old, and the pages he needed were gone.

They were in the car again by six o'clock.

There was pavement to come now—some of it pretty bad. Who went by Salles avoided the very worst—and tacked ten miles on to his journey. Fairfax went by Salles: it was not his car.

He had his reward.

The sun had retired now and was well on their right: the air was cooler, and a faint tang of salt hung in its breath: the blessed evening was coming to ease their progress.

Fairfax never forgot that last long stretch.

The sun was going down, and the shadows were growing long, and distance was creeping close. Ahead and on either hand the countryside was gone: Earth seemed to have thrown back to the days before she was tamed: Nature ran wild. Forest and furze and broom had the world to themselves. And the car shore them in two as a draper's scissors shear stuff—league after shining league, with a steady snarl. Twice they met a lorry and three times a touring car and twenty carts, perhaps, in nearly a hundred miles. . . .

They swept through St. Geours with twenty-five miles to go.

They dropped down into Bayonne, slipped across the Adour, swung to the right at cross-roads, and followed the tram-lines out.

They had to go slowly then, for the road was narrow and full. Still, they edged their way along, passing when there was room.

They floated into Biarritz at twenty-five minutes past eight. . . .

There was no room at the Carlton, but Lady Defoe was there, so they promised to squeeze Punch in.

As a porter picked up his suit-case—

"All right, sir?" queried the chauffeur.

The eagerness of his tone touched Fairfax' heart.

As he gave him a note—

"Thanks to you—yes," he said, smiling. "Good night—and many thanks."

It would have been brutal to tell him anything else.

At last Punch found Athalia, by going from pillar to post. She was staying at the *Palais*, had dined out and come back to dance.

They danced a few steps. Then he led her out of the ballroom and into the August night.

"What is it?" she said.

"He's here somewhere. Has he spoken?"

Athalia looked away.

"Not yet," she said slowly. "Not yet, but—I think he will . . . any moment, now."

Fairfax stared at the sea shifting to and fro and the line of miniature breakers curling and roaring as gently as sucking doves.

He had done it—achieved his purpose. It seemed impossible that only that morning he had stood on the quay at Dieppe and gone over the car. Yet he had done so—that morning. And now—here he was at Biarritz. And there was Athalia looking at him with steady eyes. And Beringhampton had not spoken. . . . He was—in time.

The tragedy of it was *he had nothing to say.*

There *was* nothing to say. He had meant to 'have it out.' He had torn across France like a madman to 'have it out.' Have what out? There was nothing to have out. Athalia had said as much . . . *any moment, now.* . . . In the face of that, how could he——

He began to wonder whether such a giant fool's errand had ever been run before.

Athalia was speaking.

"What is it, Punch? You didn't start a day early to ask me that."

"I didn't start a day early."

A puzzled look came into the great brown eyes.

"But you can't have——"

"Yes, I did," said Fairfax. "I got to Dieppe this morning and came down by road. I started from there at seven and got here at half-past eight."

Athalia started.

Then she caught at his arm.

"Punch, Punch! You might have broken your neck! Why—why did you come so terribly fast?"

The man hesitated.

"Why?" breathed Athalia.

Punch swung round and caught her hands in his.

"Will you forgive me if I tell you?"

"I've asked you to."

"Why, then, it's because I had to—had to get here and see you before he came. I couldn't stand by, Athalia, and watch you step out of my life without a word. I'm mad—crazy about you. I can't think of anything else. When I'm not with you everything's dull and flat, and the only way I get through is by thinking of what you look like and how soon I'll see you again. Your hair, your eyes, your temples, your precious, darling mouth—I know every tiny look of them. If I could paint, I'd paint your portrait from memory without a slip. I know your hands and the shape of your tiny nails, and I'd know your step from a million if you were going by. Oh, my lady, I do love you so. I thought I did when I asked you to be my wife, but I didn't at all. I hadn't begun to love you. But now . . . Oh, Athalia, my sweet, I've tried to play the game. You don't know what it's meant to sit by your side in the car and see your face at my shoulder and hold my tongue. I've had to hold on to myself to keep my head. When I said that but for your money I wouldn't have opened my mouth, I must have been mad. If you hadn't a bean—why, I'd go across Europe on my hands and knees and beg and pray you to let me 'bring you down.' Yes, I've got to that, my lady. Bringing you down or no—I'd beg and pray. You see, I've turned selfish. You've come to mean too much, and that's the truth." He stopped short there. Then he let fall her hands and turned to the sea. "And there you are, sweetheart—I can call you that this once. You asked me why I hurried, and now you know. If he'd spoken before I got here, I couldn't have told you this. And I felt I wanted you to know. That's all. I just wanted you to know . . . how very much . . . I cared."

For a moment the girl said nothing.

Then—

"I'm glad you did," she said gently, "awfully glad. And now I'll tell you a secret. The Athalia Stakes have been won."

"*Won!*"

"Won. Listen. The result was a dead heat."

Fairfax started.

"But you said he hadn't spoken."

"I know. Never mind. He has. And you've dead-heated—you and . . . the man I love."

Punch put a hand to his head.

"Well, here's a go," he said. "What do we do now? You can't marry us both."

With a half-laugh, half-sob, Athalia slid her arms round his neck.

"Yes, I can, my darling. You see, you're both called Punch."

ANN

LADY ANN MINTER alighted thankfully.

After the burden and heat of the third-class carriage the evening air of Suet was like a drink of water—out of a dirty mug. Still, it was water: and the journey down had been hell. After all, the tip of a beggar's finger made a desirable continent for a certain rich man.

Her husband took her arm and shepherded her out of the press.

"See now, kid," he said tenderly, setting her dressing-case down, "you jus' stay 'ere an' watch out for me. I'm off to find your trunk."

"All right, Bob," said Lady Ann Minter.

Alone for the first time since her marriage, she strove to marshal her thoughts. These, however, were mutinous. The flight of opportunity, the welter of noise and movement on the fringe of which she stood undermined her authority. It was vital that she should think quickly and clearly, that she should make up her mind. Everything was depending upon immediate decision. But the very premises were denied her. She was wild to face the facts: but the facts danced and flickered and would not be faced.

Hideous, blazing queries blinded her fumbling brain. She found herself reading them aloud.

"Why didn't I think of all this? How can I possibly bear it? What shall I do—*do*?"

And then the scorching answers.

"God knows . . . I must . . . *Nothing*. . . ."

She saw her father standing with his back to the log-laden hearth—saw his white, set face and his tightened lips. There were roses on the mantelpiece behind him, and a Morland hanging above—a spreading oak and a cottage and a jolly brown horse. . . . and a woman was standing in the doorway, holding a little boy, and a man on the horse was smiling ... and they were all alone and happy, under the spreading oak ... very poor and simple, but alone and very happy. ...

She saw her aunt on her knees with tears running down her face—saw the china ranged orderly upon the walls—smelt the pot-pourri she had made the year before. The evening sun was pouring into the chamber, planting badges of gold on plate and bowl and pitcher, turning the closet into a queen's parlour. ...

She saw the register office and the registrar's face like a mask, heard the cameras click as she and Bob passed out, felt the insolent stares of the waiter who brought them lunch. ...

The journey down had been frightful. The heat, the discomfort, the everlasting talk. ...

The coaches had been standing in the August sun and had become veritable ovens. Such air as entered them was baked instantly. Yet, the fight for seats had been savage—one woman had been knocked down, and children had been dragged and trampled. Bob had secured two places because he was strong, but one had been seized before his bride could take possession. A violent dispute had followed, while Ann stood between the seats smiling nervously and ready to die of shame. Indeed, but for the timely eviction of another inmate, the sudden activity of whose diaphragm disclosed the moving fact that he was considerably the worse for liquor, relations must have been strained beyond the breaking-point. The spectacle, however, of the wages of intemperance had proved that touch of Nature which can twitch discord into harmony, and for the next twenty minutes various appreciations of the episode revealed a cordial unanimity which was almost affecting. That a family in a corner should at the last moment have been rudely reinforced by the irruption of two small boys was sheer misfortune. In the absence of seating accommodation it had been impossible to protest against their occupation of the open windows—delicious tenancies, of which they took full advantage, boisterously exchanging reports and frequently subletting their coigns of vantage to one another. The corporal enfilading of the compartment which such arrangements necessitated had soon developed into a game, the pursuit of which their kinsfolk made no attempt to check until a particularly deliberate collision had afforded one tenant a pretext for hitting the other on the nose. The consequences of the assault had been frightful. The combatants were dragged yelling apart, the aggressor was cuffed into tears more explosive than those of his victim, both were shaken and reviled, the flow of blood was arrested by a handkerchief which had already been used as a dressing and was swaddling an ounce of bull's-eyes, hideous threats were issued, provocative comments upon upbringing were audibly exchanged. Only the production of food had at all relieved the tension, but under the healing influence of snacks good humour had more or less revived. A baby-in-arms had been given a ham sandwich—at least, the apex had been introduced into its mouth. It gnashed and sucked contentedly, while protruding shreds of fat liquefied upon its chin. A girl had abstractedly devoured plums and put the stones in Ann's lap. A married couple opposite had seemed incapable of underestimating the capacity of their mouths, thus inconceivably embarrassing their efforts to keep the ball of *badinage* rolling and distorting such retorts as they felt must be expressed into fresh dummies for their opponents' thrusts. Before the meal was over the train had run into a tunnel and, after slowing down to a crawl, come to a dead stop. Someone had giggled, and a burst of hysterical laughter had succeeded the soft impeachment of gallantry. In the midst of it all Ann had felt Bob's arm steal round her and his lips on her cheek. He had kept his arm about her for the rest of the trip....

And now—

Again she tried to concentrate—haul her thoughts into line. They came sluggishly.

Married ... she was married ... married to Bob—Bob Minter, one of her father's grooms. She had done it because she loved him. She had married him in London that morning, and——That morning? Was it possible that it was only that morning? Was it only that morning that the registrar had bowed and ...

Her thoughts began to slip away. She let them go.

She stared at her wedding-ring ... touched—plucked at it desperately.

The hideous queries and answers leapt like rams possessed.

"Why? God knows. . . . How can I? I must. . . . What? *Nothing*."

For an instant panic fear looked out of her steady grey eyes.

Then—

"All serene, kid. I've got the goods," panted Bob. He turned to a shambling porter, thrusting a truck. "Say, mate, where d'you keep your taxis?"

"Not 'ere," said the porter. "Might get a keb."

He preceded them wearily.

"You—you've got rooms, Bob?" faltered his bride.

Her husband's eyes shone as he slid an arm beneath hers.

"Course I 'ave, kid." He hesitated. Then, "I didn' mean to tell you, but . . . I won' be able to give you the 'ome you ought to 'ave—servants an' cars an' whatnot. More's the pity. But jus' this once—for this fortnight I've done my lady proud." His voice began to tremble with excitement and pride. "You've got the bes' room in Suet, darlin'—the best on the 'ole parade. There ain't a fine lady in the town that's got such a room. The Countess of 'Ampshire used to 'ave it, an' all the 'igh muck-a-mucks 'ave bit an' scratched to get it whenever they come this way. Firs' floor—looks right over the pier. . . . An' not a chair moved, nor a picture. You'll 'ave it jus' the same. You see, my aunt she keeps apartments—the best in Suet: an' when we fixed things up I wrote to 'er, told 'er on the Q.T. an' said I wanted 'er firs' bedroom—jus' for you. An' she wrote beck an' said that you should 'ave it if she 'ad to turn people out. She's a good 'eart is old Aunt 'Arriet. Givin' it us at a cut price, too—season an' all. An' we'll grub with 'er an' the girls an' Uncle Tom—I tell you, kid, they don't 'alf know 'ow to live. Why, you'll be as fat as butter 'fore we go beck to Town."

Ann's brain reeled.

'Grub with her and the girls and Uncle Tom. . . . Grub with . . .'

The station-yard faded, and the Morland above the mantelpiece stole into view—the spreading oak and the cottage and the girl standing at the door . . . and the man on the horse smiling . . . the humble intimacy of the scene—the simple happiness—the precious privacy... *privacy*....

She was outcast, of course—excommunicate. The order had been made that morning. She had signed it herself deliberately—with open eyes. More. She had done it gladly. She wanted to be expelled, that she might live with Bob—*but under a spreading oak ... in a cottage ... alone, as outcastes live* ... not—not at Suet ... not 'grubbing with Aunt Harriet and the girls and Uncle Tom.' ... She thought Bob had understood that. She had told him so plainly—a child could have understood. And yet...

The pathos of his failure hit her between the eyes. He couldn't grasp that she didn't want 'a show'—couldn't appreciate such heresy. Her words had meant nothing. Because she was his great lady, she must have as fine a show as he could compass. Other women must be made jealous of her fortune. Others could skulk in cottages and under spreading oaks; but she must go to Suet—fashionable Suet, and have the best room in the place ... looking over the pier.... It was the most loving compliment he could pay.

By a supreme effort Ann drove the consternation out of her eyes, shook off the cold clutch of Horror and squeezed her husband's arm.

"You're very good to me, Bob," she said steadily. "I think you were wonderful to think of it all. We shall—shall be grand having the best room in Suet."

Bob coloured with delight.

"Oh, it's nothin' much," he said awkwardly. "I 'spect you've often 'ad rooms pretty near as good. But I—I like to think I'll be giving you the best ... jus' for once."

He broke away and made for a cabman, who, learning his applicant's vocation, might see his way to take them on trade terms.

Ann watched him dazedly.

Nothing, it seemed, was to be spared her—nothing.

The discovery that she had made one grand, imperishable mistake stunned her: the savagery of the penalty she was to pay made her soul blench: but the ghastly, mocking irony of poor Bob's solicitude cut like a cold, wet lash. Foul tongue in cheek, the spirit of Satire was possessing his honest heart. Beneath this hideous influence, thought, word and loving deed emerged grotesque, cross-gartered. He ushered some tender travesty with every breath. The eager pride with which he strove to make Fate split its sides tore at Ann's heart. It was pathetic—with the pathos of the dying dog that whimpers to think it cannot rise to make its master sport. And just because it was so heartrending he could not possibly be told. Blow, lash, claw had to be suffered unflinchingly. He—he could not be told.

As for her love——

Ann put a hand to her head, as though to focus the truth.

Her passion for Bob was gone. The flax was not even smoking. The fire had been quenched.

Ann felt cold with shame.

Bob had been so fearful, and her love had cast out his fear. He had never doubted her love, but only whether that love could survive the strain. And she had fought to convince him, till he had been convinced. He believed heart and soul in its ability ... heart and soul.... And now—Bob had been right. Her dauntless love had not endured eight hours—*not eight hours*....

Of course she hadn't appreciated. There had been a misunderstanding. She had assumed——

The excuses leaked like sieves. The truth poured out of them.

It was she—she only that was to blame. She hadn't thought of all this. Her father had. So had her aunt. So even had Bob—poor, weak, unsophisticated Bob. With tears in his eyes, he had begged her not to smash his life; and she had smiled and kissed him and smashed it and smashed hers too.

The Sting of Death sank to a pin-prick, the Victory of the Grave to an unfinished game—beside the horror of the fare which Life was serving.

It seemed, indeed, that she was to be spared nothing.

Bob returned beaming. His wooing of the cabman had prospered, for, as luck would have it, the latter was in a holiday humour. He had been upon the point of returning to his stable, and 'Pier View' was on his way. He would drive them for nothing. He was, as Bob put it, 'a proper sport.' It soon appeared that he was a wag also.

In these circumstances it was most natural that his consent to oblige a pal should automatically promote him to the standing of a familiar. He celebrated his elevation heartily by a series of jocular allusions to nuptial bliss and intimate reminiscences of his own union, by tying a posy to his whip and desiring lustily to be informed of the shortest way to the Abode of Love.

The bystanders roared.

Encouraged by this reception, he stopped outside the station, and acquainting a policeman with the facts, begged the loan of his white gloves, his own, as he explained, 'bein' put away by me valet wiv me 'untin' things. You know wot these servants are, officer.'

He was really extremely funny.

For the rest of the way he contented himself with a lively and affectionate communion with Lady Ann's trunk—an effort which, to judge from the scandalized shrieks of mirth which followed them, went very well with such pedestrians as they passed. Indeed, their progress was triumphal.

Bob enjoyed it thoroughly, as one enjoys being rallied upon a possession of which one is justly proud. He was all sheepish smiles. Ann was all smiles, too. Her face ached with the strain. Every nerve in her body was squirming. She was upon the edge of hysteria.

"God knows . . . I must . . . *Nothing*. . . ."

Satire spat upon his hands and laid fresh hold of her tail.

Upon arrival at 'Pier View' it proved unnecessary for three several reasons, all of which were evil, to ring the front-door bell. In the first place, they did not and were not expected to use the front door. Secondly, a small boy, who was at once wearing a tight green blazer and dirty flannel shorts, swinging idly upon the area gate and contemplating the seething pageant of pleasure-seekers under the comfortable auspices of a generous complement of butterscotch, took one look at husband and wife and then fell down the steps, bellowing, "☐'Ere they are!" Thirdly, the little knot of passers-by which would long ago have collected, had the equipage but halted, began to give the driver an appreciative hearing.

Bob was out of the fly and stooping to set Ann's dressing-case by the area gate; as he turned, the small boy reappeared, followed by a large business-like countenance which gave the impression of being able to look extremely unpleasant but was at the moment wreathed in winning smiles; flanking this, rose two other feminine faces, open-mouthed, peering—one fat, snub-nosed, jolly-eyed; the other discontented and pinched; the little knot of bystanders was swelling into an obstruction; the cabman was relating an anecdote which pointed the wisdom of the removal of boots before retiring. . . .

Ann saw it all as in an ugly dream.

It occurred to her that the train-journey and this were but the prologue—the induction to the play she had commanded, the devilish comedy in which she was to play the lead. The induction had been startling, but the play . . . The play was to be the thing. Of course. Plays were. The prologue was nothing. So far she had hardly appeared. When the curtain rose on the play . . . She found herself wondering if there would be an epilogue.

Suddenly, with a frightful shock, she realized that the curtain was up, that the stage was waiting . . . *waiting* . . . that this—was—her—cue. . . .

Crowd laughs at cabman's sallies. Aunt Harriet and the girls reach the top of the area steps. Bob is busy with her trunk. Gramophone next door starts 'YES! We have no bananas.' Cabman stops his discourse, listens intently, and then says, '☐ 'Ark! The 'erald angels sing.' Crowd yells with delight. ENTER *The Lady Ann Minter*. . . .

Ann pulled herself together and got out of the cab.

Then she turned to the driver and put out her hand.

"Thank you so much for bringing us," she said most charmingly.

It was a fatal gesture—because it was the act of a lady.

The laughter snapped off short: the grins faded: the genial atmosphere stiffened with a jar.

The cabman's assurance fell from him like a shirt of mail. His drollery collapsed before a mountainous wave of respect.

He took off his shabby hat and touched the slight fingers.

"Thank you, m'm," he said humbly.

Amidst a gaping silence Ann turned to the steps.

She could hear the breathing of the bystanders, feel their resentful stares burning her face. She had spoiled sport, embarrassed, turned the frolic she should have led into a ceremony they could not follow. She had drawn the whip of her superiority, flourished it, laid it across their shoulders. Only the gramophone continued to spout its ghastly pleasantry, like a clown mouthing in a death-chamber.

'*We've broad beans like BUN-ions, cab-BAH-ges and HON-ions . . .*'

Before this master-stroke of Satire Ann could have burst into tears. She had striven wildly to rise to the occasion, only to shatter—to let the whole thing down. . . . The awful hopelessness of her position flamed. Envy, Hatred and Malice, then, had been appointed her equerries. Not only was she to suffer: she was to cause suffering, breed discontent, induce ill-will. The efforts which she must make were doomed before they were made not only to fail but to turn to her condemnation. And she could do nothing, because there was nothing to be done. She had sold her birthright, but she could not sell her birth. Her style, her speech, her plumage could not be doffed. She was a peacock in daw's feathers—and the daws would fiercely resent her condescension.

'*But YES! We have no bananas. . . . We have no bananas to-day.*'

'Would resent'? *Were resenting.* . . .

As she crossed the pavement—

"Oh, 'aughty," said someone. "Sten' beck fer the Lady Ermyntrude."

There was a stifled giggle.

Her face flaming, Ann stepped to her hostess, who was palpably intoxicated with the prospect of communion with her guest and determined unmistakably to adorn a plane upon which lack of opportunity alone had hitherto prevented her from ambling. It was important that her new niece should at once appreciate that there was not the slightest necessity for her to step down. Here and now she must be made to realize that her aunt was fully qualified to step up.

Out went her hand chin-high.

"'Ow-de-doo, Lady Ann. Pleased to make your acquaintance. I 'ope you aren't very fatigued, but it's so 'ot for travellin'." She turned to rend the bystanders. "Stare a bit 'arder, won't you? An' where's your kemp-stools? Albert, ketch up that dressin'-case before it's pinched." The small boy sprang to do her bidding. "An' don' beng it on the steps. Come in, Lady Ann." She began to descend, driving the girls before her. "I 'ope you left 'is lordship well."

"Very—very well, thank you," stammered Ann.

"Oh, I'm gled of thet," said Aunt Harriet ecstatically. "It's so nice to think of one's deer ones——" She swung round to glare at the railings. "Albert, go back an' see who threw them srimps.... 'Orrible, vulgar brutes!" She stood fairly heaving with rage. "Reelly, the people that comes to Suet nowadays, Lady Ann—well, I don't know where they was born. I didn' know there was such people. Push you as soon as look at you. Reelly, one's better at 'ome. Walkin' out's no pleasure at all. But come in, deer. Come in an' meet the girls."

She guided Ann through the passage and into a parlour.

The table was laid for a meal and there were covers for eight.

Standing uneasily together as though for protection were the two girls and two young men.

The sour-faced girl was adopting a nonchalant air. Hand on hip, eyebrows raised, lip curled, she sought self-consciously to veil her self-consciousness. Her jolly-eyed sister appeared to be upon the edge of hysteria. Her face was set in a nervous frozen grin, her hands were twitching, her eyes riveted upon the floor. The youths were, if possible, still less at ease. Both were tall and weedy. One was dark and throaty—a quality which his belief in a tennis-shirt Byronically open at the neck, with the collar carelessly arranged above that of his coat, served to accentuate. His long hair was unparted, oiled and brushed straight back. Two inches of close-cut side-whisker and an amazing length of finger-nail argued æsthetic tendencies which the soulful expression of his sallow face was intended to declare. He gave the impression of being able to groan efficiently. The other had a jaunty, more worldly air. His tiny moustache was waxed, his fair hair parted in the middle and curled into twin horns. He was clearly conscious of his superiority and, that there might be no mistake about it, was languidly sucking his teeth. His collar—a soft creation of broad black and white stripes—his red and chocolate tie, the golden kerchief flowing from his breast-pocket showed that he knew how to dress.

"These are me daughters," explained Aunt Harriet, "an' their gentlemen-frien's. May . . ."

The sour-eyed girl advanced and shook hands—then turned, flushing violently, to toy with a book.

"Ada."

The jolly-eyed girl gulped, giggled, started forward, missed Ann's hand, tried again, clutched it anyhow and withdrew.

"Mr. Barnham."

The æsthete thrust forward, stumbled, bowed over Ann's fingers and turned confusedly away.

"Mr. Alcock."

Mr. Alcock delighted in showing how things should be done. Here was a brilliant opportunity of at once asserting his superiority, astonishing Ann, who would be thankful to find such unexpected *savoir-faire*, and dispelling any skulking idea that to carry off such an encounter was beyond his powers. He stepped forward briskly.

"Pleased to meet you, indeed," he said warmly. "□'Ow's Piccadilly?"

It was a difficult question to answer.

Before Ann had found a reply, there was the appalling explosion with which laughter which has been denied its usual channel forces the narrows of the nose. The strain had been too great. Nature had asserted herself. Ada had broken down.

Before her relatives' horrified gaze, she abandoned herself to succeeding paroxysms of mirth, to which, to his undying shame, Mr. Barnham began sniggeringly to subscribe.

The devastation of gentility was too awful.

Mr. Alcock blenched, recovered, turned slowly purple and broke into a gleaming sweat. Ann regarded him as though fascinated. Two red spots of dishonour burned upon May's cheekbones. Aunt Harriet was making a rattling noise.... All the time convulsion after convulsion shook the destructive to her foundations. And Mr. Barnham shook also.

"*Aida!*"

The rasp in her mother's tone brought her up short. The former was glaring unutterably.

As her daughter's abominable emotions began to subside, Aunt Harriet turned to her guest.

"Hoverwrought," she said in the tone of one who is publicly excusing whom she intends privately to flay alive. "Takes after 'er father. Shell we go upstairs, Lady Ann? I'm sure you'd like to take a look at your room, an' we can 'ave a quiet chat."

"I'ld love to," said Ann.

As she came to the door, she glanced round.

Mr. Alcock had slunk to the window and was savagely employing a service-dressed brother of the golden kerchief. Ada, red-nosed and bloated with exertion, stared blearedly upon the ground. May was regarding the cornice with smouldering eyes. Mr. Barnham appeared to be about to prophesy no good, but evil.

"So—so long," said Ann pleasantly.

The others stared back.

"Me deer," said Aunt Harriet, labouring up the stairs, "I want you to feel that this is a nome from 'ome. Merriage is a wrench. One leaves a lovin' 'ome for a strange country. An' you do feel strange. I remember me own merriage. Down we goes to a little one-eyed place with never a soul as knew wot a lady was. I tell you I felt that lonely I could 'ave cut me throat. But you've no call to do that. You're among frien's 'ere that feels as you do an' likes the ways you like. I give you me word, Lady Ann, vulgarity makes me sick. An' there's so much of it to-day."

Arrived at a door upon the first floor, she opened it and passed into a large, dingily furnished bedroom facing the sea. The brown wallpaper was bruised and soiled: the threadbare carpet was overlaid with cheap rugs: a voluminous muslin valance swaddled the dressing-table: wardrobe, washstand and bed recalled the several sale-rooms whence they had come: a rusty horse-hair couch sulked in a corner: spotted engravings of Royalty being baptized or married or churched hung upon the walls: a cord of one of the Venetian blinds had broken, and the slats were splayed: a window of the bay was open and admitting something of what seemed to be the uproar of a gigantic fair.

"There," said the proud hostess, mechanically laying folded hands upon the abdominal wall. "Simple, but tasty. I remember so well the firs' time the Countess of 'Ampshire was 'ere. 'Mrs. Root,' she says, 'people 'as an idea that we titled must 'ave display. Completely wrong. Now, my bedroom at 'Assocks is jus' like this—quiet, but distanggy.' "

"It's delightful," said Ann, looking round. "I—I don't feel strange at all."

"Couldn' if you tried," was the triumphant reply. "It's so—so res'ful." She sank on to a chair. "An' now, me deer, make yourself at 'ome. This is your private room in 'Oliday 'Ouse."

"You're very kind," said Ann.

"Don' mention it."

The abrupt injunction was disconcerting. It was not meant, of course, to be obeyed. On the contrary. . . . After searching desperately for words with which to flout its blunt authority—

"I—I wonder where Bob is," faltered Ann. "If I could have my dressing-case . . ."

"Now, don't you go makin' any toilet," said Aunt Harriet. "We'll be goin' out presently. Not that I don't like changin'," she added hastily, "because I do. But Tom—my husban's that slack. In course I'm afraid I've fell away, but there you are. Where's the good of me makin' meself tidy, when 'is idea of dressin' is to take 'is collar orf?" She sighed heavily. "But there, there," she added. "We all 'as our crorse to bear."

"Well, I'll just wash my face and hands," said Ann. "One gets so dirty in the train."

"Just as you please," said her hostess. "I'm afraid it's waste o' time—the pier's that filthy—but it'll freshen you up."

She fought her way past the dressing-table and thrust her head out of the window.

"Albert," she yelled.

"'Ullo," rose the small boy's voice.

"Don't say 'Ullo' to me," snapped Aunt Harriet.

"Whatsay?"

His great-aunt drew in her breath.

"Where's Bob?" she demanded.

"Gone to 'ave a drink with the driver."

"Well, leave that there trunk an' fetch up Lady Ann's dressin'-case."

"Whatsay?"

Albert's inability to hear unwelcome tidings was a maddening complaint.

His great-aunt looked volumes.

"You 'eard well enough jus' now," she said in a shaking voice.

"Bob tole me to wait 'ere."

"An' I tell you to fetch up Lady Ann's case."

"Whatsay?"

Aunt Harriet left the window and erupted from the room.

Albert put the road between himself and 'Pier View.'

Ann took off her hat and flung herself face downward upon the bed. . . .

"Why didn't I think of all this? *God knows*. How can I possibly bear it? *I must*. What shall I do—do? *Nothing*."

It occurred to Ann suddenly that it was all intensely funny. The comedy of the situation was rich. Albert—Aunt Harriet—Mr. Alcock alone would have brought down the house. Surely, her sense of humour . . .

Somebody laughed—wildly.

Ann perceived that here was another of Satire's subtleties. Nothing so obvious as tragedy was to be her portion. She was to be tormented by a roaring farce—a farce that was founded on tears and broken dreams and all the cureless agony of passionate regret. It was the Dance of Doom, if not of Death.

When Aunt Harriet reappeared, lugging the dressing-case, she was manifestly conscious that, but for her guest's whimsy, she would have been spared great provocation, distasteful exercise and—most important of all—a menial task. She certainly managed to smile, but it was a crooked business. She felt that her mask had slipped.

So soon as Ann was ready, the two descended—thoughtfully. The ladylike bond of union which Aunt Harriet had forged seemed to have stretched. All Ann's efforts to contract it but served to emphasize its slenderness.

Mercifully, Bob was in the parlour, exchanging cheerful reminiscences with a jolly, fat man who proved to be Uncle Tom.

Her husband presented Ann, with shining eyes.

For a moment the fat man looked at her. Then he inclined his head.

"Your servant, me lady," he said respectfully.

"Rot," said Ann. "You're my uncle," and kissed him then and there.

"Oh, you peach," said her uncle, and kissed her back. With his arm about her, he addressed the rest of the company. "Jus' leave us alone a few minutes, will you?" he said. "There's one or two 'ymns we want to run over together."

This allusion to a recent scandal in which a local pillar of the nonconformist church was involved naturally evoked great merriment.

Ann tried to be thankful.

It also inspired Mr. Alcock.

"Break away, break away, there," he cried.

Uncle Tom screwed round his head.

"Percy, me lad," he said, "you 'aven't a chance. This little girl likes 'em fat."

Squeaks of delight contributed to another explosion of mirth.

They sat down to tea hilariously. . . .

"Do you 'unt at all?" said Mr. Alcock, presenting a dish of shrimps.

"I've given it up," said Ann.

"☐'E means by night," said Uncle Tom.

The laughter was renewed.

"Oh, give over, pa," wailed Ada. "You've give me the 'iccups."

It was too true.

Seats were left: remedies were commended: the victim was conjured—to no purpose. Spasm succeeded spasm with sickening regularity.

"'Old your breath," said Bob.

Ada inspired and sat like a graven image.

The others watched her in a silence pregnant with expectation.

Her eyes began to protrude. . . .

"Stick it," said Bob. "Stick it."

A dusky flush began to steal into her face: sweat gathered on her brow: she was squinting. . . .

At last she let her breath go with a loose rush.

For a moment she breathed peacefully. Then a belated spasm convulsed her frame.

There was a rustle of consternation.

Suddenly, with a blood-curdling roar, Mr. Barnham smote upon the board.

In a second all was confusion.

Ann started to her feet: Aunt Harriet screamed: May recoiled against the wall: Bob and Mr. Alcock regarded their compeer open-mouthed: Uncle Tom, who had been in the act of drinking, was coughing and cursing and wringing tea from his moustache.

What was more to the point, Ada stopped hiccuping.

When Mr. Barnham pointed this out, the fact was coldly received.

"Enough to make anybody stop anything," snarled Aunt Harriet. "Don't you know 'ow to be'ave?"

"In course I do," said Mr. Barnham. "You never see me do that before."

"No, an' don't you never let me see you do it again," was the tart reply. "Nasty, vulgar 'abits."

"But I done it to stop 'er 'iccups," protested the ill-used youth.

"I don't want to know why you done it," observed his hostess. "You done it—an' that's enough. You oughtter be ashamed of yourself. . . . May, give Lady Ann a cut of beef."

With goggling eyes, Mr. Barnham proceeded in some dudgeon to the consumption of a hunk of dry bread, presumably with some vague idea that this mortification of the flesh would stimulate a recognition of his injury.

Conversation revived.

Mr. Alcock spoke of sport, commending the pursuit of lawn tennis with the air of one who has tried everything and come to the reluctant conclusion that that pastime is a better antidote to *ennui* than any other.

Uncle Tom recounted a dispute which had arisen in the saloon bar of *The Goat* regarding elephantiasis. His narrative slid naturally enough into a vivid comparison of such cases of this complaint as had come under his notice or that of the other patrons of the saloon bar. Aunt Harriet, even more naturally, proved able and willing to supplement his list with personal experiences so distressing as to suggest that an inscrutable Providence had chosen her among women to be harrowed in this peculiar way.

May related how someone had 'passed the remark' that a new char-à-banc service was to be instituted between Suet and Lather, and asked Ann if she was fond of motoring.

Ann replied with enthusiasm.

"I think it's tremendous fun."

"D'you 'ave the Blue Fleet in Dorset?"

"I—I don't know," stammered Ann. "Do we, Bob?"

"Yes, dear," said Bob. "That bounder wot 'it your coopy was one o' the Blue Fleet."

There was an awful silence.

"Your coopy?" said Uncle Tom.

"Er, yes," said Ann desperately.

"Nice, tight little car, too," said Bob. "Wish I could give 'er one now."

"A.C.?" ventured Mr. Alcock.

"'A.C.'?" said Bob. "Forty-fifty Rolls."

There was another silence.

"Must 've bin delightful," said Aunt Harriet shakily. "Still, there's things beside cars."

"Rather," said Ann heartily.

"Such as wot?" said Uncle Tom.

"Well, all isn't gold as glitters," snapped his wife.

"That's true," said Mr. Barnham sagely.

"Woddyer mean?" said his host. "Wot's true? A Rolls moter coopy's good enough fer mos' people."

"Well, an' who said it wasn't?" said May.

"Look 'ere," said her father. "Your mother said there was things beside cars."

"So there is," said May. "Fine clothes an' fine relations."

She laughed spitefully.

"Shut up, May," said Ada. "She never said she 'ad a coopy. It was Bob wot started it."

"That's right," said Bob, red in the face. "I said it, an' where's the 'arm?"

"No 'arm at all," said his aunt silkily. "If the troof was known, I spec' she 'ad two or free cars."

Her husband suspended mastication and stared at Ann. Then he spoke through the cud.

"Didjoo?" he demanded.

"No, indeed," said Ann swiftly. "I think I was jolly lucky to have one."

Uncle Tom nodded approval.

"You were that," he said emphatically. Ann breathed again. "Why, my ole dad thought 'imself mighty lucky to 'ave 'is own tip-cart, an'——"

"Don't be stoopid, pa," said May. "Grandpa was only a common man."

Her father gasped. Here was parricide.

"I mean," said May sweetly, "he wasn't a nurl."

"I'll bet he was just as good," said Ann.

"So 'e was," cried Uncle Tom. With an effort he emptied his mouth. "You 'ear?" he raved, turning upon May. "You 'ear, you undootiful girl? 'Ere's a lady wot knows a nurl when she sees one an' don't 'ave to go to Boots' Lendin' Library to find out wot 'igh life means. An' she says 'e was as good. 'Common man'!" The iteration of the objectionable phrase re-pricked his piety. He wagged a cautionary forefinger. "You jus' be careful, young woman. Don't you go gettin' ideas above your station. Jus' because you go orf to dances an' cinemas o' nights an' keep a tame mug 'andy to buy you cheap sweets—that don' make you no better than wot you are. *Ladies is born.* . . ."

Never was enemy so hoist with his own petard.

Never was the seasoning of bitterness so sloshed into the pot.

Never was a silence so ominous as that which followed the reproof.

May's face was purple, her eyes narrowed to green points of steel. Aunt Harriet was sweating with indignation:

her mouth worked. Ada looked scared. As though to belie a particularly hang-dog expression, Mr. Barnham muttered and snorted beneath his breath. Mr. Alcock sneered upon his finger-nails. Bob was smiling sheepishly. And the unconscious author of the unsavoury stew sat back regarding the company with eyes that saw nothing but a forgotten deference to authority awakened by the old lion's roar.

Ann tried not to tremble.

Were there no lengths to which Satire would not go? Had Irony no mercy? God! What a tune they were calling! All hell was fiddling in the orchestra—and she had to pay . . . pay . . . .

A sudden peal at the bell saved a situation which was under sentence of death.

"That's Mr. Mason," said Ada. "I 'ope 'e's brought Miss Gedge."

She rose and left the room.

The cold, strained silence slid into the blessed hush of curiosity.

Then—

"*I ain't nobody's darlin', I'm blue as can be*," feelingly rendered by an indifferent baritone, floated into the room.

"That's 'im," shouted Uncle Tom gleefully. "Come in, yer bounder. There ain't no room, but we can't keep you out."

Mr. Alcock and Mr. Barnham laughed half-heartedly.

Mr. Mason entered, tripped, recovered himself, gave the threshold an awful look, placed his hat upon the hand which Mr. Barnham was extending, side-stepped to the fireplace, pressed an imaginary bell and said, "Waiter bring a non-skid 'ammock and a moonlit night: I've just been married."

Even Aunt Harriet laughed—rather reluctantly. In fact, good humour was bundled into the room, neck and crop.

Mr. Mason was tubby and of a cheerful countenance. He was neatly dressed in a sponge-bag suit which was too tight for him, a low double collar, a spotted bow tie and sand-shoes. A cane dangled from his pocket and a faded carnation drooped from his buttonhole.

Miss Gedge was stout, frankly vulgar and, but for a cast in her eye, would have been a good-looking girl. She was the personification of contentment and goodwill. A droll pertness of manner enhanced her charm. She had, moreover, a most infectious laugh. This her squire exploited vigorously. The two carried all before them.

There were but eight chairs, but the shortage, so far from presenting difficulty, smoothed an irregularity away. Lady Ann took her proper place, namely, her husband's lap, while Ada, with many giggles, subsided into that of Mr. Alcock.

The tambourine was rolling. . . .

The flow of hatred had been arrested: soon the leak was being plugged—with the very underlinen of Sensitiveness, delicate, rosy mysteries, ripped from a girl's back.

"Yes," said Mr. Mason. "Children is bits of 'eaven. I was a very large 'unk. I remember Mother sayin' so when she found 'er boots in the oven. She didn't put it that way, but . . . Besides, look at the burf rate."

Amid shrieks of laughter, he was conjured to 'give over,' whilst a glowing Bob squeezed Ann surreptitiously.

"Oh, isn't 'e awful?" panted Miss Gedge. "An' when we're out 'e does pass such dreadful remarks. Las' Saturday afternoon a gentleman's 'at blows off. 'Stop it,' cries someone. 'Not me,' says 'Erbert, 'I've lef' me gas-marsk at 'ome.' "

There was a gust of merriment. As it died down, a fat guffaw of delight announced Uncle Tom's perception of the point.

" 'E ought to go on the 'alls," said Mr. Alcock. "Make 'is fortune."

Mr. Mason shook his head.

"Why," he said, "I should be stole in a week. An' there'ld be pore Mabel——"

"I should worry," said Miss Gedge. "But you can't 'ave your 'Untley an' eat it too, can you, May?"

"Not likely," said May. "Look at pore Mrs. Stoker."

"There's a tregedy," said Aunt Harriet. "An' three children an' all."

Mr. Barnham, who had been awaiting his chance, groaned eloquently.

"So when 'e talks about the stage," continued Miss Gedge, "I says, 'You go, me little friend,' I says, 'and 'ere's 'appy days. But don't you call roun' for me on Monday evenin', 'cause this is where you get off.'☐"

A round of applause acclaimed this admirable sentiment.

Mr. Mason blinked very hard.

"Ah, well," he said, "I s'pose it'll 'ave to be 'oly orders after all." He adjusted his collar, peered at an imaginary book and looked up earnestly. "Brethren, we will now sing *Cease thy ticklin', Jock*."

This justly occasioned great laughter.

As it subsided—

"Oh, I've bought a new straw," said Miss Gedge. "A regular Kiss-me-quick. Not that I wanted to, but since Benk 'Oliday the other ain't gone with my scent. I wore it to 'Astin's, you know, an' 'Erbert's brother was 'oldin' it when 'e come over queer. Of course, memories is very sweet, but . . ."

Amidst squeals of delight—

"She 'ad 'im on the brain," explained Mr. Mason.

The paroxysm which succeeded Uncle Tom's appreciation of this remark was so prolonged as to suggest that his labouring lungs were in need of assistance, and there was a general feeling of relief when he was able to assure his anxious ministers that he would let them know when he was dying.

As order was restored—

"I say, is this a smoking-carriage?" said Mr. Alcock, and looked round, grinning, for approval.

Once the ball was rolling, the question usually went. The great thing was not to ask it too soon. 'And when men have well drunk, then . . .'

The laughter was renewed.

"I should 'ope so," said Uncle Tom, taking out an enormous calabash.

Cigarettes were produced.

Mr. Barnham made bold to offer his case to Ann, who declined smilingly.

"She'll 'ave one with me," said Bob.

He lighted a Gold Flake and, after inhaling luxuriously, put the cigarette to her lips. . . .

Ann winced. Another tender intimacy clapped in the common stocks. . . .

May accepted a cigarette from Mr. Mason, who had an unfinished cigar. Together Ada and Mr. Alcock enjoyed the cigarette till lately reposing behind the latter's ear.

Beneath the soothing influence conversation became less boisterous. Little coteries sprang up. Miss Gedge and May exchanged murmurous confidences. Mr. Barnham listened to Aunt Harriet. Uncle Tom and Mr. Mason discussed 'closing time.' Ada played with Mr. Alcock's hair and squeaked or whispered according to the nature of the sweet nothings with which he plied her. Breathing endearment, Bob fondled and kissed Ann's fingers and presently pleaded for her lips.

"They won't mind," he insisted. . . .

At length Mr. Mason looked round.

"Well, ladies and gents," he said, "what's the pier done? I think an evenin' with the movies with a little footwork in between the shows'll just about see me 'ome."

The suggestion was greeted with action.

Chairs were drawn back, laps shaken and smoothed, pardons begged.

Ann was feverishly considering how best to announce that she was weary and would like to retire, when Bob put in his oar.

"An' this is my show," he said expansively. "I'm goin' to stan' treat to-night."

There was a murmur of deprecation.

Quick as a flash—

"Well, I'm sure that's very 'andsome," simpered Aunt Harriet.

"Now, look 'ere, Bobbie lad," said Uncle Tom, "don't you go rushin' in. Ten to one's a bit thick. Jus' 'cause it's your day out, that ain't no call for you to go treatin'——"

"Why not?" cried Bob. "Why, I want you all to remember this day, I do—the 'appies' day o' my life. Ten? I wish you was fifty. I've becked a winner to-day—drawn the firs' prize in the bigges' sweep on earth. . . . Look at 'er standin' there! Ain't she a peach? An' you want me to 'old me 'and for a matter o' thirty bob!"

"'Ooray!" cried Mr. Mason. "'Ooray! An' mind—the firs' Benger's with me."

Laughter and cheers confirmed the acceptance of hospitality.

Feeling as though she had dashed herself against a wall, Ann stammered something about getting her hat.

"Oh, it's right opposight," said Ada. "We never wear 'ats jus'——"

She stopped with a jerk.

Aunt Harriet filled up the hole.

"I'm afraid it soun's very lax, Lady Ann, but, you know, this year the residents proper 'ave to a great extent given up wearin' 'eadgear of nights. In fac', I think we should be remarked on . . ."

"Oh, I don't mind in the least," said Ann. "In fact, I like it much better."

After all, what on earth did it matter? What did anything matter? She was married . . . married to Bob . . . tied for life . . . *life*: and she was boggling about going uncovered!

They passed out of the house. Aunt Harriet delaying the procession to enjoin a sickly charwoman to clear, wash up and set the table for six.

"For *six*," she repeated meaningly, trusting thereby to promote such operation of mental arithmetic as would convince Mr. Barnham and Mr. Alcock that they were not expected to return. "Oh, an' Mrs. Perch—I've measured the beef."

"Very good, Mrs. Root," said that lady, breathing through her nose. "I'll bet you 'ave," she added under her breath. "Rotten ole toad."

When the door was shut, she shed a few tears of chagrin. It was a beautiful bit of beef.

The pier was indeed conveniently close. In less than a minute they stood before its gates.

The negotiation of the turnstile offered opportunities of humour, none of which were missed. The surly controller was rallied, rose and was appropriately mocked. His impotent indignation, hastily but vigorously served, followed them down the pier.

After the fresh sea air the breathless reek of the cinema was stale and stifling. It was the Saturday evening of a blazing week, to whose rare invitation the audience had healthily responded. Ann could have choked. She sat between Bob and Uncle Tom, with the former's arm about her and her left hand in his.

A melodrama was being shown: some of the scenery was superb— a forest at dawn, a cool reach of some river with sunlit woods about its banks, the spreading lawns of a great mansion blotched with the silhouettes of stately trees. The dazzling luxury of the interiors, the perfection of their appointment, the admirable manner of the men-servants, the smooth rush of the cars turned the fruit of memory into the grapes of Tantalus.

Ann sat dumb before the cruelty of Fate. It was true, then—she was to be spared nothing. Every slender tack that could be hammered was to be driven home—punched into her heart.

She had a terrible yearning to express her agony. She wanted to moan and twist her hands. She wanted to fall upon her knees and clasp her head. She wanted to breathe "My God.... My God.... My God...." She wanted to stammer her woe—change this fantastic hell into the similitude of human sorrow—picture it in words and tears—wrap it in the napkin of blessed, familiar speech.

Bob was importuning her.

"Give us a kiss, sweetheart."

Fainting, she gave him her lips.

"Now, then, break away, there," rasped an attendant. "If you can't wait, there's plenty of room outside."

It was not the man's fault. Complaints had been received and forwarded. Orders had come down that morning that any abuse of the obscurity indispensable to the performance was to be sternly checked. It was, of course, rather a delicate matter. Custom, if not prescription, was to be set by the ears. Still, the remark was well received—with hysterical laughter.

A wave of hot blood surged to Ann's temples. Her mind staggered. When she came to, she found herself praying for death.

The reflection that a week ago Bob would not have—had not done these things preened its grim self before her. Ann realized suddenly that familiarity was breeding assurance, if not contempt. From being 'my lady' she had become 'my—my missus.' More. For the first time since their engagement Bob was among his own. Hitherto he had been upon parade. Now he was relaxed—comfortable. His own had received him. He was sliding into their ways—naturally. It was not a case of infection, of evil communications corrupting manners. They were his—*his* ways. Of course. His ways. He saw no harm—there *was* no harm in them. They were wholesome enough. Only—they were not her ways....

The melodrama came to an end, and they filed out. The sheet had announced an interval of fifteen minutes.

The *salle de danse* was crowded. They thrust and were thrust within its walls.

Bob could not dance. Mr. Alcock, however, was clearly treading firm ground. The assurance with which he spoke made this still more manifest.

"Em I to 'ave the pleasure, Leddy Enn?"

What did it matter? What did anything—— Besides, how could she refuse?

They danced to a rousing fox-trot—as well as they could. There was little room, and steering was nothing accounted of on Saturday nights. Couples went as they pleased. Many seemed rapt—unaware that they were not alone: others heaved and revolved, careless of collision and greeting every bump with incorrigible cheer: some frolicked openly, to the unveiled disgust of the more intense, who sneered upon them as they passed.

By such as were not dancing Ann's presence upon the floor was instantly remarked. As she went by, she saw heads nodding, arms being caught, fingers pointing, ribs being nudged. The infection spread to the floor. Couples began to stare—to draw apart. Very soon she and Mr. Alcock were dancing in a little space of their own. As if by magic, this revolved with them. Had he pleased, Mr. Alcock could have left the space standing. That he did not so please was natural enough. The youth was intoxicated. His thirsty vanity, ordinarily but scurvily found, was in its cups. His superciliary muscle was strained to breaking-point: his eyes were almost closed: his sneer, the droop of his parted lips beggared description. It was his hour.

The dance ended with a crash, and the two returned to their party.

As Ann was desperately raking its environs for Bob—

"Well, Lady Ann," said Aunt Harriet, "what d'you think of our floor?" She laid her hand familiarly upon the girl's arm. "Not so bad for ole Suet?"

"I—I think it's very good," said Ann, observing with horror that the space, which had momentarily disappeared, was beginning to surround her again.

Aunt Harriet saw it, too, and raised her voice.

"You know, Lady Ann, I'm so glad to 'ave you at last. I've got so much I want you to 'elp me with. You know, livin' all the year round in the country, one's ideas seem to get into a groove. In course, Taown's the 'ub. There one's in touch with things. 'Otels and emporiums is up to date. People 'as *got* to move. One's only to take a walk down the street or pop into a laounge. . . . But 'ere—nothin'. An' after a bit, Lady Ann, stegnation sets in. I tell you," she added, with a mischievous laugh, "I'm not goin' to give you no rest. You'll be wore out before I'm through."

"I'm—I'm sure I shan't," faltered Ann, trying to smile and wildly conscious of an unnatural hush. "Indeed, I——"

Mercifully, the band recommenced its labours.

"Shell we take another turn?" said Mr. Alcock.

Ann lifted up her head.

"To tell you the truth," she said, "I'm a little tired." She looked round anxiously. "I wonder where Bob is."

"Gone to 'ave a drink," said Ada.

"Let's go an' fin' them," said Aunt Harriet.

They passed out after the manner of Royalty, a lane being made.

Mr. Alcock was dispatched in quest of the revellers, while Mr. Barnham, now sole warden of virtue, took up a central position and stared about him with an air of apologetic defiance.

After a suspiciously long absence, his colleague returned to say that the other squires were not to be found.

"They're gone to the Arms, the greedies," decided Aunt Harriet. "That's where they're gone. Never mind."

A rich clearance of Mr. Barnham's throat declared that he was labouring of plan.

"Let's take a stroll down," he suggested, "an' ketch them as they come back."

Economy had driven him to speak.

A premature return to their seats meant that the girl who sold chocolates would offer her tempting wares. This offer he would be bound in decency to frank. The acceptance or rejection thereof would rest with May—and Mr. Barnham did not trust May....

His misgivings were well founded.

"Oh, who wants to stroll?" said May. "Let's get back before the crush. I'm sure I've been trod and shoved enough for one night. Something crool, people are."

It was not magnificent: it was not even war: it was pure oppression—hitting the poor in spirit below the belt.

Aunt Harriet acclaimed the suggestion, and the move was made.

Two minutes later Mr. Barnham was eased of two shillings. He parted, sweating, with a hunted look in his eyes that went to Ann's heart.

She found herself wondering what, when he had married his bully, his life would be like. She saw him mute and shrinking before the eternal abuse, standing jaded and hungry without his own house, trying to summon the courage to enter in, dreaming of the happy days when he could buy exemption with a two-shilling piece....

For a blessed instant her mind left her own tragedy to suck at his. Then it leapt back, buzzing....

Aunt Harriet was purring hypocrisy, lying, dressing her lies in dirty splendour, fouling well after well. Ann responded mechanically, conscious that her spiritless dissembling would not have deluded a child, physically and mentally unable to play up to such form. An innocent-looking chocolate had caused Miss Gedge's jaws to conglutinate—a comical condition of things which she was turning to generous account, throwing May and Ada into convulsions of girlish laughter. Mr. Alcock was confiding to Mr. Barnham confessions of a well-dressed man....

A frightful feeling of loneliness flung into Ann's heart—a new kind of desolation, of which her philosophy had never dreamed. Sympathy was clean gone. Nobody, nothing within sight meant anything to her—or she to them. A desert island had animals and trees and skies and yellow sands: an empty house had silence and memories and dreams to offer: she had things in common with a wilderness—would have got on with Death. But this ... There was an awful emptiness about this crowded hall, a ghostly dreariness about this blithesome flow of soul which scared and terrified. 'As the hart panteth after the water-brooks ...' She was parched—mad with thirst. The muddiest trickle would have served. . . . But the saving fountains had stopped playing, the once innumerable rills were dried up.

At last the lights were lowered, and the talk died down.

Ann tried to shuffle her thoughts and find a way.

Instantly her brain told her that there was no way to be found.

She fobbed the tidings off and began again.

A way. She must find out a way. Where to? A way out—*out*. Suicide, Flight presented themselves and were set upon one side. Flight presented itself again—almost immediately. Ann permitted herself to consider Flight. . . . With a shock she realized that now, if ever, was the time. The hall was in darkness: Bob was not there: before Aunt Harriet could follow, she would be clear of the place: outside, it was night and there were crowds to mingle with: pursuit would be vain. . . . With a hammering heart, Ann began to wonder if there were night trains to Town. . . . Then, with a hideous leer, Flight faded away. *Her things—her money—her hat, even, was at 'Pier View.'* To get them was out of the question. The house was locked: Aunt Harriet had the key: if the charwoman was yet there, she did not know Ann by sight: besides—— Oh, it was hopeless, of course . . . hopeless.

Ann decided desperately that she must talk to Bob. She must try to explain—teach, if possible, the moment he reappeared, before a worse thing befell. She could not face that awful parlour again. Aunt Harriet alone. . . . Besides, the meal would be of the nature of a wedding-feast. Its prelusive character would be insisted upon. Jocular references would be made: sly digs administered. It would be hideous—revolting. Ann's flesh crept.

The moment Bob came she must ask him to take her outside—away, out of the crowd to where they could have a talk. Perhaps they could get a room somewhere, out on the skirts of the town. He wouldn't understand, of course. To repulse the kindly advances of his own kin! Deliberately to jettison 'the best'! All his instincts would jib at such heresy. But to-night—for a week, perhaps, she could override those instincts. As for the future——

Three figures appeared, boggling, at the end of her row. Then they began to push their way along.

Mr. Mason came first, announcing in apprehensive falsetto that if anyone pinched him he should call the women police. Uncle Tom followed, heaving with merriment and inquiring cheerily if there was room for a little one. Bob came last, laughing very much and repeatedly asking his companions if they were right for 'Emmersmith Broadway.'

Cries of 'Shut up!' and 'Sit down!' resounded.

An attendant came bustling. . . .

Bob subsided into his seat and mopped his face.

Then he laid a hand on Ann's knee.

"Well, Beauty, 'ow's things?" he whispered.

He reeked of liquor . . . reeked.

Something deep inside Ann seemed to give way.

"Didn' min' my leavin' you, did you, sweetheart? Just 'ad a quick one or two to celebrate. They're a couple of 'earties, they are—'Erb Mason an' Uncle Tom. I tell you, kid, you've got orf with them all right." He slid an arm about her and held her tight. "An' I don' wonder, by gosh. There ain't much left to the others when you're around."

Uncle Tom was speaking excitedly—from a great way off. His breath . . .

"Bob, Bob! She's bin showin' 'em 'ow to dance. Danced about with young Alcock, an' the others give 'em the floor." He slapped his thigh. "Glory, but I wish I'd bin there to see 'er put it across them—see my peach of a niece showin' ole Suet wot's wot." He thrust an arm through Ann's and covered her hand with his. "Strike me dead, sonny, but you're a lucky dog. I tell you—— Hullo!"

Ann had fainted.

The fresh air revived her immediately, but, though she implored the others to leave her husband with her and return to their seats, they would not hear of it. After a little, she abandoned the attempt. There was no reason why they should not have returned. Indeed, the girls were obviously disappointed. There was no reason at all—except that she was doomed. That was most clear. Every slightest chance was to be crushed. She had signed on and she was to go through the hoop. Resistance was futile. That terrible ring-master, Satire, knew his job.

They proceeded leisurely towards 'Pier View.'

Mr. Mason and Miss Gedge left them at the pier gates. Bob parted with the former effusively, swaying a little as he turned. Could she have done so, Ann would have begged them to stay. The two were scrupulous: they had authority: she trusted them. Miss Gedge was kind, human, no fool. Mr. Mason's vulgarity was but a pasteboard blade. . . .

As the area steps were won, two figures emerged.

These proved to be those of old friends, Mr. and Mrs. Joe Allen, of Bung Street, Plaistow, who, finding their call ill-timed, were upon the point of departure.

The encounter was cordial in the extreme.

A kill-joy might have suggested that Mr. Allen was under the influence of drink. The way in which concluding words of sentences occasionally rebelled against the deliberate precision with which he enunciated their predecessors might have aroused suspicion in a bigot's mind. So might the colour of his nose—and other things. But—he was an old friend; and among friends . . .

The Allens were bidden delightedly to supper; Mr. Barnham and Mr. Alcock were cavalierly sped.

The party descended carefully, Ada and May tarrying for a moment with their lingering swains presumably to temper the cold wind of dismissal and make further assignations.

Arrived at the door of the parlour, Ann shook off the sense of nightmare and begged to be excused.

Aunt Harriet crushed her entreaty, as a boa-constrictor his prey.

Food. That was what she wanted. A good bite of food. Ann had eaten nothing at tea—she had watched her. Nothing. That there fainting was nothing but want of food. Ann must trust her. She knew. Hadn't she been a bride? How well she remembered how when—— But in *course* Ann wasn't hungry. Why, that was the surest sign. Food. A nice cut off the joint and a glass of stout. Why, she remembered when she was married. . . .

Her hostess was determined that Ann should grace the board. The latter gave way listlessly. What did it matter? What did anything matter? What——

She took her seat dully, with despair sunk in her eyes.

She sat on her uncle's right and within his reach. From the opposite side of the table Mrs. Allen regarded her beadily. A plate of beef was given her and butter and bread. Stout was poured into her glass. They bade her eat and drink. She did so obediently. If they had bade her sing, she would have lifted up her voice. She was beaten. She had passed the end of her tether. Her spirit was broken down.

The meal proceeded.

The presence of the Allens was providing a merciful distraction from her estate. She had not the heart to be grateful. It was, she knew, only a temporary release—a postponement, big with hell. Satire was playing with her, as a cat plays with a mouse.

Conversation warmed. The output of geniality was amazing. Righteousness and peace kissed each other.

Aunt Harriet expanded. Uncle Tom broadened. Bob began to laugh indiscriminately. With increasing difficulty, Mr. Allen remembered bygone days.

As the joint reconstruction of a more than usually side-splitting episode was concluded—

"Dearie me," croaked Aunt Harriet, wiping the tears from her eyes, "'ow many years is that ago?"

Mr. Allen regarded Uncle Tom. To survey and measure the past was beyond his powers.

"Now, don't go addin' up milestones," said Uncle Tom. "I'm an optimis', I am. There's a good few tides come in since that little lark, but I don't feel no older."

"You would if you lived i' Plaizow," said Mr. Allen.

"No, I shouldn't," said his host. "'Cause I should blow down to jolly ole Suet a bit more often—an' 'ave one with me ole pals."

He laughed jovially.

"Yes, you would," said Mr. Allen. "The iron o' the city would enter in-in-injerso."

He looked round defiantly.

"I don't know about the iron," said Uncle Tom hilariously, "but I'd see the Scotch didn't. I bet that'ld go the right way."

"Trust you," said Aunt Harriet.

"Yes, an' touch the spot, too," added Uncle Tom, shaken with merriment.

"Oh, did you ever?" said Mrs. Allen, deliciously shocked.

"Yes, you would," said her husband, throwing back. "When you saw the people bein' groun' to powder an' the rich swillin' idow."

The reference was obscure. Possibly Mr. Allen was imperfectly remembering the fate of the Golden Calf and confusing his allusion with the imagery of oppression.

For all that, it carried.

"That's true," said Uncle Tom soberly.

"Is the distress very prenaounced?" said Aunt Harriet.

"Wicked," said Mr. Allen. "Women an' children's life-blood is bein' suggaway."

As though to neutralize such drainage, he drank deep and mournfully.

"Wot's four poun' ten?" he continued. " 'Ow far does that go? 'Ho,' they says, 'but look at wot you 'ad before the War. Why, we've doubled your pay,' they says. Per'aps. But wot they don' say is, 'An' we're chargin' you double, too, for the necesserities of life.' An' you ask if there's blussuggy goanon."

"But surely," said Bob, "it ain't the blokes as pays the wages as shoves the prices up. They 'as to fork out, too."

Mr. Allen braced himself.

"So they says," he said darkly. "That's their bettle-cry. But it's a deliberate 'ave. They're all in league, they are. The rich man's 'and is agains' the pore, an' always 'as been." He smote upon the table. "Walk down Bon' Street, brother, an' take a look at the cars. See 'ow the idle rich lives an' moves an' 'as their vile bein'. Caount the Rolls-Royce." He paused dramatically. "But don't you go gettin' in their way. You may 'ave 'elped to pave it wiv blood an' teers, but it's not your street—'cause you're only a common man."

There was a frightful silence.

Suddenly May burst into ecstatic laughter.

Mr. Allen, who was about to drink, stared at her, tumbler in hand.

As the transport subsided, he set down his glass.

"An' wot 'ave I said," he demanded, "that you fin' so 'ighly divertin'?"

"Oh, nothin'," said May, looking to the cornice, as though for help to fight her mirth. "I was only laughin' at me thoughts." She hesitated. Then, "I 'appened to pass the same remarks this afternoon—*an' got ticked orf for them.*"

Uncle Tom shifted in his chair.

"You said your granpa was a common man," he said uneasily. "You said——"

"I said 'e wasn't a nurl," retorted May. "An' you said it wasn' for me to speak disrespec'ful of urls 'cause I wasn' a lady born, an' you'ld rather 'ave the opinion of a *nurl's daughter* than your own's any day."

Before Uncle Tom could focus this perversion sufficiently to discern the lie upon which a distasteful knowledge of his first-born told him it was depending—

"A nurl's daughter?" said Mr. Allen, glaring at Ann.

"Oh, that's all over," said Aunt Harriet nervously. "She's one of us now. After all, burf's an accideni'."

"Oh, she's one of us, of course," said May. She laughed spitefully. "I'm sure it's a privilege—the way she shares our food an' gentlemen friends." Her voice began to quiver. "An' I'm sure she'd 've brought 'er Rolls-Royce coopy down—if she'd 'appened to think of it."

Mr. Allen's forehead and cheeks approached the colour of his nose. He began to breathe stertorously.

"Rolls-Royce?" he said hoarsely. He pointed a shaking finger. Instinctively Ann recoiled. "She 'as a Rolls-Royce? An' I've been breakin' bread at the same table wiv one ooze fathers 'as graoun' the pore to 'eap up riches?" He threw himself forward. "Where's yer Rolls-Royce come from? Aout of the pennies earned by toilin' slaves. Aout of——"

"'Ere, shut yer face," said Bob, rising. "Wot d'you know about it? Jus' 'cause she's a lady——"

Mr. Allen started to his feet.

"Wot do I know?" he repeated, with blazing eyes. "I know the terruth. That's wot I know. I say 'er wealth 'as bin stole aout o' the maouths of starvin' baibes. The widder an' the orphin 'as bin robbed to——"

"An' I say you're a liar," roared Bob.

Ada began to cry, and Aunt Harriet laid a hand upon Bob's arm. He shook her off. Everyone was on their feet. Uncle Tom was at Allen's shoulder. Trembling in every limb, Ann clung to the back of her chair.

Bob continued furiously.

"She never robbed nor stole in all 'er life. Nor 'er father before 'er. It's easy enough for those as don' want to work to 'oller an' carry on 'cause there's dukes an' earls ooze fathers 've made good an' saved, instead o' blindin' their money at the nearest pub."

Mr. Allen surged forward, blaring.

"I'm a liar, am I?" he mouthed. "Jus' 'cause I'm not afraid to strip the troof? She never stole, nor 'er father? P'r'aps not. You wouldn' 'ave no call to steal if your gran'father 'd bin a thief . . . an' murdered an' stole an' saved so as she could 'ave a Rolls-Royce to 'ide 'er nakedness."

Bob hit him on the mouth. . . .

Uncle Tom was between them—shouting. He had Mr. Allen round the waist. The two were lurching and struggling violently. Mr. Allen was cursing in a thick guttural. Blood was welling from his lip. Black in the face with rage, Bob was labouring fiercely to shake himself free. Ann, frantic, was hanging on his arm, beseeching him to come away. Aunt Harriet, who had been something of an expert and knew that dead weight told, lay upon his breast with her arms round his neck. Ada, whimpering, had him by the coat.

Finger to lip, May watched the affray with gleaming eyes. Remembering her husband's prowess as an indifferent heavy-weight, Mrs. Allen regarded Ann with a supercilious stare.

"Get 'im away!" yelled Uncle Tom. "Out o' the room—upstairs! Now then, Joe. Don' lose yer dignity. 'E'll be sorry to-morrer."

"'E'll be sorry ternight," howled Mr. Allen. "You saw 'im strike me. You saw——"

"Yes, I saw," shouted Uncle Tom. "But, you know, you arst fer trouble, Joe. You 'adn't got no call to make it personal. Never min'.

You siddown an' 'ave a drink." He screwed his head round. "Will you get 'im away?" he raved. "I ain't a 'Ercules."

"Oh, Bob, Bob!" wailed Ann. "Bob, for God's sake come away. Surely, if I don't mind, whyever should you? What does it matter? We know it isn't true. Bob, if you love me, leave him and come away."

Bob never heard her.

"☐'E's insulted my wife," he raged. "You 'eard 'im. That dirty red-nosed skunk 'as laid 'is tongue to my girl. Lemme go, Aunt 'Arriet. I tell you, it's me or 'im. An'——"

Ann's voice rang out.

"D'you want to kill me? D'you want me to die of shame?"

Her husband stopped struggling and turned.

"Look 'ere, kid," he expostulated. "You can't expec' me to sit still an' 'ear——"

"You haven't. You've hit him on the mouth. And I say that's enough—*I* say so."

The pronoun stood up above the uproar.

Uncle Tom started: an oath Mr. Allen was savaging died on his lips. Aunt Harriet released her nephew and stood up, staring.

Ann continued steadily.

"Are you going to question my right?"

Bob's eyes fell.

"Of course," he said clumsily, "of course, if you like to——"

"I do. I want to go. It's my wish. I want you to take me away—out of the house—now. Come, please."

"Out of the 'ouse?" said Bob.

"Out of the house," said Ann. "And—at once. Come."

She turned to the door.

No one said anything at all. The quiet, cold air of one having authority tied up their tongues. They felt suddenly diminished. A wave of detestable respect had swept them off their feet. Blood had told.

Without turning, Ann passed out.

Bob followed his wife, crestfallen enough. . . .

There was a moment's silence.

Then—

"Dear me," said Aunt Harriet, trembling with rage and mortification. "Might be a craowned queen. 'Take me away—aout of the 'aouse—naow . . .'□"

She laughed hysterically.

"Woddid I say?" cried Mr. Allen, smearing the blood from his lip. "Dirt. That's wot we are—dirt. Dirt for 'er to shake orf 'er gilded feet. Wot if we 'ave——"

"Yes, I notice you didn't say that when she was 'ere," snapped Aunt Harriet. "Very quiet you was. Anyone might 've thought you was frightened."

"*Frightened?*" screamed Mr. Allen. "Gimme my 'at. I'll show yer whether I'm frightened."

With a filthy oath, he flung Uncle Tom aside, clapped his hat upon his head and lunged to the door. . . .

They heard him ricochet down the passage and bawl up the area steps.

"Naow you've done it, 'Arriet," breathed Uncle Tom.

Bob heard him bawl, too, and stopped in his tracks. He was on the pavement perhaps two houses away.

Ann heard the challenge, too, and lost her nerve.

She caught at Bob's arm and tried to pull him along.

"Come on, Bob! Come along. Don't take any notice of him." Bob resisting, she tried to drag him with her. "For God's sake, Bob . . ."

Before the terror in her voice the last vestige of her authority collapsed. She became again the weaker vessel, meet to be protected—and avenged.

Bob shook her off and turned.

She flung herself upon him, but he tore her hands away.

She reeled against the railings, shaken and fainting. . . .

She saw the two men meet and heard the smack of a blow. They parted—then drew together again, assuming grotesque postures like animals about to spring. Again they closed for an instant, ducking and slamming like madmen. Broken spurts of cursing were jerked to her ears. . . .

They were in the road now—immediately opposite 'Pier View.' A street-lamp showed her the blood on Allen's face. His mouth was smothered. . . .

Figures began to rise out of the shadows. The light of the lamp was illuminating some of their heads. Somebody panted past her hotfoot. A little bunch was crammed in the area gate—Aunt Harriet and . . .

Bob seemed to lift himself up. Then he fell headlong backwards, towards the pavement. His shoulders reached the gutter, and his head just made the kerb. This brought his face forward, with a click. For a moment he lay as he had fallen—as one who wishes to remain recumbent and yet, ridiculously, to regard his feet. Then his head slid slowly sideways. . . .

As the crowd surged up, Ann stumbled forward and fell on her knees beside the corpse. Then she asked for water and began to loosen its tie.

People were nudging one another. She knew it. She could feel their curious stares and the awkwardness of the hush that fell wherever she went. She did not care at all. This was quite different. Bob had need of her. . . . Bob . . .

Two police came hastening. One was a sergeant. The crowd fell back respectfully.

The sergeant fell upon one knee and flashed his lantern on the dead man's face.

"Who done this?" he cried, looking up.

Again the crowd parted to reveal Joe Allen holding on to the railings with his coat-sleeve across his eyes.

The sergeant addressed his subordinate.

"Take 'im," he said shortly.

He drew a whistle and blew five or six short blasts. Then he turned to Ann.

"Was he your friend, lady?"

Ann started violently at the tense, staring open-mouthed into the sergeant's eyes. Then she caught the groom's head and peered at the quiet face. For a moment she held it between her palms; then very gently she suffered it to roll back into its old position. . . .

Ann sank back on her heels and stared at the sky.

Slowly the Morland took shape—the spreading oak and the cottage and the jolly brown horse . . . the girl standing in the doorway, holding the little boy . . . and the man on the horse, smiling . . . all alone and happy—under the spreading oak . . . very poor and simple, but very, very happy. . . .

A dry sob shook Ann—the first of many.

Presently the tears began to stream down her cheeks.

She continued to stare steadfastly up into the sky, till the bystanders followed her gaze and tried to see something.

ELEANOR

COFFEE was served. Finally, liqueurs were offered. A moment later the servants withdrew silently, leaving the quartette to their cups.

The six shaded candles threw down upon the table a gentle light. This the silver and rosewood gave back vastly enriched. From a decanter before the host a fine old port rendered a comfortable glow. An onyx ash-tray and a match-box flashed by each painted plate; at either end of the table was a gold box of cigarettes; between the two men lay cigars; fruit was within reach; the board was not crowded, yet seemed to be pleasantly full; upon the sideboard were remaining champagne, water, coffee and the little group of liqueurs.

The dinner had been perfect, the service superb; but then you had come to expect that at 20 Park Place. It was the Willoughbys' fault; from the day they were married they had always spoiled their guests.

Herrick looked across the violets at Eleanor Cloke.

"Kitchen, cellar, table and service," he said, "all one long last word. Nell, how do they do it?"

Miss Cloke shrugged her white shoulders.

"You can search me," she said hopelessly. "But don't dwell on it, or I shall burst into idle tears."

Madge Willoughby set down her cup.

"Why?" she demanded.

"Same as the Queen of Sheba," said Herrick hastily. "You know. She thought she knew how to live; but when she saw Solomon's idea of comfort——"

"Tell her," said Eleanor Cloke.

"I am," said Herrick. "Give me a chance.... Well, what really broke the Queen's heart was the poisonous reflection that for the rest of her life the King of Sheba would be saying, 'My dear, why can't we have so-and-so? *Solomon has.*' "

His hostess leaned forward, with parted lips.

"D'you mean that you're . . ."

David Herrick swallowed.

"Don't rush him," said Crispin Willoughby. "The roof of his mouth's dry." He turned to his faltering guest. "Moisten the lips, old bean, and let it come with the breath."

"I mean," said Herrick desperately, "that we're—we're thinkin' of joinin' up."

His hostess sighed contentedly.

"At last," she said.

Crispin turned to Miss Cloke.

"My dear," he said, "be careful. Have you ever seen him unshaved?"

"That," said Eleanor, "is a pleasure to come."

"Pleasure?" said Crispin. "Oh, she has got it bad. Never mind. Was you took ill gradual like, or was it all of a suddin that you came over queer?"

"To be perfectly frank," said Eleanor, "I've always liked the look of him."

Willoughby put up an eye-glass and inspected his prey.

"There is something rather winsome about that sheepish grin of his, isn't there? D'you see what I mean, Madge? That David's-my-name-but-call-me-Boris-look."

"What a shame," said his wife. "David, if I were Nell, I should be very proud."

"I am," said Eleanor. "When he seized me——"

"Oh, you story!" said David. "I never——"

"Shut your face," said Crispin. "Go on, Nell. When he seized you . . ."

"I never seized her," cried Herrick. "I—I hadn't time. Your butler——"

"You see," said Eleanor, "we arrived together to-night. I was just going to ring when he said that I looked like a fairy-tale. Well, that was all right, so, instead of ringing, I gave him a baby stare."

"Oh, the hussy!" raved Herrick. "The——"

"Be quiet," shrieked his host and hostess.

"The next minute," said Eleanor coolly, "it was all over. And, when I came to, the door was open and I was in his arms."

"Oh, she's slurred it," said Crispin. "She's slurred it. What was all over?"

Eleanor smiled bewitchingly.

"You must ask your butler," she said.

Crispin lifted his glass and looked at his wife.

"My sweet," he said, "your very good health. There's no one like you in all the blinkin' world." His guests cried their approval, and the tenderest look stole into Madge Willoughby's eyes. He drank, smiled and set down his glass. Then he turned to Miss Cloke. "Nell," he said, "you're a darling. I'd rather have you on my right than any woman I know. Yet, sweet as you are, you're a fortunate child. David may be peculiar, but he'll never let you down."

"What d'you mean—'peculiar'?" said Herrick.

"That," said Eleanor, "is what I'm burning to know."

"Oh, it's nothing to worry about. Be careful of him when he's in beer, and if ever he says he's a life-belt and tries to put himself on, don't argue, but send for the police."

"They say," said Eleanor, gurgling, "that marriage tends to shatter all sorts of illusions."

Crispin laid a hand upon his heart.

"My dear," he declared, "I'm sure that yours will but substantiate your dreams."

"With which," said Madge tremulously, "we grey-beards look towards you."

Solemnly she and her husband toasted their guests.

Herrick cleared his throat.

"Nell," he said, "I give you the verb 'to love.' *Je t'aime, tu m'aimes, il s'aime, mais nous aimons Madge tous les trois.*"

He raised his glass.

"'*Il s'aime*'?" said Crispin. "Put down that port."

"We'd better include him," said Eleanor. "Besides, he's—he's rather a dear."

She blew her host a kiss, and the toast was honoured.

"A little more of this," said Mrs. Willoughby, "and I shall break down."

"I—I'm sure I should have seized her," said Crispin brokenly.

"Well, now," said Herrick, squeezing the end of a cigar, "what's the first thing to do?"

"Broadcast your folly," said Crispin. "Put a notice in *The Times*, announcing her unaccountable determination to become your wife. If I were you I should kill two birds with one rock and add that you won't be responsible for her debts. You never know."

"The next thing," said Madge, "is to decide roughly upon a date. Let's see. This is March. What about some time in May?"

"That's all right for me," said Eleanor. "As at present arranged, I get back from Nice——"

"My dear good child," said her hostess, "you can wash Nice out. You've got to get your *trousseau*."

The lovers regarded one another.

"Can't she get that at Nice?" said David. "I mean, I'd thought I'd go too. Give the east winds a miss an' play a little pat-ball an'——"

"Nice?" said Crispin. "You won't have time to get to Worthing and back. You haven't the remotest idea of what you're up against. As a rule, a full-dress wedding takes over two months to produce, and that means going full blast the whole of the time."

Herrick shifted uneasily.

"Must—er—must it be full-dress?" he ventured. "I mean——"

A shriek from Madge and Eleanor cut short the protest.

"But, of *course*," cried his hostess. "You must be married at St. Margaret's, with six bridesmaids."

"That's right," said Crispin. "And flowers on the organ. I'll order the confetti. The best way is to get it by the hundredweight."

Herrick tugged his moustache.

"You're sure," he said humbly, "you're sure, Nell, you wouldn't like quite a quiet show? You know. Sort of hidin' our light under a bushel."

"Positive, darling," said Eleanor. "I want to splurge. Besides, we can go to Nice any old time. Can we have a guard of honour?"

"There you are," said Crispin. "They're squabbling already."

"Look here," said Madge, laughing. "Within limits of reason each of you's anxious to do what the other wants. Am I right?"

"My heart's desire," said David piously.

"Liar," said Eleanor. "Go on, Madge."

"Very well. I've got a plan. Certain things, like her *trousseau*, are left to the woman, and certain other things are always left to the man. Now, that's a bad arrangement, because the woman gets what she wants and the man pleases himself."

"Why's that bad?" said Eleanor suspiciously.

"Because, if they're to be happy, the woman should get what he wants, while the man should please her."

Finger to exquisite lip, Eleanor regarded her swain.

"Yes, I've got that," said the latter. "It's rather subtle, but——"

"It's love," said Madge. "That's all. If Nell gets a frock and you don't like it, she'll loathe the sight of it."

"That's right," said Crispin. "And if you get a pair of boots and they frighten her, the very thought of the swine'll make your gorge rise."

"Therefore," continued Madge, bubbling, "the usual practice must be reversed. The things that a man does will become Nell's business, while David must choose and manage what's usually left to the girl."

There was a pregnant silence.

Then—

"My dear," said her husband, "I take my hat right off. What a truly tidal brain-wave. David, we'll go and look at chemises to-morrow morning."

"No, you won't," said Madge. "But we shall—David and I. And you and Nell will go and get David some boots."

"But I don't want any boots," cried David. "Besides——"

"What d'you mean?" said Crispin. "You can't be married in your socks. To-morrow morning Nell and I are going down the Edgware Road to choose your wedding foot-joy—a good-looking pair of roomy, elastic-sided, banana-coloured boots; and if we should see a nice pair of trousers . . ."

The rest of the sentence was lost in a roar of laughter.

When order had been restored—

"They must each," said Madge shakily, "make a list of what they need and where they'd like the things got. Who's your bootmaker, David?"

"Stoop."

"Very well. Nell and Crispin'll go to Stoop, and Nell'll order some boots. Stoop's got your last, and Crispin, being a man, will keep her straight. In the same way, you and I'll go to Zyrot's and you shall pick out some hats. They can be tried on me, and I'll supervise your choice."

"That's all very well," said David, "but I know Crispin's ideas of humour, and——"

"I give you my word," said his host, "I'll do you a treat. Nell shan't get a blinkin' thing I wouldn't be glad of myself. It'll be for her, of course, to choose the engagement ring." He turned to Eleanor. "Oh, you shall have a snorter." The unfortunate Herrick blenched. "I think, perhaps, you'd better have two—just in case you lose one."

Madge Willoughby began to shake with laughter.

"If she does," blurted David, "she'll have all grey flannel *lingerie*—with brass buttons."

"Oh, I'm sure you wouldn't do that," said Eleanor. "That would be unkind. Besides, a sponge-bag kilt wouldn't suit you."

So soon as he could speak—

"It's all off," cried David wildly. "I absolutely refuse to agree to this lop-sided idea. I won't have anything to do with it. Her—her imagination's too vivid. And with that overfed serpent to egg her on . . ."

It was fully two minutes before his protest was overcome.

"As for the jobs," said Madge tearfully, "that they usually do together, we can be a Court of Appeal. Take the wedding, for instance. Well, I think it should be full-dress—not because Nell wants it, but because it's only decent."

"I agree," said Crispin warmly. "I've been through the hoop; why shouldn't David?"

Herrick raised his eyes to heaven and set his teeth.

"Madge," he said weakly, "why did you marry the brute?"

His hostess rose with a laugh.

"Love," she said. "He wanted me to, you see, and I wanted to do as he wanted."

The absurd arrangement worked well.

The Willoughbys' taste was irreproachable.

Madge had learned how to dress in Boston, Mass., and possessed an uncanny instinct for anticipating *les modes*. Crispin's sartorial opinions were respected in Savile Row. He had, moreover, a genius for organization. Under his direction the 'production' of the wedding proceeded like clockwork. An eye to colour made Madge a born decorator, and, where furniture was concerned, while they were yet herded in the showrooms, she could tell the sheep from the goats. David's half-timbered cottage at Hammercloth Down began to look as it had looked when James the First was young.

Herrick and Eleanor Cloke were admirably served.

As for their patrons, they were tickled to death. Whether sitting as a Court of Appeal or supervising the lovers' selection of the wherewithal to take the matrimonial field, they called an hilarious tune. Born with large ideas, they indulged them generously. Happily for their *protégés*, the latter were rich. . . .

If Crispin and Madge made the running, David and Eleanor were well up. An afternoon at the dressmaker's suited Madge down to the ground, but the lady herself made such a dazzling mannequin that David would not have been human if he had found the hours long. In the same way, Crispin shouldered his burdens with the most infectious good humour, continually reducing Miss Cloke to a condition of mirth which verged upon abandon and throwing shop after shop into sniggering confusion. The climax was reached at the hosier's, when Willoughby suddenly found himself unable to speak anything but the most imperfect English, enthusiastically supported by an excited flow of French. Indeed, but for his solemn promise never to repeat such simulation, their pilgrimages would have ended that day, for, as Eleanor observed that evening—

"The laws that seem to govern men's clothes are difficult enough without any international complications."

Herrick inspired audibly.

"That's a good one," he said. "I suppose the laws (sic) that govern women's clothes (sic) require rather less intelligence than does the sucking of eggs. Of course, my office is a complete sinecure. I'm not dressing you at all. Apparently I'm not—not competent. A woman's headgear alone seems to be a life study. If I make the most patent suggestion, all the women in the place nearly burst themselves with laughter: and when I ask why, the only answer I get is that I 'shouldn't like it like that.' And sometimes Madge adds that 'the line'ld be wrong.' And when I ask, 'What line?' she says, 'The line of the hat.' Not 'lining,' mark you, but 'line.'"

"Well, I expect it would."

Herrick put a hand to his head.

"'*Et tu, Brute,*'" he murmured. Then, "Look here. Supposing I was an architect, and you wanted to choose a house. And every one you liked I said, 'You can't have that because the point's wrong.' And when you said 'What point?' I said, 'The point of the house.' Well, after about thirty, you'ld want to lie down and scream."

"Your wretched things," wailed Eleanor, "are every bit as bad. Yesterday I chose a grey suit—at least, I chose the cloth. And I said I'ld bring them the buttons. As it happened, I'd seen some that morning—blue pebble buttons——"

"Good God!" said Herrick.

"Exactly," said Eleanor. "That was what Crispin said. And when I asked the cause of the excitement, I was told that I 'didn't understand.' I ask you."

"At least," said Herrick faintly, "we don't change our rubric once a year."

"Once a month," corrected Willoughby. "You wait. How many hats did you get to-day?"

"Three," said David. "One's a topper—all blue and white straw. Looks as if someone had rolled on it and then bought it half a pint of gooseberries to keep it quiet."

"What?" screamed Eleanor.

"It's all right, darling," cried Madge. "It's a dream. They're not gooseberries at all. They're cherries—blue cherries, and the shape's rather like one—I wonder if you remember; I wore it at Henley last year, and it had a crushed strawberry——"

"Time," said Crispin. "Maudlin memories of discarded headgear are bad for my heart. I only introduced this ghastly topic to illustrate the fugacity of women's raiment. The hats you chose to-day will be out of date before they're married."

"I don't think so," said Madge. "I'm trying to buy well ahead. Of course——"

"One moment," said David. "D'you mean to say that there's even a possibility of such a thing?"

"Well, I'm a little bit anxious about that velvet toque. You see——"

A howl of dismay interrupted her.

"My favourite?" cried David. "The wicked one that dips over the left eye?" He threw up his hands. "Why, properly cared for, there's years of wear in that hat."

"Years of wear?" shrieked the girls.

"Years," yelled Herrick. "An' then it could be done up."

There was a roar of laughter.

"You see?" said Crispin. "He hasn't the remotest idea. Never mind. To-morrow Nell and I are looking at furnished flats."

Eleanor made a little mouth.

"Much," she announced, "against my will. A house would have been much nicer. Still, I accept your ruling."

"My dear," purred Madge, "I know what servants are. You're sure to strike some wash-outs in your first twelve months—real old soldiers, I mean. They're like vultures. They can smell a newly married couple five miles off. And a house is so unwieldy."

"I know, but——"

David put in his oar.

"Give me an undress wedding, and you shall have your house."

"Not on your life," said Eleanor. "Besides, if you really loved me you'd do as I want."

"Ugh," said David, "she's wheedling me." He cleared his throat. "Nothing doing," he said sternly. "Besides, if you worshipped me, you'd—you'd hang upon my lips."

"I think," said Eleanor demurely, "I think I—I might . . . in a house."

"I'll back the lady," shouted Crispin. "I'll lay five to one—six—ten . . . ten sovereigns to one sovereign the lady gets her way."

"Taken," said Madge. "David, stick to your guns. The Court of Appeal's behind you. Besides, I've had some. If you take a house before you've got the right servants you'll be buying trouble in red."

Eleanor gave her *fiancé* a melting look.

"David darling," she murmured, "don't you think that this once we could upset the Court of Appeal? After all, we've got to live in it—you . . . and I."

She blushed exquisitely.

Herrick writhed.

"Be strong," shrieked Madge, "be strong. Think of the housemaids saying they can't stick the stairs and the cook complaining of the damp and the charwomen——"

"Ch-charwomen?" stammered David.

"Charwomen. Relays of them—when all the servants have gone. And the silver at the Bank because you've no one to clean it, and poor Nell in tears counting your shirts, and answering the back-door yourself. . . . At least, a flat has only one door."

David addressed himself to Eleanor.

"My sweet," he said, "not even for an undress wedding will I give you a house. In your own interest——"

Here a salted almond hit him upon the nose.

Mrs. Willoughby regarded the ceiling.

"Ten sovereigns to one," she murmured. "Dear me, this is very fortunate. David, how much was that hat you didn't like?"

"What, not 'The Lost Chord'?"

"That's right."

"Nine and a half guineas," said Herrick. He turned to Crispin. "Nine and a half guineas for a piece of rope—wound round and round—painted red and white—with a chunk of wood on each end."

"But how ravishing," said Crispin. "Was it real rope, or only imitation?"

"It was a gem," said Madge. "We'll get it to-morrow, David, before we look at the cooks."

The conference was typical and one of several.

The four fleeted the time pleasantly, hunting in couples, conferring perhaps twice a week. Once Madge had protested that the arrangement was false, that her jest was being carried too far. The betrothal, she hinted, was being shorn of its rights; the privacy of courtship was being invaded; halcyon days were being stolen away. Her objection was tumultuously quashed. With one consent Eleanor and David insisted that all was well. They declared that they were not children, that chances of present discord were being eliminated, that future harmony was being assured. They also expressed their gratitude in certain terms. Madge was reassured. Crispin, being a man, said and thought nothing at all. And, as is always the way, some people, who were not concerned, said and looked volumes.

This was inevitable.

The engagement had attracted attention to a notable pair.

Miss Cloke had been bridesmaid to Royalty, was immensely liked and of great beauty. Herrick had played polo for England, and was known and respected on the Turf. His beautiful filly, Cretonne, was fancied for the Derby. Her victory would undoubtedly be cordially received.

As for the Willoughbys, they were celebrities pure and simple. They had been conspicuous as man and maid. Captain Willoughby, bachelor, was a V.C. Miss Madge Dinwiddy had been the darling of New York. The two had married for love and nothing else. Two personalities—one brilliant and the other steadfast—had made two simultaneous mutual appeals, each of them too powerful to be withstood. Before the respective onslaughts Crispin Willoughby and Madge had gone down incontinently.

Mayfair had roared its approval then and there, and its approval had never waned.

So far as the two were concerned, the result of their union was natural enough. Each began to assume something of the other's outstanding quality. A sheen stole upon the nap of Crispin's steadfastness. The charm of Madge's brilliance began to crystallize.

American by birth, the lady would have graced any company. She was tall and beautifully made. Some said her neck was too long, but I do not think so. Be that as it may, it was the neck of a goddess. The Willoughby emeralds had never looked half so well. Soft brown hair and laughing eyes, a fine colour and an exquisite mouth went to the making of a countenance you never forgot. Her air, her easy dignity, her flow of excellent talk—above all, that precious radiance which could coax flame from smoking flax would have ennobled a hunchback. Wherever she went, Madge Willoughby was constantly aerating the wine of life. Often enough she turned it into champagne.

Crispin was thirty-five and a handsome man. Tall, quiet, pleasant, grave-faced, he suggested a strength and depth of character not to be met every day. The suggestion was true. The deeper you dug, the finer the ore you came to. But, until his marriage, the mine had to be worked. His style, his manners were perfect—and always had been; he inspired astounding confidence. But he had been reserved—shy. Only among his familiars would he let himself go. . . . Five years with Madge had altered everything. The man had shed his reserve and given his spirits their head. His humour came bubbling. Invariably he led the dance. And Madge watched him leading with the gentlest light in her eyes. . . .

The opposition of two such fair planets, no less than their several conjunction with stars almost as bright, was bound to excite remark.

Eyebrows were raised; whispers were repeated; nudges were covertly exchanged. Soon an impatient confidence that smoke so thick must be the greasy harbinger of conflagration set tongues wagging.

It was on the evening of the nineteenth of April, as Mrs. Willoughby and Herrick were returning by taxi from choosing a breakfast set, that the latter threw his cigarette out of the window, took the lady in his arms and kissed her upon the mouth.

"*David!*"

She shook him off and shrank into her corner, trembling violently.

Herrick took out his handkerchief and wiped his face. This was unnaturally pale.

"I'm sorry," he said quietly. "I beg your pardon. I—I don't know why I did it. I think—I think it was your perfume. I shall smell it all my life, dear . . . your faint perfume."

"*David!*"

The horror of the girl's tone was reflected in her beautiful eyes.

The man nodded.

"Yes, it's true," he said. "I've fallen in love with you."

"Oh, David . . ."

She began to wail tremulously, twisting her fingers as though in an agony of mind.

"I'm only human, Madge; and if you could see yourself I think you'd understand. I've tried, dear. I know all it means. I've tried and fought and jammed my nose to the stone. But it's not the slightest good."

"But Nell," cried Madge. "Nell..."

Herrick shrugged his shoulders.

"I know. It can't be helped. I'm sorry. She's awfully sweet. But—— Oh, Madge, there's something about you that takes a man by the throat... something that——"

"Stop, David, stop! You must be out of your mind. You can't mean—— Oh, for God's sake tell me you're only pulling my leg."

"I wish to God I could," said Herrick miserably. "But I can't, my lady, I can't. I love you, and there you are." Madge caught her breath and clapped her hands to her face. "I'm wild—crazy about you, and that's the truth. Of course it's hopeless—grotesque. You're Crispin's wife, and Crispin's one of the best. But I don't suppose I'm the first that's loved his wife.... You'll tell him, of course. And say if he wants to kick me, I won't try and cramp his style. He's every right in the world. But I don't think he will, because he'll understand. He's a man, you see... and he knows that it's pretty easy to fall in love with you."

"But Nell, David, Nell.... Don't you see what this means to her? You're letting her down most frightfully. Why, man, it'll break her heart. If it wasn't for Nell, I wouldn't care a kick. We'd have a straight talk, and after a month——"

"Month?" echoed David, with a bitter laugh. "Shows how much you understand. 'After a month.'... Good God, Madge, this isn't an evening out. I'm finished... bent... broken.... You've shown me the precious fountain. I've drunk its water out of your blessed palms. I've drunk—*drunk*, my lady.... And you only drink once. I'm badged—branded, Madge, branded as your man. With me you stand for womanhood. Your smile, your voice, your hair, the light in your wonderful eyes——"

"Oh, stop, stop," wailed Madge. "How can you talk like this? You know it's not the game. You know you're wronging Nell... and Crispin... and me. If I've given you cause, God knows I never meant it. If..."

Her voice broke, and she began to weep silently.

Herrick set his teeth.

"We're nearly home," he said. "Shall I tell him to drive round the Park?"

"Yes—no—yes," sobbed Mrs. Willoughby. "And—please don't talk any more."

David gave the order and flung himself back in his seat. Presently with a shaking hand he lighted a cigarette. . . .

By the time they were back at Park Place, Madge was reasonably composed.

She descended quickly, waved her hand, and let herself in with a rush.

Herrick told the cabman to go to the Club.

Crispin was in the library, seated upon the floor, with a pipe between his teeth, brushing the Sealyham.

His wife burst in tempestuously.

"Crip, the most awful thing has happened."

"Impossible," said Crispin calmly. "My word, how lovely you look. Of course, the way to see you is to sit at your feet."

His wife sat down by his side and put an arm round his neck.

"Crip," she said, laying her cheek against his. "David's gone off the deep end."

"What?" cried Crispin. "Gone and got sozzled by day?"

"No, no, no. Far worse, Crip. He thinks he's in love with me."

"The devil he does," said Crispin. "Not that it isn't natural, but what a stew and a half! Where's Nell come in?"

"He swears she doesn't," cried Madge. "That's the frightful part. Whatever are we to do?"

Her husband knitted his brows.

"Of course, he'll get over it," he murmured. "That's certain enough. Just as the others have. But in this case we're up against time."

"Exactly," said Madge. "Right up against it. A week in the country might help, but he can't have a couple of days. Whatever happens, Nell must never suspect."

"By Jove, no." He turned and looked at his wife. "Hullo, you've been crying, sweetheart." His lips tightened. "Did he—make a fool of himself?"

"Only for a second. He caught hold of me and kissed me. But I didn't mind that. Besides, he apologised directly. And he told me to tell you that if you wanted to kick him he was at your service." Crispin grinned. "But he said he didn't think you would."

"Why?"

"He said that, being a man, you'd understand."

"Ah."

There was a moment's silence.

Then Crispin kissed his wife, smiled into her eyes and fell again to brushing the terrier, who was patiently lying on his back with his legs in the air.

"Where is, er, Paris, at the moment?" he demanded lazily.

"I haven't the faintest idea. Probably at the Club."

"And Œnone?"

"Probably at home. Why?"

"I was thinking they'd better not meet till David's got his orders. Of course, the marriage must go through. They're perfectly matched and they'll be ridiculously happy. If there were anything doing—I mean, if you were on, it'ld be a different thing. Nell wouldn't stand an earthly—no woman would." Mrs. Willoughby squeezed his arm. "But as you're not, old lady—well, unrequited love doesn't wear as well as it did when 'burning Sappho loved and sung.' Personally, I'm not at all sure that it was ever very durable. But that's beside the point, which is that our job is to knock it out quick."

"I agree," said Madge, abstracting her husband's case and taking a cigarette. "But how on earth can we do it?"

"Ask him to dinner to-night. I'll go out. Somewhere about the fish tell him tenderly that you wouldn't be seen dead with him. That'll put him off and, what's far more important, wound his pride. Add, for instance, that you don't like the way he eats." Madge began to shake with laughter. "And say, 'to be perfectly frank,' that you've always been much surprised that Nell didn't seem to mind."

"I can't, Crip. Besides——"

"You must. It's the only way. Then, having got so far, say, 'as a matter of fact,' you're not at all sure that she hasn't noticed something. That'll make him sit up. It'll also make him ask questions. You'll beat about the bush till you get to the sweet. Then say you'll tell him when the servants are gone."

"Go on," said Madge, bubbling.

"When you're alone, extract his word to say nothing, and then tell him bluntly we've a sort of idea that she's looking at somebody else. Refuse to say who it is—that shouldn't be difficult—but say he's a pretty strong man. Add casually that of course it isn't everyone that could hold a girl like Nell and that, 'to tell the truth,' you and I'd always said that the one thing we were afraid of was that he wouldn't be strong enough to hold her affection."

"Yes, yes,"—excitedly.

"Well, that's all. He'll snort and blow a bit. He may even grind his teeth. But if you do it well, you'll bring it off. First you wound his pride and then you slap its face. No matter what he says, I'll bet he leaves this house mentally swearing he'll show us whether he can hold Nell. . . . As for his loving you, sweetheart, you'll have blotted that frenzy out."

For a moment his wife looked thoughtful.

Then she got upon her feet.

"Crip," she said, gently smoothing his hair, "you've got a lightning brain."

"I've got a peach of a wife," said Crispin Willoughby. He smacked the Sealyham's flank. "Haven't I, Boodle?"

The terrier sneezed his assent.

Husband and wife laughed.

Then—

"I'd better telephone now," said Mrs. Willoughby. "There's only one thing you haven't thought of, Crip. Obviously David and I can't continue our raids. How's that to be explained? Nell will want to know why."

Crispin removed his pipe and regarded its bowl.

"I know," he said. "We'll say Aunt Millicent's ill and burst off to Como at once. A couple of weeks in Italy'll suit me down to the ground."

"And me," said Madge. "Give me the home of romance."

"But not its occupant?"

"No—unless she can show a good title."

Husband and wife smiled.

Arrived at the door, Madge paused.

"I suppose you must go out," she said wistfully.

"I must, my darling. This is a one man show. Besides, I think my job is to get hold of Nell. You don't want her blowing in to spoke your wheel."

"My word, no," said Mrs. Willoughby.

"I'll say you're tired and take her to see the play."

"Right."

The door closed.

For a moment or two Crispin continued to brush the Sealyham. Then he rose to his feet and picked up the letter on which he had been sitting. He re-read it carefully.

> *You ask me why I never turned up this morning. I can see no earthly reason why you shouldn't know. Convention has offered me fifty, but they're none of them sound. If either of us was a fool, if the understanding which*

you and Madge share was less perfect, finally, if you were almost any sort of man but the sort of man you are, it would be different. As it is. . . .

Crispin, my dear, you can add a scalp to your belt. I don't suppose for a second that you even know you've got a belt; but you have, and—it's pretty full. Any way, mine's the latest. . . . And that's the inconvenient truth.

As for David, I'm dreadfully sorry, because he's one of the best. I'm afraid he's silly enough to worship me, and now I'm letting him down. Heavens, how I'm tearing things up! But there you are. . . .

You need have no fear. I don't propose to assault you by word or deed. I'm not going to throw my arms round your neck or tell you I love you better than anything on earth. BUT MY IMPULSE IS TO DO BOTH. *So now you see, dear, why I never turned up this morning.*

NELL.

The royal box at the Imperial was available. So, incidentally, were more than half the stalls. The occasion, however, was demanding privacy.

So soon as the curtain rose, Crispin opened the door and ushered Eleanor into the withdrawing-room.

"Crispin, why have you done this? You know what I said."

Standing still by the table, the girl made a pathetically beautiful picture. Her simple white frock, her short hair, her little folded hands, her high colour, the piteous droop of her lips—above all, the tense dog-like devotion of her big brown eyes lent her the air of a child that has pleaded guilty and come to judgment.

Willoughby steeled his heart.

"One can say things," he said, "which it isn't easy to write. Sit down, Nell."

He flung himself into a chair and crossed his legs. Then he took out a cigar and lighted it carefully.

"As a matter of fact," he said, "your letter was rather a godsend."

Miss Cloke started.

"A—a godsend?" she stammered.

"A godsend," said Crispin comfortably. "But let that pass. I'll tell you why presently. To tell you the truth, I was always a little afraid of something like this." Eleanor opened her mouth, shut it, hesitated and then sat down. "I couldn't very well say so, but when Madge first suggested that we should hunt in pairs I thought it was playing with fire. You see, as you hint in your letter, I—well, I've had some, Nell. It's a difficult thing to say, but . . ."

The sentence slid into an apologetic snigger.

"You're rather—rather popular?" said Eleanor, using an odd, strained tone.

"Exactly. Heaven knows why, but you wouldn't believe the number of, er, applications I've had in the last five years."

Eleanor's eyes flashed.

"What fools women are," she said.

"And men," said Crispin, with a generous air. "And men—often enough. In the present case, I wasn't afraid for myself because, though you're awfully attractive, Nell, I'm—I'm funny like that." He laughed self-consciously, uncrossing and recrossing his legs. "You know, I've got one simply appalling fault."

"One—yes?"

"Well, I'm frightfully critical—particular."

There was a frozen silence.

Then—

"Where," said Eleanor in a choking voice, "where do I fall short?"

Crispin shifted uneasily.

"Don't let's go into details," he said. "It'll only——"

"Please."

"My dear Nell, you are so attractive and you've got so many——"

"That'll do," said Eleanor Cloke. "And now please tell me exactly where I fail."

Crispin hesitated. Then—

"Perhaps it's as well," he muttered. "You see. . . . Nell, my dear, it's your walk."

"My *what*?" shrieked Eleanor.

"Your walk—carriage, my dear. In repose you're immense. Standing by the table just now, you were simply it. But when you move—I don't know what it is, but you, er, you don't do yourself justice. You're inclined to . . . to . . ."

"Waddle?" said Eleanor mercilessly.

"Not exactly waddle, but. . . . Well, perhaps you would call it 'waddling.' But it's nothing to write home about. The trouble is I'm afraid it's occurred to David."

"What has? My wal—waddle?"

"Your walk. I may be wrong, but. . . . Nell, it's your only blemish, but, as it happens, the one thing David's noticed ever since I've known him was the way a woman walked. When you two said you were engaged, you could have knocked me down. But apparently——"

"He happens," said Eleanor icily, "to have affirmed on more than one occasion that I had the bearing of a queen."

Crispin shrugged his shoulders.

"Love is blind," he said shortly. "But of course I may be wrong. Still, if it isn't that, I don't know what it is. If you wash that out, you're practically flawless," and with that he leaned back, thrust his cigar between his lips and smoked luxuriously.

"What do you mean," said Eleanor " '—if it isn't that'?"

Crispin started. Then he rose to his feet and began to pace the room nervously.

Eleanor Cloke watched him with smouldering eyes.

After two or three turns he stopped in front of her chair.

"I said your note was a godsend. Well, so in a way it is. Nell, if you value your happiness, you'd better give David up."

The girl stared.

"Thanks very much—why? Are you afraid my waddle will get on his nerves?"

"I'm afraid," said Crispin, "it has." Eleanor smothered an exclamation. "At least, if it hasn't," he added, "then something else has. Nell, I'm grieved to tell you, but he's looking elsewhere."

"Who to?"

Crispin shook his head.

"I've not the faintest idea. But I'm pretty sure he's cooling. Now he's not the man to cool off unless somewhere around there's another brighter fire. Of course, we—I may be wrong."

"Madge thinks so?"

Crispin threw away his cigar, picked up a chair and sat himself down with the table between himself and Eleanor Cloke.

"Look here," he said, "if you want to be happy, Nell, you'll take my advice. *Back out before it's too late.* If you and he marry, you're done. Madge and I've always been afraid that you wouldn't be able to hold him. Well, it looks as though we were right. . . . You're awfully sweet, Nell, and David's one of the best. He'd never go looking for trouble—he's not that sort. But he's an attractive man, and there are plenty of girls. Only a strong personality—a charm that fills up his life—will ever hold David Herrick."

"I see," said Eleanor slowly, nodding her head. "And my charm's not strong enough?"

"I'm frightfully sorry, Nell, but I'm afraid it isn't. The mercy is that you haven't burned your boats."

There was a long silence.

From behind the closed door a sudden swell of applause came to their ears, subduing for an instant the faint roar and jingle of the traffic, the toots of innumerable horns, and even the staccato clamour of a fire-engine's tongue. Then the demonstration died down, leaving the distant racket to snarl and grumble over the bone of silence as a beast frets jealously over the consumption of its prey.

At length—

"Well, I'm greatly obliged," said Miss Cloke, with a dry laugh. "It was a good thing I wrote, wasn't it?"

"It was Fate," said Crispin piously. "'There's a divinity that shapes our ends, Rough-hew them how we will.'"

"No doubt," said Eleanor. "Any way, you've opened my eyes—wide. . . . By the way, have you got my, er, application or did you leave it on the piano?"

Crispin began to search his pockets.

"I had it," he murmured. "I remember thinking when I was dressing 'I must not leave that about.'"

"Never mind," said Eleanor in a shaking voice. "I expect the servants have found it and thrown it away."

"Here it is," said Crispin triumphantly.

Eleanor snatched the letter and thrust it into her bag.

Then she rose to her feet.

"If you don't mind," she said, "I think I'll go. Don't let me take you away. I'm only sorry to have put you to so much expense."

"My dear," said Crispin, "the thought that I've opened your eyes makes it cheap at the price."

"It is obvious," said Eleanor, "that the great thing in life is to know oneself."

"That's the idea," cried Crispin, thumping the table with his fist. "You've got it in one, Nell. And it's never too late to begin."

Speechless with indignation, Miss Cloke regarded him.

Then she recovered her face and began to shake with laughter. . . .

Crispin watched her open-mouthed.

At last she pulled herself together and passed to the door.

"Poor . . . old . . . Madge," she said deliberately.

Crispin swallowed.

"Oh, it's nothing," he said. "She's only rather tired."

"I'm not surprised," said Eleanor. "I think I should be—*rather tired* . . . after five years."

The next second she was gone.

Captain Willoughby took out a handkerchief and proceeded to mop his face. Then he stepped to a mirror and adjusted his tie.

"And they think they're acting," he muttered, jerking his head towards the box. "Well, well—it's all in the day's work. . . ." He fell to pulling his moustache. Suddenly he burst out laughing. "What a game Life is!" he cried. "I try to protect my own skin, and they give me the V.C.; I deliberately scrap my reputation to do a girl a good turn, and—and it costs me a jolly good friend and seven quid." He lighted a cigarette and picked up his coat. "I wonder how Madge has got on," he continued musingly. "And perhaps it'ld be as well if I had a look at the play. I can't reappear till it's over, and she might ask what it's about."

He hung up his coat, extinguished his cigarette and entered the box.

The wedding of David Herrick and Eleanor Cloke took place early in May and was a brilliant success.

The bride looked extraordinarily beautiful, and if the dignity of her gait was slightly affected, that was a fault upon the right side.

At the reception the bridegroom, who had eaten no lunch, ate nothing at all. I imagine he had decided that the occasion was one upon which no risks should be run.

Captain and Mrs. Willoughby were among the guests.

The tongues which had recently wagged fairly spouted the 'Amens,' and afterwards slobbered over the 'enchanting atmosphere of a true love-match.' Subduing a feeling of nausea, Madge and Crispin agreed enthusiastically.

The relations, however, between the Herricks and Willoughbys seemed to leave something to be desired. The old familiar affection seemed to have been superseded by a boisterous cordiality which was rather too hearty to be true.

These conditions prevailed until the month of July.

It was then for the first time that Mr. and Mrs. Herrick spent twenty-four hours apart. And that was against their will—they were really absurdly in love. But Eleanor had a cold, and Tattersall's Sale Ring may be a draughty place. . . .

For all that, Madge Willoughby was there, and she and David had an engaging talk—so engaging, in fact, that the mare which he had come to Newmarket to buy became the property of another at less than half the figure to which Herrick was prepared to go.

That same July morning Mrs. Herrick received a note.

> NELL DEAR,
>
> *I gave you back your letter because you asked for it, but to part with it went against the grain rather more than did anything else I had to do that night. You see, next to Madge, I love you rather better than anyone else, and I was so pleased to know that, next to David, you felt the same about me. Besides, to be strictly truthful, it was the only 'application' I'd ever had. . . . Still, perhaps it's as well.*
>
> *One or two confessions you'll value.*

> *First, before your delivery of the word 'waddle,' I almost broke down. I never could have believed that so much withering contempt could be compressed into so homely a dissyllable. Secondly, I never missed one of your thrusts; they were superb. Finally, never to my dying day shall I know how, when first you were standing by the table, I resisted the temptation to take you in my arms. Before we got down to it, I mean. Nell, it—was—irresistible. . . . Yet, I came through. Truly, 'There's a divinity that shapes our ends, Rough-hew them how we will.'*
>
> CRISPIN.

As her husband came in that evening—

"Well, my darling," cried Eleanor, "what d'you know?"

"Little enough, old lady. I lost the mare, but Madge and Crispin were there, and they helped me home. They want us to dine to-morrow. Will you be fit?"

Eleanor sat up in bed.

"I'd love to," she said. "But d'you think we possibly can? I've put the Festivals off."

"Good Heavens, yes. I mean, they're practically relatives, aren't they—Crispin and Madge?"

"Practically," said Eleanor. "And much—much more intelligent."

SUSAN

NICHOLAS JOHN KILMUIR, DUKE of Culloden, turned his letter about. Presently he fell into a reverie.

He was a quiet, good-looking man a short thirty-six years old. As luck would have it, he looked an aristocrat and perhaps because of this, was seldom recognized. His features were fine and clean-cut, his shoulders square, his head well set on. He was tall, moved perfectly, rode as though he were part of his horse. His gentle brown eyes and pleasant voice, above all, his steady, grave smile, made many friends. In France, his men had reverenced him as a god. His tenantry did not reverence him, because reverence was not among their faculties, but the bluntest crofter would have died for him as a matter of course. Culloden understood this devotion and valued it as it deserved. He spent ten months of the year at Ruth Castle and full four-fifths of his income upon his estate. And since in this world much is expected of a duke, the remaining fifth had to be gingerly expended. Thanks to his loyalty to his own, Culloden was a comparatively poor man. He could not, for instance, afford to keep a car....

At the present moment he was rather awkwardly placed.

His operation had been an expensive business. To judge by the surgeon's fee-book, dukes' appendices were twice as refractory as those of commoners. Again, his bill at the nursing-home had been worthy of his rank. More. He was to have convalesced upon an old friend's steam-yacht: then at the last moment his host had fallen sick and the cruise had been cancelled.

Staying at his Club in St. James's, Culloden, who was really hard up and had been medically forbidden to return to the isolation of Ruth for at least six weeks, did not know what to do.

It is not surprising that an invitation which in the ordinary way he would not have cared to accept seemed to have fallen from heaven....

c/o Comte Boschetto,

Château Chiennile

Cannes.

DEAR NICK,

I know it's not your practice to batten on people you've never seen in your life, but I really think for once you'll have to climb down. My dear fellow, you MUST. You're going spare: to judge by your blasphemous incoherence, the weather in England is foul: the vacuum within you demands consolation in the shape of complete relaxation appropriately leavened with nice, gentle exercise. Very well, then. Join me.

Listen.

The Boschettos are mad to have you, of course, but don't let that stop you. They mayn't be pre-war, but they're insanely kind. Their one idea is to do their guests about fifteen times as well as they've ever been done before—in an inoffensive way. What's more, they actually bring it off.

First, they leave you alone. We make up our own parties, go as we please. I get up when I like. I retire when I like. I eat and drink what I like, when I like. I do what I like. I come and go as I happen to feel inclined. In fact, so long as you sleep in, they don't care what you do if only you're happy. I'm one of the few who make a point of seeing the Countess about every other day just to tell her how much I'm enjoying myself. Whereupon she almost weeps upon my neck and wails that there are always sandwiches and champagne in the **salon bleu** *from eleven a.m. on, but that if I prefer port I've only to ask for it.*

Secondly, I thought I knew a thing or two about the contents of the top-drawer, but I didn't. My son, I'm a blinkin' tenderfoot. Luxury? I tell you, before I came here I couldn't spell the word. Of course the château's palatial—you never saw such a place. Over thirty bathrooms. My bedroom faces south and is about forty feet square. Fifteen cars all going all day long and half the night, and the stables full of ripping good ponies and hacks. Three motor-boats. As for the servants, I didn't know there were so many in France. They literally swarm. I have a valet to myself, and so, I believe, has everyone. And the women have maids. Two private bands—three, I think. Dancing all night—if you like. If I want a car or a cocktail or a Corona or any imaginable thing, I just call the nearest wallah, and there it is. God knows what it costs—I should think about two thousand a day—pounds, not francs, pounds. But apparently that doesn't matter. I tell you, it's indescribable. . . .

Hospitality like this seems to be proof against abuse. Short of larceny, you can't abuse it. Your duty towards your hostess and your duty towards yourself are synonymous terms. The most dutiful guest is the most self-indulgent. Naturally, such an establishment has attracted a motley crowd: still, there are no flagrant undesirables, and most of us mean well. Bertram Scarlet has just left—amid lamentations. The Pemburys are coming. So you see. . . .

I play golf all day, have a rubber of bridge before dinner—small tables, of course—and do a little dancing afterwards. Eleven o'clock usually sees me out. I ran into the Fairies the other day on the links and after a lot of bickering persuaded them to come along after dinner. They and Bertram and I and one or two others made up our own party and had a good evening. When they said 'Good-night' to the Countess, she thanked them effusively for coming and begged them to leave the Carlton and stay here instead. She'd no idea who they were. They left dazedly in a Hispano limousine with two chauffeurs, wondering whether it was all a dream, I tell you, the whole thing is incredible—has to be seen to be believed.

So COME.

Yours,

TEDDY MANDEVILLE.

Culloden lowered the letter and gazed into the street.

It did seem an obvious way out. But for his title, he would not have thought twice . . . but for his title.

The man could not endure to traffic with his name. In spite of golden opportunities, he was not a director of a single company: and, as he steadfastly refused to rent his style, so he declined to exchange it for board and lodging. If he was invited for himself, he was delighted to accept; but every new invitation was carefully weighed, and nine out of ten of them were found wanting. He need not have spent ten months of the year at Ruth Castle. In point of fact, had he pleased, he need not have spent ten days of the year at home. Bachelor dukes are apt to be in demand. . . .

The present offer of hospitality was slightly different. It seemed that commoners were welcome—not so welcome, of course. 'They're mad to have you.' Still, Bertram Scarlet and the Fairies—Teddy Mandeville himself seemed to be *personæ gratæ* at Chiennile. Besides, no one, apparently, was wanted for himself. The Boschettos were purely beneficent. All was fish that came to their net. All they were wanting was a thundering catch. If this included turtle, so much the better: but that was all.

There was no doubt about it. Not to avail himself of such a timely chance would be the act of a fool.

He wired to Mandeville that night—

Seriously shall I arrive on Monday next?

In due season he received a reply—

Every time.

Monsieur Auguste Labotte adjusted his tie. Then he slid elegantly into the pink dress-coat which the servant was holding, told the man offensively to be gone and assumed a courtly pose before the pier-glass. After a careful survey of his points, he clicked his heels, bowed low, took on a jaunty air and, clasping an imaginary partner proceeded to shake his shoulders with every circumstance of abandon...

He was in the act of kissing his finger-tips—a delicious, careless gesture, by which the fragrant caress was apparently tossed into the air to wreak who knows what havoc, when he observed that the symmetry of his eyebrows left something to be desired. Simultaneously he remembered that his aggrandizement of the left had been interrupted and never resumed. He repaired the omission delicately....

Again he reverted to the pier-glass, to be inspected.

This time his scrutiny could find no fault in him.

Here was Chivalry *allegro*. The rude paraphernalia of virility had been doffed: the hardy victor of the field was turning to tenderer, more luscious conquests.

With a happy sigh, Labotte reflected that, disguise it as he would, his sportsmanship emerged always. No one could miss it. If anyone did—well, that was what the pink coat was for.

He opened the door of his room and descended thoughtfully....

The *salon rose* was crowded.

Two pretty Englishwomen were sitting on the club-kerb, sipping cocktails and exchanging back-chat with a handsome jolly-eyed Frenchman and a tall Italian, whose manner suggested that he might adorn diplomacy. As a matter of fact, he had. A Frenchwoman of great beauty was relating her impressions of the Trooping of the Colour and lending both English and ceremony a peculiar charm. Two Englishmen, soldiers, were listening delightedly. A jovial, broad-shouldered Spaniard was vividly recounting his prowess upon the tennis-court and throwing his hearers into convulsions of mirth. A well-set-up Frenchman, one-armed, was lighting a cigarette: this belonged to an Italian lady: between the two of them the simple attention put on the courtly livery of a forgotten age. A tall American girl, with grave grey eyes and a proud mouth, was standing close to an alcove. A common, unhealthy-looking youth, with a loose lip and an aggressive stare was expelling smoke from his nostrils and languidly conversing with Count Boschetto, a stout, nervous little man, with vacant eyes and an everlasting smile. The latter was most deferential and was working extremely hard. Six or eight other guests were about their striving host, listening greedily to the youth and thrusting toothsome banalities into the discussion, as though in the hope of attracting attention to themselves. From the alcove, heaving with emotion, the Countess was surveying the scene with a beatific smile. Her proportions were immense: her splendour, barbaric. Her snow-white hair was almost hidden beneath an enormous tiara, while the size and number of the pearls about her neck was almost frightening. Bracelets flashed upon her tremendous arms: rings winked from every finger. Her dress was of purple and gold. Her shoes were of gold, with high purple heels.

The Duke of Culloden stood beside her, addressing her quietly from time to time. She whimpered irrelevant replies, sometimes tremulously voicing her thoughts. "Oll my gues-s-s," she would falter.

"Oll my deer guess-s-s. They were so naize to make vull my salons—the salons of an ole daungkih as me."

It was pathetic.

Culloden felt as once he had felt in an asylum, watching a mad architect gleefully supervising the construction of a new wing. The poor wretch was intoxicated with his own importance, and the bricklayers were calling him 'Sir' and laughing until the tears rolled down their cheeks.

The peer felt suddenly ashamed. He was subscribing to this tragic pantomime, taking advantage of an idiot's whim. He was—

Another picture rose up before his eyes. He saw the halls deserted, the ball-rooms empty . . . saw his host and hostess in melancholy state, the servants idle, yawning, kicking their heels . . . heard the bands droning music to which no feet danced . . . perceived with a shock the awful dreariness of riches with none to gather them.

Culloden decided that the woman beside him was no fool. It was her glory to kill the fatted calf. She was labouring under no delusion. She knew. She actually thanked her guests, begged them to batten upon her, meant what she said.

After all, his visit was neither more nor less than a happy deal. It suited the Countess' book, and it suited his. What he found especially pleasant was that for once in a way his title was cutting no ice. He was not being named: no one was being introduced. Teddy Mandeville was perfectly right—they really left him alone. He might have been Albert Binks, of High Street, Clapham.

He had arrived at Chiennile that Tuesday afternoon—a day later than he had said, but that was because there had raged a storm in the Channel and the present expediency of humouring his stomach had been impressed upon him. Upon his arrival he had found that Mandeville had left the château. It seemed that the latter had been wired for on Sunday night. His Grace considered, frowning, that, even if he could not advise, Teddy might at least have left him a note. However. . . .

A major-domo had received him and had shown him his rooms. It was clear that, for all his respect, the man had had no idea that he was not conducting a commoner. Culloden was faintly surprised and immensely relieved. The last thing he wanted was the carpet down. Still, it was curious. None of the servants knew. Yet—'They're mad to have you.' Possibly Teddy had paved this admirable way....

Labotte entered the room.

For a moment he stood, looking round. Then he joined the circle about Boschetto.

He at once perceived that the latter was doing his best to please and decided to exploit the endeavour. He therefore directed attention to the poor labourer by laughing and nudging his neighbours and presently mimicking the manner of his host.

"Yess, yess," cried Boschetto, by way of hearty agreement with the unpleasant youth's remarks.

"Yess, yess," echoed Labotte, grinning.

"Yess, yess," repeated Boschetto unconsciously.

"We 'af no bananas," said Labotte.

His host flushed painfully, endeavouring to contribute to the laughter in which his loose-lipped patron joined.

"You know," continued Labotte, taking the stage and indicating his host, "'e says to me one day, 'Labotte, I 'af feer I am dull. I weesh that I could mague my guess-s laugh.' An' I say to 'im, 'My frien', you do this more better than you know.'" There was a shriek of laughter. Labotte looked round grinning. "Am I not right—yes?"

Boschetto fell away, chuckling in a queer, strained way, while Labotte engaged the youth in a discussion of the gaieties of Town.

Culloden stepped to Boschetto and began to admire the room.

"Indeed, it's all so admirable. Not only the château, but the establishment. It's a privilege to be here. You think of everything. I tell you, Count, I know some people in England who think they can entertain, but if they could see this they'd go and jump off somewhere. Why are you so kind to us all?"

The Count blinked at him.

"Thank you," he said tremulously. "Thank you."

The American girl was speaking.

"To-day," she said, "he took me for such a lovely drive. Didn't you, Count?"

Her host drew himself up.

"I' af enjoy every minute," he said most earnestly.

The girl appealed to Culloden.

"You see?" she said. "He won't let anyone thank him. He gives us all the very time of our lives——"

"I am dull," said Boschetto.

The girl took his arm.

"What awful rot," she said. She turned to Culloden. "You ought to hear him on Europe. I wonder how many people in this room——"

"Yes, but you was an angel," said Boschetto gravely.

He glanced at his watch, begged to be excused and made his way to a servant with an anxious air. . . .

"Who," said Culloden, "are the young chevaliers?"

The girl smiled.

"The one in pink," she said, "is Monsieur Labotte—a man, as you have seen, of singular taste and charm. The other—well, surely you know who that is."

"I haven't the faintest idea."

"Aren't you English?"

"I'm a Scotsman."

"Worse and worse," laughed the girl. "My good sir, that is the Duke of Culloden."

Two days and two hours had gone by, and Nicholas John Kilmuir was enjoying himself very much.

He was royally lodged, admirably served, superbly fed. What was still more to his taste, he went incognito. 'Incognito'? No one had the remotest idea who he was—except that he was *not* the Duke of Culloden. To turn to smaller mercies, the weather was brilliant, and his time was his own. Moreover, his conscience was clear—whenever Boschetto saw him, a pleased light crept into the dull, strained eyes. . . .

But that was not nearly all.

First, there was the spectacle of an impostor, whose arrival on Monday had been taken for that of His Grace, deliberately exploiting the error, accepting the fervent homage of a perfectly poisonous crowd and generally playing such 'tricks before high Heaven as make the angels weep.'

Secondly, there was Susan Armitage Crail. . . .

"I should like," said Nicholas John, "to ask you to dance. But a recent bereavement. . . ."

Miss Crail raised her sweet eyebrows.

"I've heard some excuses," she bubbled, "but that's the very best. It suggests shades of mourning of which the average relict never dreams."

"He wasn't a relation," said Nicholas. "Only a—an intimate connection. And I'm not really mourning. We got on admirably for many years, and then at the last he got above himself. Indeed, he caused me much pain, before—before he . . . passed over."

Miss Crail frowned.

"Why not 'died'?" she demanded. "Don't say you're——"

"Can appendices die?" said Nicholas.

Susan Crail stared and then fell into silvery laughter.

Kilmuir regarded her gravely.

There was about this girl a natural dignity which no manner of mirth could subvert. The pride of her red mouth was gone: the grave eyes were fairly dancing with merriment; she was unconscious of anything save that she was amused. Yet—hers was the amusement of a great lady. And of such was her charm. More. The girl had depth, quality: she did not require to be amused. There seemed to be things other than dalliance which were dreamt of in her philosophy.

"What should I do without you?" said Nicholas John.

"I expect you'ld play Bridge," said Susan.

The man shook his head.

"I suppose I should read," he said. "I've nothing in common here with anyone else."

"You haven't tried," said Susan. "That little French girl with the glorious mop of hair. . . ."

"Can you see me?" said Nicholas John. "Do we look as if we should get on? I tell you I can't—er—chatter. I'd like to tell you what beautiful arms you've got, but I can't put it into words."

"Hush," said Susan. "You mustn't say things like that."

"Why?"

Steadily grey eyes met brown.

"Because they ring true. I know now that you think I have beautiful arms. I haven't, but that's beside the point. I know you think I have. If anyone else said so, I should know they were telling the tale. But you—you mean what you say."

"I hope so. But that's no reason. Why shouldn't I——"

"I don't know. It's difficult to say. Somehow it's—it's dangerous ground. You see, to-day a man can say anything—at least, they do. I hate it, but it's the fashion . . . *anything*. But there's always a button on the foil. They don't mean a word of it. If they did . . . Well, I should take the veil. But they don't. And that's the saving clause in an odious document. But you're different. You mean what you say. Your foil hasn't got any button. And so—it's dangerous."

Kilmuir digested this, frowning.

"In a word," he said, "I mustn't make personal remarks?"

"That's right," said Susan. With a sudden, childish gesture she touched his arm. "You don't mind my telling you?" she said.

The sweet simplicity of heart that prompted gesture and word took Kilmuir by the throat. She was a child—this great lady, an exquisite, unspoiled child. Gentle, fair, wise—smothering up her nature because it was not safe for her nature to be abroad. His impulse was to take her hand and kiss it. He wanted to, immensely. But he mustn't—because she was a child.

In an instant, in the twinkling of an eye, their positions had been reversed. A moment ago he had been sitting at her feet. Now her hand was in his, and she was looking up trustfully into his eyes. She was a child.

"No," he said, "I don't. In fact, I'm much obliged. Let's—let's shake hands, shall we?"

They shook hands gravely.

Locked together, two couples rocketed out of the ballroom, whirled past Miss Crail and Kilmuir and, as the tune ended, crashed in a heap on a divan. They sorted themselves uproariously.

"What about a little courage?" said 'the Duke,' drying his neck. "And a mouthful of goose-grease, just to help it down?"

"Are you steel so thirsty?" queried his partner.

"I am when I look at you," was the ducal reply.

Labotte suspended his handkerchief as a curtain between the two girls, as though to screen the speakers from inconvenient gaze. To do this, he passed his arms upon either side of his partner. The latter, an English girl, sought to duck beneath his sleeve. Instantly he lowered his arm. In a moment the screen was forgotten, and the business became an affray between Gallantry and Virtue.

"See, see," cried Labotte, grinning. "I 'af catched a leedle mouze in a gage. She will get oud, but she does not know 'ow." The girl slid to the ground, and her captor slid with her. "You see?" he announced. "It ees no good at oll. You are a preesner for life."

The pretty scene concluded with a violent struggle from which the lady emerged with a torn dress—a mishap which occasioned shrieks of laughter and a volley of innuendo.

The four departed hilariously in search of champagne. . . .

"D'you like all this?" said Nicholas. "I don't mean the scene we've just witnessed, but the manners of which it's the fruit."

"What d'you think?" said Miss Crail.

"I think you hate it. I think you like gaiety, and as this is the only sort going you make the best of it."

"You're wrong," said the girl. "I could live on a desert island and be completely happy."

"Then why do you stay here?"

"Well, for one thing, I haven't an island. Secondly, I haven't any money. I live with an aunt, who keeps me and is at present on a yacht. When I saw the passenger-list, I begged to be excused. So I've been left here till she returns. If I'd the nerve, I'd strike out a line for myself, but I've always lived soft and I can't type a letter, so what can I do?"

Kilmuir regarded the end of his cigarette.

"How long have you done this?" he said.

"Nearly two years now. The idea is to get me married and out of the way. But I don't go very well. Two or three men have been kind enough to bid, but one was married already and the others. . . ." She shuddered. "My aunt says it's my fault," she added, "and so it is! I don't push my wares. . . . I'm not so bad as I was. At one time I was quite hopeless. But I'm better now. At least I give people a chance—to be nice or nasty according to how they feel. I'm afraid even now I'm not very good at horse-play, but I shall probably learn."

"Don't," cried Nicholas. "Don't."

The girl looked at him.

"All right," she said. "I won't. I promise I won't again. I don't know why I did. Yes, I do," she added abruptly. "I know why I did."

"Why?" said Kilmuir.

Susan Crail started.

Then, suddenly, she fell into long strained laughter.

"From your curious tone," she said, "I perceive that I have been maudlin. You know. Not offensively blind, but sorry for myself. It's just that extra half-glass, you know. You think 'I won't drink it,' and then you get talking and——"

"Rot," said Nicholas John.

"Oh, but how rude," said Susan. "Never mind. You'll believe me one day. Didn't I talk about a desert island? Yes, I thought so. I always do. But I'll bet you never said what the last man said. You're much too solemn."

"What did he say?"

"He said it wouldn't be a desert island long, especially if I went in for goatskin shorts."

"My very words," said Kilmuir steadily.

There was a long silence.

Susan was beaten and she knew it.

Hastily she shuffled her cards. These were frightening.

Without thinking, she had told him her story, because she valued his esteem. She valued his esteem, because she loved him. She had told him her plight and, without thinking, she had told him its remedy—*marriage*. She had actually rammed it home—without thinking. Suddenly she had realized. . . .

Horrified at what she had done, she had striven frenziedly to undo it . . . somehow—*anyhow* . . . no matter at what cost. And he had watched her efforts and feinted and knocked them out.

There was nothing for it: she must begin again.

"I shall pinch you in a minute," she said. "I tell you, the reaction has set in. The muzzy feeling is passing and I'm beginning to feel ready for anything. Don't say I didn't warn you."

Labotte arrived—a very *deus ex machina*.

He came straight to the two, stood before Susan, spread out anticipative hands and began to oscillate to the one-step which had just commenced. An impudence of raised eyebrows and the shadow of a superior grin argued a confident familiarity which could afford to dispense with a formal invitation to dance.

With a heart of lead, Miss Crail acceded brightly to the unspoken request.

As she launched herself, she flung out the words of the melody in the approved darkie fashion.

And you never know whether she will,
And you never know whether you may,
    But hold her tight,
        With all your might,
    By the small of her back,
        On a moonlight night,
    And you won't be left,
        'Cause you must be right—
THOWAT-T-T'S the way!

They flashed the short length of the salon, whirled through the open doors and disappeared. . . .

There is an old saying that you cannot have it both ways. If you decide to discourage heaven, then you must be prepared to encourage hell. Whether or no Susan had offended Kilmuir, she had exalted Labotte—a supererogatory and rather dangerous elevation.

He began to improve the occasion almost at once.

"I do not know why I 'af not resgue you more soon. I think I am a gread fool. There is the nices' leedle 'orse in oll the place sidding with a gread dull fellow an' I 'af lose my dime in tryin' to school so many mules. *Tant pis!* I tell you, we are goin' to 'af a good dime now. We are goin' to go well this evenin'—my naize leedle 'orse an' I."

His buoyant tenderness was hideous, but Kilmuir was standing in the doorway, and they were dancing towards him.

Susan threw back her head and laughed wildly.

"Your horse?"

Labotte tightened his hold.

"From the firs' dime I 'af see you, you 'af been my naize leedle 'orse. Bud olways before, you 'af been shy from me. 'Ah,' I 'af say, 'bud thad is a good fault.' You know, a man like much bedder when a girl is not oll over 'im at once. An' so I say, 'Gently, my frien', tread gently your naize leedle 'orse: an' one day she shall whinney when she shall 'ear your face——"

"And eat out of your hand?"

It is doubtful whether the sage heard what she said.

Intoxicated with the triumph of his compelling personality, dazzled by the richness of the pasture his brilliancy had won, considerably affected by the elegance with which his imagery had betrayed at once the sportsman, master and swain, Labotte was out of earshot.

He whirled her past Nicholas in an eloquent dithyramb of motion to which she deliberately subscribed.

"My naize leedle 'orse," he crooned, "oll while I 'af make spord with the mules I 'af see olways my leedle 'orse in the dail of my eye. An' ad night I 'af dream about 'er, an' now... 'Af I not say that we shall go well this evening? Eh? An' do we not? Eh? Was I nod righd then, sweet-bit?"

Craning his neck, he leered into her eyes.

As they swung round, Susan was able to see that the doorway was empty. Kilmuir had gone.

"Now then I will teach you 'ow. You mus' turn your 'ead sweetbit, and our leaps shall brush themselves. It will, of gourse, be an agsiden'. I shall not 'af know that you were to move. An' no one shall know neither... But we shall know an' be 'appy—my leedle——"

"Let's stop," said Susan, suiting the action to the word.

Labotte wagged his head.

"I know a leedle salon," he chanted rhythmically, " 'alf-way on the stairs."

As the girl turned, he laid hands upon her. It was his way. He always smeared his prey. The suggestion of an embrace appealed to him. For one thing, it looked so well. It argued a certain proprietorship—a seignory, such as other men did not enjoy; it suggested the existence of a familiarity which, short of a scene, his victim could seldom rebut: it enhanced his reputation as an irresistible dog. For another, he found it agreeable.

He slid an arm about her shoulders and squeezed her hand, as though by way of shepherding her in the required direction.

"D'you mind not touching me?" said Susan.

Labotte started, and the greasy hands fell away.

Then he rapped his knuckles.

"Ah, then," he simpered, "you mus' be more gareful, block-face. You mus' nod go to frighden your leedle 'orse."

Susan passed out of a door and sat down in the hall. This was empty, but it was not remote.

Labotte stared.

"Bud," he blurted, "we 'af arrange to go——"

"I sit here," said Susan.

Labotte sat down by her side and took out a cigarette. His grin had faded into a supercilious and rather unpleasant regard which sat uneasily upon his insignificant face.

"And," continued Miss Crail, "I'ld be glad if you wouldn't refer to me as 'your little horse.' It suggests an intimacy which does not exist between us; it's vulgar and it's bad form. I don't suppose that any of those reasons will appeal to you, but you can take my word for it they're pretty sound."

Labotte regarded her open-mouthed.

After a moment the blood began to pour into his face. Very soon this was completely suffused and glistening. The scarlet of his ears suggested that they were on fire. As for his eyes, these had become small slits of grey-green flame.

He shut his mouth with a snap.

"What?" he breathed through his teeth. "I—*I* am vulgar?"

"Intensely vulgar," said Susan, producing a cigarette. "Get me a match."

For a second Labotte hesitated.

Then he rose, crossed to a table and returned with a box of matches.

"Thank you," said Miss Crail. "Now you can go."

Labotte drew himself up.

"I 'af nod the use to be commanded," he said. "I am a gennelman, an'——"

"Don't be silly," said Susan. "Because it suited me to dance with you, that doesn't make you a gentleman. And now, if you take my advice, you'll run away and play—while there is time. Otherwise, I may be tempted to put you where you belong."

The macaroni appeared to have lost the power of speech.

His world was rocking before him.

A woman—a fury, of course—had had the hideous presumption to turn him down. His advances had been rejected: his condescension had been actually flung in his face: he had been offered gross, gratuitous insult. The dove he had deigned to nourish had turned serpent. The female he had demeaned himself to favour had turned and rent him—*him*, Labotte, knight and sportsman. . . .

The indecency of the affair made his brain reel.

Dazedly he put a hand to his head.

"No one 'as never speak to me so—nevare," he announced dramatically. "Eef you was a man——"

"Be thankful," said Miss Crail, "that I am not. Why, you wouldn't ride for weeks," she added pleasantly.

Labotte blenched. The reflection, however, that sex cannot be changed at will steadied him almost at once.

He took a pace backward and bowed.

"I go," he said stiffly, "bud nod begauze you 'af say so. No." Susan began to shake with laughter. "The only reason wot I 'af got ees that I will blease myself. Oh, yes. Eet ees very fine to laugh," he added violently. "It ees a gread jork to make slaps when you are very safe that they cannot be render: but eet ees you shall waid, Mees Crail, an' fin' whether you shall 'af make these blace too 'ott for you to 'old."

He turned and sauntered away with such nonchalance as he could muster.

When he was out of sight, Susan went to her room, sank into a chair, buried her face in her hands and burst into tears.

Upon the next floor Nicholas was pulling his moustache and covering his third mile upon an Aubusson carpet of great beauty.

Three rooms away Labotte was savaging a pillow.

"*Sapristi!*" he mouthed. "*Mais je vous montrerai, Speet smoke, qu'on ne gagne rien à insulter un sportsman.*"

Nicholas very nearly returned to Town.

The man was shocked. At one and the same moment he had made two striking discoveries—severally harmless enough, but jointly corrosive. The first was that Susan Crail was a waster: the second, that he loved her very much. What made things infinitely worse was that, as women go, she was a queen. Spotted silk is so much worse than stained sackcloth. Unearthing more bitterness, he reflected that never again would he be offered the blessed opportunity of wooing without his title to promote his suit.

He avoided Susan but watched her, taking care to conceal his disappointment and wearing it on his sleeve.

Susan could have wept, was careful to appear blithesome and got away with it.

Labotte was as good as his word.

His vanity had been outraged. Very well. All the chivalry of the man rose up in condemnation of the foul deed. His hate had to be served. After surveying his dirty armoury with a malevolent stare, he turned his attention to his opponent's harness.

Almost immediately he perceived a vulnerable spot.

Miss Crail was a lady, and ladies had an aversion to figuring in scenes. Indeed, to avoid a scene they would endure almost anything....

Labotte licked his lips.

If he approached her privately, he would be told to go away. Very well. Supposing he approached her publicly—short of a scene, she would have to submit to his approach. More. If he addressed her, sat by her side, made loud, innocent conversation—no one would see anything inconsistent with courtesy in that. Everybody would think that he was dancing attendance. But he and she would know that she was being whipped....

Susan's luck was clean out.

Five times in three days he contrived to sit next to her at meat: twice he had managed to be driven in the same car: seven times he had asked her to dance. She had not done so, but it was not too pleasant—this pestering. Labotte's attentions would have been odious at any time: now they were nothing less than a direct insult. When upon the third day at dinner he steered the conversation to the points of a 'naize leedle 'orse,' mentioned nice clean legs, a soft mouth and well-rounded quarters as essential features and then asked Susan if she did not agree, the latter felt cold with rage.

Most of the women saw there was something amiss and, reluctantly respecting Susan, were faintly amused. The more quick-witted of the men began to smell trouble. The jolly-eyed Frenchman looked very hard at Labotte: the Spaniard had frowned and lost the thread of his discourse: the tall Italian had stared and then asked Susan to dance. But that was all. The way of a man with a maid had to be patently outrageous to warrant intervention. . . .

Deep in a shadowy corner of the *salon vert* Susan was contemplating her state and wondering, if she fled, how far four hundred and fifty francs would go.

Six feet away two Englishmen were talking.

For a moment or two she listened idly, too much depressed to care at all for their words.

Then her brain leapt.

"Sponge knows who he is."

"He would"—contemptuously.

"He didn't go so far as to claim his acquaintance, but he says he's Kilmuir of Kilsay. He added that he knew his wife intimately—spoke of her as 'Kitty Kilmuir.' "

"And I bet if she came here she wouldn't know him. What a sweep the man is!"

The two moved away, and the voices faded.

His wife. . . . Kitty Kilmuir.

Wondering why she had assumed that Nicholas John Kilmuir was unmarried, halting curiously between relief and dismay, Susan started to her feet. . . .

Then she sank down again and stared at the floor.

Her impulse had been to find Kilmuir at once and tell him the truth. Not all of it, of course, but enough to make him her friend—a present help in her trouble. But Susan Crail was no fool. Life was a stern creditor. If she invoked the sympathy of the man she loved, touched his strong hand, called up the kindness of his steady brown eyes—these things would have to be paid for in blood and tears. As it was, even if Labotte vanished, she would still have to try to forget. . . . Nicholas Kilmuir. There was a scourge waiting. Was it worth her while, for the sake of a little relief, deliberately to load the cords? Wasn't it better to——

"No," said Susan suddenly. "It isn't better. What is better is to take what you can get. I can't take him, because somebody else has done that. But I can be with him and see him and hear his blessed voice. Damn what the future holds. The present's the thing."

She rose and stepped out of the shadow—almost into the arms of 'the Duke of Culloden' and Labotte.

The latter bowed low.

"Good evening, Miss Susan Crail."

"Good evening."

'His Grace' stared. Then—

"Oh, 'elp," he said. "Any more for the throne-room?" He bowed grotesquely. "Good sunset, sweeting. What doth the night-light say?"

"Too late," said Susan pleasantly. "I've a letter to write."

"Splendid," said 'the Duke.' "We'll tell you what to say, shall I?" He linked her arm in his and turned to Labotte. "If I'm not back in half an hour, Saddle-soap——"

Labotte raised his eyebrows.

"I do nod think," he announced, "you will be zo long." Suddenly his eyes gleamed. "But there," he added, "I do nod know. Perhaps . . . I tell you, when she was naize, she was vairy, vairy naize." He closed his eyes and vented a happy sigh.

Susan felt rather sick.

"O-o-oh," said 'the Duke,' approaching a face which appeared to have been recently buttered. "And how does he know?"

"I don't think he does," said Susan, seeking to disengage herself. "Please let me go."

"And why was she 'vairy naize'?" continued 'the Duke,' detaining her.

"You'd better ask him," said Susan, trying to pass it off. "He seems to know. And now let me go, please. I've got this letter to write."

'His Grace' skipped to a doorway and spread out his arms.

"Block the other one, Saddle-soap: and we'll give her a run," he cried, and, with that, he switched off the lights.

Then curtain rings rasped, and, except for the rosiness of a dying fire, the room was black.

Susan stood paralysed.

She was going to be kissed, of course. That went without saying. She wondered dully whether she was going to be scratched. Labotte.... Perhaps he would only pinch her.

With a shock she realized that she had better move. To stay where she was would be fatal. If she could change her position . . .

With a beating heart, she began to steal to one side, straining her ears.

Suddenly she stood still as death.

Something—someone was almost touching her. She could hear his breathing. She was right under his hand. And she was trapped. Her knee was against a chair, and she could not move. Any second now . . .

The form sheered off. Whose-ever it was, he had missed her by a hair's breadth.

Trembling all over, Susan began to edge away from the chair. . . .

A piercing scream of agony shattered the silence—the sort of scream which is associated with torture—the scream of a human being under the pain of hell.

Susan's heart stood still.

The scream slid into a flurry of howled oaths, the nature of which suggested that Labotte was out of action. If he was, there was a doorway clear. . . .

Susan was there in a flash.

She and Kilmuir passed out together.

"Steady," he said quietly. "Now turn round, get behind me and appear to be looking in. Then they won't connect us with this little play."

As he parted the curtains, the lights in the room went up, and four or five guests and servants appeared in the other doorway.

Labotte was sitting on the parquet, rocking himself to and fro, nursing his bridle-hand and addressing 'the Duke of Culloden,' who was leaning against a sofa convulsed with laughter.

"I tell you I 'af not see why jus' begozz you are duke that 'as nod give you the raighd to starm' to my 'and laike there was fifdy tousan' dun of storns in your boode an' then you gannot bray bardon bud mus' laugh laike you gry an' make that you 'af nod starm' to no one's 'and. I suppose it is I wot 'af march oll over my own 'and—yess! Bah! I make myself to be your frien', I let you to call me Zaddle-zorp an' show you the rorpes of these place, an' then you starm' to my 'and and when I say, 'See 'ow you 'af done,' then there was a gread forny jork that I am 'urt. I tell you I do not gare ooze duke you are . . ."

By one consent Miss Crail and Nicholas turned and made their way out of the press.

"So perish all traitors," said the latter. "As the actual executioner, my use of that pious expression is traditionally becoming."

Susan stared.

"You?"

Kilmuir nodded.

"I was there all the time," he said. "None of you saw me. I was wondering where I came in, when the lights went out. I happen to be able to see rather well in the dark, and just as I passed you I saw our little red-back making for where you stood on his hands and knees. ... I admit I'm not very proud of myself. I should have preferred to thrash him in daylight and a public place, but you—you had to be considered. ... I was going to harry the—er—Duke of Culloden also, but Saddle-soap made such a noise that I hadn't time. That he should credit his accomplice with the assault is sheer good fortune. I never dreamed of such an elegant *dénouement*." He led the way to a closet at the end of the *salon gris*. This was deserted. "And now, why did you rush upon your fate three days ago? Why did you try to discredit yourself in my eyes? We'd only just made friends."

"Did I succeed?"

"To a certain extent. Won't you sit down? That's right." He took his seat by her side. "I've changed my mind now."

"What d'you think now?"

"I think you wanted to put me off," said Nicholas. "And I want to know why."

"You remember what I told you—about my life?"

"Every word."

"Well, I spoke without thinking, you know. I don't know why. I've never done it before. And suddenly I realised that. ..."

"Yes?"

Susan hesitated. Then—

"I knew a woman once," she said, "who was always tied up for money. And she used to come to Aunt Beatrice. She never asked her right out, but she used to tell her the awful plight she was in and say if she couldn't get someone to lend her two hundred dollars she'd have to kill herself and—and look volumes. ... Well, it wasn't pretty."

"No," said Kilmuir. "But how does that apply?"

"I realized the other night that I'd done exactly the same—told you in so many words *how you could rescue me*. ... You see, I didn't know then that you were married. If the woman had come and told me how poor she was, it wouldn't have mattered, because I had nothing. But Aunt

Beatrice had the means. In the same way, my telling you my plight doesn't matter now, because you can't help."

There was a long silence.

At length—

"Surely," said Nicholas gently, "you knew me better than that? Surely you needn't 've thought——"

"You're a man," said Susan. "You don't know how frightfully sensitive about marriage a woman can be. Many a girl's thrown away happiness rather than let a man even suspect—quite wrongly—that she's setting the pace."

"I'm inclined to think that still more have set the pace rather than run the risk of throwing away happiness."

Susan laughed.

"And, what's more," continued Kilmuir, "the latter have all my sympathy."

"Listen to the man," said Susan.

"Supposing," said Nicholas John, "I had been a bachelor. You naturally thought I was, because there are still men left who travel with their wives. I happen to have a good reason for not being one of them. Next time I go abroad I hope my wife will be with me. But that's by the way. Supposing I had been a bachelor and, as such, eligible—to pull you out of your slough. And supposing I'd decided that I loved you and had asked you to be my wife. . . . And supposing you'd thought it good enough. . . . D'you mean to say you'd 've actually turned me down?"

"Undoubtedly," said Susan.

"Why?"

"They call it," said Susan, " 'self-respect.' You might have sworn that you loved me, but I should have been terrified that it was only *Noblesse oblige*."

"Surely a woman can distinguish pity from love?"

"A wife could, because she'ld be in a position to apply all sorts of tests. But that's not very much good. I mean, it's a bit late . . ."

Kilmuir took out a cigarette.

"Three days ago," he said slowly, "you told me I meant what I said." Susan started. "That what I said rang true. Yet I might have sworn that I——"

"I know," said the girl desperately. "But the terror of making a mistake. . . ."

"Aren't you digging too deep?" said Nicholas. "If somebody offers me a drink and I feel thirsty, I jolly well take it. So long as it's honest liquor, I don't bother about their motives. If I assume anything, I assume that they wouldn't ask me if they didn't want me to have it."

"You're not going to compare marriage to a Martini?"

"They're much the same. A happy marriage is like a slap-up cocktail, the effect of which never passes off. . . . Well, if a man doesn't offer another a tenpenny drink unless he wants him to have it, d'you seriously think he's going to offer his heart, his home, his name, his fortune, his future to any daughter of Eve that ever was foaled—unless he wants her to have 'em?"

"Prosper Le Gai did."

"Only to save Isoult's neck. And, though she knew that, she took him. What's more, my lady, it was a great success."

Susan began to shake with laughter.

"That was an unfortunate instance, wasn't it?" she said. "You know, you're too well read. I should have got away with that with most of the people I know."

"It's a question of Greeks meeting," said Nicholas John. "Or deeps calling. We've more or less the same tastes. I think you like the dawn and the silence of high places and the roar of the woods when the wind is laying on——"

"And the thud and suck of the surf and the baby talk of a brook and great cotton-wool clouds in the sky and a wind you can lean against. . . . Oh, I should think I do."

For a moment the girl was transfigured.

Sitting upright, her grave eyes shining, her lips parted and her sweet pretty head thrown back, she might have been some Nereid out of some Odyssey. His eyes ablaze, Kilmuir regarded her, fascinated. . . .

Then she lowered her head, and the light in her eyes died.

"But that sort of life's not for me," she said abstractedly.

"Look here," said Nicholas John. "D'you want that sort of life?"

"What d'you mean?"

"What I say—as usual," said Kilmuir. He waved his hand. "Would you like to wash all this out? Would you like to get down to Nature? Spend nine months of the year under her wing? Sell this mess for a birthright? Know the rain on your face, and——"

"Are you offering me a land-agent's job?"

The man looked at his finger-tips.

"It's more of a stewardship," he said. "There's a post at my place in Scotland which you could fill—most admirably. It's been vacant—oh, twenty years now, because I could never find the right person to take it on."

Susan put a hand to her head.

"It—it sounds like a fairy-tale," she said. "A girl—steward. . . . Of course, you're making this up—creating some sinecure out of compassion for me."

"No I'm not," said Kilmuir. "The post's going. Quite a good house, and about—about six hundred a year. Fuel. I could have filled it, of course: but I didn't want someone who'd get fed up in a week. D'you think you could stick it? It's lonely up there—after this: and the dawn's a bit late in the winter, and—I've known it pretty cold."

"D'you think I'ld mind that? But what d'you know of me? What makes you think I could manage? I don't even know myself. In fact, I'm sure I couldn't. I don't know what stewards do. I couldn't control and order—I'ld try to learn, of course, and I'ld simply love the life. I'm choked here—tied and cooped and sickened and choked. I hardly saw a city before I was twelve years old. I was born and bred up in Maine. My grandfather's place was there. . . ." She hesitated—then burst out suddenly. "Six years ago he died, and everything crashed. They sold my saddles and my very own mare with the others I used to ride. I couldn't prove she was mine, and if I could have I hadn't got any money to buy her corn. They sold the curtains I'd made to hang in my rooms, and lamps and mirrors and pictures I'd saved up to buy. They sold everything—house, woods, farms, hills, valleys. . . . And I who'd been mistress of it all was sold too. At least, I was put up for sale. But then you know that. . . . And all because my grandfather had forgotten to sign his will. . . . What was I saying? Oh, I know. Well, now you see why your fantasy dazzles me so. But don't let's talk about it any more. I know it's out of the question, and you know it too. Don't think I don't appreciate——"

"Why is it out of the question?"

"Oh, for a thousand reasons. I should have no authority. A woman——"

"I am obeyed—up there."

"I don't care. A woman can do many things, but she can't fill a post like that. You know you're only saying it out of pure——"

"I'm not," said Kilmuir steadily. "It's always been held by a woman. The last . . . died . . . twenty years ago." His voice became very soft. "She was the sweetest lady—with the gentlest smile. She never gave an order in all her blessed life, but I think if she'd asked the waves to stop their fretting there would have been a calm. I've seen her tend a horse that the grooms were afraid to feed; I've seen wild birds on her shoulder; and once I saw a drunkard pour out his store of whisky on the ground before her eyes. I tell you the roughest fisherman hung upon her will. You see, she always understood. She never taught, yet everyone learned of her: she was so humble, yet she was found a queen. Her laugh—well, Eve may have laughed like that, before the apple. . . . And then . . . one day . . . she died. . . ." He took out a letter-case and discovered a photograph. Then he rose and stood in front of the girl. "For what it's worth, that's a picture of her."

Susan stared at the beautiful, eager face. . . .

A crazy truth, such as one finds in dreams, kept thrusting into her brain.

Sharply she flung up her head.

"*Your mother?*" she whispered.

Nicholas nodded.

"I want you to take her place. . . . You see, I'm—I'm not married, darling." Susan started violently, and the man set a hand on her shoulder. "I'm—I'm not that Kilmuir."

"O-o-oh!"

For a moment she stared at him wildly. Then she closed her eyes, let her head fall and buried her face in her hands.

Nicholas continued steadily.

"It isn't much to offer—a share in my lonely life. But it won't be lonely any more if you'll accept it. I never thought I should marry. I never thought I'd find anyone I'd care to see in her place. And then . . . at last . . . I saw you. . . . And the moment I saw you, I knew . . . I'm poor, you know, but if you'd been worth twenty millions, I'd 've asked you to be my wife. You see, I love you, my lady: and so I can't help myself. I love your beautiful temples and the droop of your precious lips: I love your grave grey eyes and your sweet pretty ways . . ." He hesitated. Then, "I warn you, I won't be able to give you much of a time. I can't even afford a car, Susan. At least, I haven't been able to yet. But I think, if we were careful, perhaps . . ." He took her wrists and drew her hands from her face. She continued to hang her head. "Oh, my blessed lady, I want you so much: and, as you don't mind the cold and the quiet, don't you think you could——"

"*Noblesse oblige*," wailed the girl. "*Noblesse oblige.*"

"Oh, you darling," cried Nicholas, lifting her to her feet.

Susan flung up her head and stared at the face of her squire three inches away.

With his arms about her, Nicholas smiled back.

"I confess," he said, "I'd 've liked to feel that you loved me, but I'd rather you took me out of pity than not at all."

A child put her hands on his shoulders.

"Do you really love me?" she whispered.

Nicholas smiled down.

"No," he said. "I'm doing it out of pity."

A radiant, mischievous look leapt into the child's grey eyes.

"I don't believe you," she said, and put up her mouth.

Ten glorious minutes had passed, and Susan and Nicholas were standing in the *salon bleu*, drinking each other's healths in rose-coloured Clicquot. Ten or twelve fellow-guests were hard by, flicking their several appetites with the same beverage. Among them, their recent difference adjusted, were 'the Duke of Culloden' and Labotte. The latter's hand was bandaged and reclining in a sling.

A servant entered with a card.

This he took directly to 'the Duke.'

The youth glanced at it and frowned.

"Say I'm not here," he said.

The servant bowed and turned away.

"Stop," said Nicholas John.

The servant hesitated, and a hush fell upon the room.

"Bring me that card."

With an apologetic glance at 'Culloden,' the fellow did as he was bid.

Nicholas picked up the card and read the name.

"Where is *Monsieur le Comte*?"

"*Monsieur le Comte est couché.*"

"*Et Madame?*"

"*Madame aussi, Monsieur.*"

"Then show this gentleman in."

"*Bien, Monsieur*," said the man, and made his escape. . . .

Amid an electric silence Nicholas picked up his glass and drank comfortably.

Susan was touching his arm.

"Nicholas! What are you doing?"

Her lover turned with a swift smile.

"I want him to meet you, lady."

"But——"

Labotte was before them, speaking acidly.

"Your frien' 'as nod seem to unnerstan'——"

"Address yourself to me," said Kilmuir.

Labotte stared. Then he looked Nicholas up and down.

"I am nod a servant," he said.

"No," said the other. "I knew that by your coat."

Labotte drew himself up.

"I do nod know 'oo you are," he said loftily, "an' I do nod gare, but eet ees good you shall know that in France when a gennelman 'as gommanded it was nod use to gommand the opposide in 'is faze. You 'af 'ear my frien' dell that 'e was nod to be seen an' then you mus' put your lorng norse to a thing which 'as not belong to you at oll an' make jus' the same business as my frien' 'as nod wand."

"And what," said Nicholas, "is it to do with you? Why don't you let him—Hullo, he's cleared."

Labotte swung round. Then he spread out his hands.

"Ov gourse 'e 'as gorn," he cried. "Eet ees you wot 'ave drive 'im away. 'E 'as say 'e is nod to be seen, an' then you mus' . . ."

Here a nice-looking man with a merry eye was ushered into the room.

As he stepped forward—

"Hullo, Berry," said Nicholas, taking his hand. "Nice of you to come up."

"Yes, isn't it touching?" said Berry.

Nicholas turned to Susan, staring, big-eyed.

"This, dear, is Major Pleydell—a very old friend. Berry, this is Susan—Miss Susan Crail. She's just promised to be my wife."

Berry Pleydell smiled. Then he took Susan's hand.

"My dear," he said, "this is most fortunate. You can do me a little service. Listen. When I was last at Ruth—about four years ago, I sent a good-looking pair of bed-socks to the Castle dairy. Well, I had to go before the wash came back, and in spite of repeated applications to His Grace the Duke of Culloden my property has never been restored. Now, when you get there, go through his rotten things, and——"

"*The Duke of Culloden?*" cried Susan. "But . . ." The sentence died there, and she looked from one to the other with fright in her eyes. Then she addressed her swain. "Are *you*," she breathed, "are *you* the Duke of Culloden?"

"Yes, dear," said Nicholas John.

To style the sensation 'profound' conveys nothing at all.

Susan felt rather faint. Her fellow-guests, standing like drugged sheep, seemed to be bent upon at once avoiding one another's gaze and ascertaining one another's demeanour. Only their eyes shifted, their heads and bodies remaining perfectly still. As for Labotte, the consciousness that he had publicly insulted a Duke, harrassed a future Duchess, and for the last seven days conspicuously licked a rank impostor all over seemed to have affected his reason. He staggered to a doorway, collided with and ricochetted from the jamb, kicked the latter savagely, screamed and disappeared. . . .

Major Pleydell was speaking.

"But didn't you know?" he said.

Susan could only shake her head.

"Bless my soul," said Berry. "Never mind. Let's drown it in drink. Besides, it's not his fault. Only . . ."

"What?" said Susan.

Berry laid a hand on Nicholas' shoulder.

"Well," he said, "if it isn't because of his title, what are you marrying him for?"

Susan and Nicholas laughed.

"*Noblesse oblige*," they said.

THE END

Milton Keynes UK
Ingram Content Group UK Ltd.
UKHW040432140224
437791UK00007B/553